Fascism and the Right in Europe, 1919–1945

Pearson
Education

We work with leading authors to develop the
strongest educational materials in history,
bringing cutting-edge thinking and best learning
practice to a global market.

Under a range of well-known imprints, including
Longman, we craft high-quality print and electronic
publications which help readers to understand and
apply their content, whether studying or at work.

To find out more about the complete range of our
publishing please visit us on the World Wide Web at:
www.pearsoneduc.com

SEMINAR STUDIES   IN HISTORY

Fascism and the Right in Europe, 1919–1945

MARTIN BLINKHORN

An imprint of **Pearson Education**

Harlow, England · London · New York · Reading, Massachusetts · San Francisco · Toronto · Don Mills, Ontario · Sydney
Tokyo · Singapore · Hong Kong · Seoul · Taipei · Cape Town · Madrid · Mexico City · Amsterdam · Munich · Paris · Milan

Pearson Education Limited
Edinburgh Gate
Harlow
Essex CM20 2JE
England
and Associated Companies throughout the world.

Visit us on the World Wide Web at:
www.pearsoned.co.uk

First published 2000

ISBN 978-0-582-07021-9

British Library Cataloguing-in-Publication Data
A catalogue record for this book is
available from the British Library

Library of Congress Cataloging-in-Publication Data
A catalog record for this book is available from the Library of Congress

Transferred to Digital Print on Demand 2011

Set by 7 in 10/12 Sabon Roman
Printed and bound by CPI Group (UK) Ltd, Croydon, CR0 4YY

INTRODUCTION TO THE SERIES

Such is the pace of historical enquiry in the modern world that there is an ever-widening gap between the specialist article or monograph, incorporating the results of current research, and general surveys, which inevitably become out of date. *Seminar Studies in History* is designed to bridge this gap. The series was founded by Patrick Richardson in 1966 and his aim was to cover major themes in British, European and world history. Between 1980 and 1996 Roger Lockyer continued his work, before handing the editorship over to Clive Emsley and Gordon Martel. Clive Emsley is Professor of History at the Open University, while Gordon Martel is Professor of International History at the University of Northern British Columbia, Canada, and Senior Research Fellow at De Montfort University.

All the books are written by experts in their field who are not only familiar with the latest research but have often contributed to it. They are frequently revised, in order to take account of new information and interpretations. They provide a selection of documents to illustrate major themes and provoke discussion, and also a guide to further reading. The aim of *Seminar Studies in History* is to clarify complex issues without over-simplifying them, and to stimulate readers into deepening their knowledge and understanding of major themes and topics.

NOTE ON REFERENCING SYSTEM

Readers should note that numbers in square brackets [5] refer them to the corresponding entry in the Bibliography at the end of the book (specific page numbers are given in italics). A number in square brackets preceded by *Doc.* [*Doc. 5*] refers readers to the corresponding item in the Documents section which follows the main text.

AUTHOR'S ACKNOWLEDGEMENTS

I should like to express my gratitude to the many Lancaster University history students, both undergraduates and postgraduates, whose work over three decades has contributed so much to my understanding of, and views on, the matters discussed in this book; to the staff of the Lancaster University Library for their unfailing helpfulness; and to the Seminar Studies editors and the Longman editorial staff for their care, professionalism and patience.

PUBLISHER'S ACKNOWLEDGEMENTS

We are indebted to the following for permission to reproduce copyright material: Mary Evans Picture Library for the eight black and white plates.

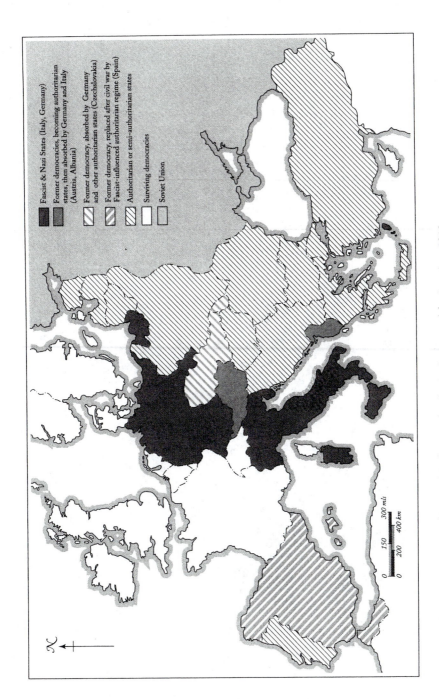

Legend:

- Fascist & Nazi States (Italy, Germany)
- Former democracies, becoming authoritarian states, then absorbed by Germany and Italy (Austria, Albania)
- Former democracy, absorbed by Germany and other authoritarian states (Czechoslovakia)
- Former democracy, replaced after civil war by Fascist-influenced authoritarian regime (Spain)
- Authoritarian or semi-authoritarian states
- Surviving democracies
- Soviet Union

0   150   300 mls
0   200   400 km

Map 1   Europe, summer 1939, showing the advance of authoritarianism and fascism since 1919

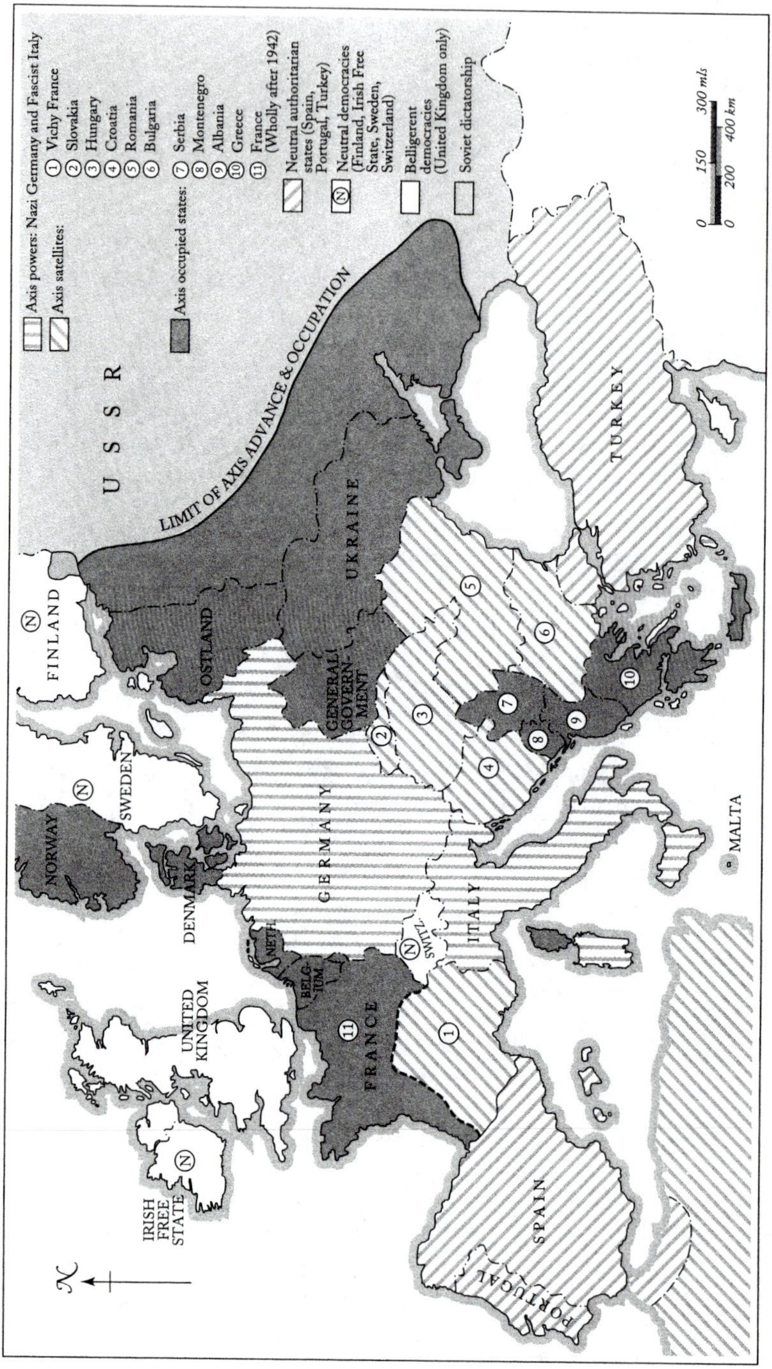

Map 2   Europe, 1941–42

PART ONE   BACKGROUND

CHAPTER ONE

PROBLEMS OF STUDYING FASCISM

Let us begin by imagining three political maps of Europe. The first bears the caption 'January 1920', immediately following the promulgation of the Versailles Treaty and some months after the overthrow of short-lived Soviet regimes in Hungary and Bavaria. The second is dated 'Summer 1939', a few weeks before the outbreak of the Second World War in Europe. The third is labelled 'Winter 1941–42', showing the continent at the peak of Nazi Germany's European hegemony. On all three maps, each country is coloured according to its official constitutional status: communist states red, constitutional democracies white, and right-wing dictatorships black. Looking at the first map, we immediately see that west of the red of Soviet Russia, and perhaps with the exception of a decidedly grey Hungary, Europe is completely white. The second map, however, presents a very different picture: the Soviet Union is still of course red, but the white area has retreated to roughly the northwestern quadrant: France, Switzerland, the Benelux countries, the Nordic countries (including Finland and Iceland), Britain and Ireland. The rest of Europe stands out as black. Portugal, Spain, Italy, Germany, Austria, dismembered Czechoslovakia, Poland, the three Baltic states, Hungary, Yugoslavia, Romania, Bulgaria, Albania and Greece are all now subject to one or another form of right-wing authoritarian regime. Moving our gaze finally to the third map, we see that now only Britain, Ireland, Iceland, Sweden, Finland and Switzerland remain as white islands in a vast blackness whose eastern boundaries, furthermore, have been pushed hundreds of miles into the otherwise still stubbornly red Soviet Union.

Clearly, Europe between 1919 and the middle of the Second World War witnessed a broad historical process whereby the liberal democracies of the immediate post-1919 period were challenged, and in many cases overturned, by what for the moment we may loosely call right-wing forces. Moreover, and as the second of our three maps showed us, most of this process occurred before the outbreak of war in 1939, even if German arms then carried it further. In part because the first truly dramatic example of this tendency (though not actually the very first) called itself 'fascism', and because Fascist Italy then attracted enormous interest and publicity throughout Europe and the wider world, that term came at the time to be loosely applied to many other right-wing movements and regimes, and indeed has sometimes been applied to the whole interwar period: the so-called 'era of fascism'. Contemporary observers of left-wing or liberal persuasion can scarcely be condemned for seeing all or most of the right-wing ideas, movements and regimes of their day, however they might differ in detail, as members of one family; all appeared hostile to representative democracy, free trade unionism, and the essential liberal freedoms of speech, publication, movement and assembly, while under all such 'fascist' regimes, not only were free institutions suppressed but also those who upheld them were liable to be persecuted.

It would be wrong to lose sight of these common features, or too readily to accuse of over-generalization or inaccuracy those who viewed them as variant manifestations of a single – and malign – phenomenon. Such a view of 'fascism' conveys the spirit of its time, possesses its own quite genuine validity, and transmits to our own age at least as much contemporary 'reality' as any other. Nevertheless even the most casual glance at interwar Europe ought to be enough to convince the student of history that beneath the hastily applied label of 'fascism' lay a very broad range of ideas, individuals, organizations and regimes, the diversity of which historians are obliged to recognize. Some of these embraced the name 'fascist' with enthusiasm, while others rejected it. Some preferred the label 'national socialist', raising questions concerning the relationship between these two forces. Some took 'fascism' very seriously, stressing those features which they believed distinguished it from other elements of the far right; others used it selectively and even cynically, to disguise conservative realities with a usually thin veneer of something more radical.

Given this diversity, some Europeans during the interwar years, at first chiefly on the conservative right but, mostly rather later, also on the liberal centre and the socialist left, preferred to stress the *differences* rather than the *common characteristics* within the contemporary right. For conservatives, the aim in doing so was to distance themselves from something with which, fairly or not, they were often linked, but which they distrusted; for liberals and socialists, the goal was to achieve a subtler understanding of the right's complexities, the better to resist the threat it posed them. Either way, such observers insisted that fascism, chiefly by virtue of its radicalism, was intrinsically *different* from other forms of right-wing expression, organization and government, however authoritarian these might be. With this, of course, albeit for their own reasons, self-confessed fascists were in full agreement: their cause, in their eyes, was above all *revolutionary*.

A similar emphasis upon the differentiation between 'fascism' and the rest of the right has also come to dominate the scholarly study of fascism since the Second World War. This has been especially true since the 1960s, when 'fascist studies' truly began to take shape as the academic heavy industry which it remains today, more than half a century after the destruction of the Third Reich. Over the past thirty years, armies of political scientists, sociologists, social psychologists, and historians of various kinds have sought to isolate the essential, distinguishing features of fascism, their goal being a generally acceptable definition of an elusive phenomenon nowadays usually termed 'generic fascism'.

The quest for the Holy Grail of 'generic fascism' has seldom been less than intellectually stimulating. Central to it, nevertheless, are problems which – notwithstanding recent claims that a 'new consensus' on the subject may be emerging [2 *p. 14*] – stubbornly refuse to go away. Most serious scholars studying fascism agree that the term must be used with some attempt at precision – though one, Gilbert Allardyce, did suggest some years ago that since this was impossible, it should be abandoned altogether as an analytic category [1]. (Since inviting the luminaries of 'fascist studies' to do this was on a par with asking turkeys to vote for Christmas, it is unsurprising that Allardyce's suggestion fell on unreceptive ears.) Yet for all the effort expended, no agreement or consensus *has* yet emerged on how the term 'fascism' should be used, or indeed on exactly what it is that so many have been attempting to define. Is 'fascism' a set of *ideas and goals*? Is it a particular type of political *movement* embodying a distinctive political '*style*'? Is it, rather, a type of *regime*, irrespective of the kind of movement or movements which may have helped to create it, or of how it came into existence at all? Is it possible to produce a single definition which will encompass all of these things (and more)? And what about the relationship of fascism with nazism? Are 'fascism' and 'national socialism' essentially synonymous as analytic categories, variations on a single theme, or actually quite different? Is 'fascism' historically defined by its period, and post-1945 'neo-fascism' something quite distinct, or – a very real question today – is fascism, once having been created, an enduring phenomenon? These and other difficult questions remain to taunt us.

This is a work of history, written by a historian, which sets out to investigate these issues in as down-to-earth a manner as their complexity permits. It aims to explore the intellectual and cultural origins of fascism, its emergence and development between the two world wars, the reasons for its successes and failures in pursuing power, and its relationship – as a body of ideas, as a species of political movement, and as a system of power – with other forms of right-wing authoritarianism and radicalism. Little attempt will be made here to force fluid historical phenomena into the kind of rigid, or perhaps it would be better to say static, analytic categories that a quest for 'generic fascism' too often seems to require. Indeed, the book's central theme or argument may be said to be precisely that fascism needs to be understood in terms of its *metamorphosis* as it moves (sometimes) from theory to movement and then (more rarely) from movement to regime. It is this process and its implications which have largely dictated the book's structure, and which inform the modest attempt to end it, not so much with a *definition* of fascism, as with a *template* against which fascism, and its relationship with the right as a whole, may be examined.

Nevertheless, whatever we may ultimately conclude, it is necessary to establish some terminological points of departure. As is implicit in much of what has already been said, my starting point is that it *is* possible to identify a collection of ideas and goals, many with their origins in pre-1914 Europe, but maturing after 1919, which we may broadly call 'fascist'. Very broadly speaking, these ideas were, in their various settings, ultra-nationalist and sometimes, though not always, racist; their exponents viewed their respective nations, and in all probability Western civilization as a whole, as 'decadent' and in need of cultural revitalization; they sought to replace liberal, parliamentary, democratic institutions, seen as epitomizing decadence in the political sphere, with some kind of authoritarian system manned by a new ruling elite; and all, bitterly anti-Marxist, sought a 'national' revolution that would bind society together within a new social order. Fascists thus claimed to stand well apart from other, even extreme rightists in wanting far more than the deployment of authoritarian means to defend the existing social order.

Identifying ideas and goals as 'fascist' is all very well, but we also need to consider the relationship, in a variety of national contexts, of these ideas to the movements that espoused them, to the individuals who joined or otherwise supported those movements, to other political organizations who shared some but not all of their outlook, and to the various right-wing dictatorships which fastened upon Europe between the early 1920s and the end of the Second World War. It is here that the clear distinctions perceptible in the ideological sphere start to become problematical. Some political movements wholeheartedly embraced 'fascist' ideas and pursued most or all of the goals implied by them. Others, spontaneously or by calculation, operated more selectively, adopting only some unambiguously fascist ideas and goals, and tempering them with powerful elements of a more conventional conservatism. Yet others shared with out-and-out fascists little more than a common hostility towards democracy and the left, viewing fascism as scarcely less suspect and threatening.

Most problematical of all is the question of what constitutes a fascist *regime*. On the one hand, some regimes with little in the way of a prior 'fascist' ideological or organizational input adopted much of the appearance, 'style' and even substance of fascism. On the other hand, it might be suggested that beneath the glossy surface of the Italian Fascist regime there lurked an essentially conservative reality so marked as to define its very character: thus Italian Fascism, the prototypical model by which 'fascism' must surely be measured, paradoxically may have been less 'fascist' than it claimed and even appeared. Especially to the extent that this last point possesses validity, the question arises: where, then, does the National Socialist Third Reich fit in any general analysis of fascism? What, more particularly, was the relationship of Nazi excesses and above all the Holocaust to 'fascism'? The purpose of this short book is to make some sense of this complex and bewildering collection of conundrums.

European fascism is, and always will be, inextricably associated with the years between the end of the First World War and the end of the Second. Yet while very much the product of its age, and unimaginable as a potent force without the combined impact of the First World War and the Russian Revolution, many if not most of its intellectual and ideological genes are traceable back to the Europe of the late nineteenth and early twentieth centuries. It is to this very different Europe that we must now therefore turn.

CHAPTER TWO

FORETASTES OF FASCISM IN PRE-1914 EUROPE

It is essential to be cautious when speaking of 'foretastes of fascism' before the First World War, in an age when the word 'fascism' had yet to be coined and most of the conditions which enabled fascism to flourish had yet to come about. There must be no suggestion that any discernible prewar 'roots' of fascism were roots *only* of fascism, or on the other hand that their existence in any way rendered inevitable either the appearance of fascism or, where relevant, its success. Like any important historical phenomenon, fascism was the product of both long-term and more immediate factors, without either of which it could never have existed in recognizable form. This section considers some of the former. And since the beginnings of fascism – whatever else it may have become – lay in the realm of culture and ideas, it is with these that we shall begin.

EUROPEAN LIBERALISM AT THE CROSSROADS

The century before 1914 in Europe has often been labelled the 'liberal century', or something along those lines. By the turn of the century, almost the whole of Europe west of the Russian Empire was governed by political systems containing at least some degree of parliamentary representation; with the introduction of the Duma following the 1905 revolution, even Russia might have been thought to be moving, however uncertainly, in a similar direction. Most of urban Europe, at least, may also be said to have enjoyed a liberal *culture*, boosted by rising literacy and revolutionized communications, and characterized by ideological pluralism, a varied press, a vigorous literary, artistic, musical and theatrical life, and so on. Economically speaking, both urban/industrial and rural/agrarian Europe by this time were integrated into a capitalist economy wherein property could be freely bought and sold, while both employers and, increasingly, labour were permitted to organize in furtherance of their interests. Although traditional landed aristocracies still carried considerable social and indeed political weight, both their ranks and their power were subject to more or less continuous erosion and challenge from members of the financial, commercial, industrial and professional middle class [19].

Closer scrutiny nevertheless reveals a more complex picture. For all the proliferation of parliaments and widening of suffrage, most European countries in the years immediately before the First World War were still some way from being fully developed *democracies* and many could not yet claim to possess genuinely representative or responsible government. For example, in the German Empire, founded in 1871, while the (all-male) suffrage was broad and elections more or less honestly run, governments were answerable to the emperor rather than to the national parliament, the Reichstag, and through it the electorate. Much the same was true in the Austro-Hungarian Empire. In Italy, a self-consciously 'liberal' state, anything approaching universal male suffrage arrived only in 1912. As Italy entered the war in 1915 it was still unclear whether the country would be able to negotiate a difficult political transition, namely from the 'oligarchic' liberal system introduced following Unification in 1861 to a modern, mass democracy. Spain possessed universal male suffrage from 1890, but elections were manipulated by the ministry of the interior and political bosses known as *caciques* – practices which, naturally with important national and local variations, operated throughout southern and southeastern Europe: in Italy, Portugal, Greece, Romania and the other young Balkan nations. Women were still disenfranchised throughout the whole of Europe except, after 1906, in Norway and Finland, the latter an autonomous part of the Russian Empire. Generalizing, one might suggest that much of Europe in the years before 1914 remained under the political control of elites – part aristocratic, part wealthy bourgeois – who accepted parliamentary *liberalism* because they could control it, while still resisting outright *democracy* for fear that that control would be lost.

At least two major challenges to this elite dominance were emerging, both reflections of a rapidly urbanizing, more complex, faster changing, and less easily controlled social order. The first was pressure simply for greater and more authentic democracy: depending upon the particular setting, more genuinely representative and responsible government, extension of the suffrage, more honest elections, etc. The second, overlapping with but distinct from the first, was the challenge of organized labour and the political left, much of which was wedded, at least in theory, to the idea of overthrowing capitalism by revolutionary means. Even in those countries such as Britain and France that were managing to accommodate themselves reasonably well to mass politics, the question of whether this challenge could be contained within a liberal-parliamentary framework was a very real one.

While for some, especially on the liberal and moderate left, the burning question was the ability of liberalism to open out and mature into full-scale democracy, for others the transformation and especially the 'massification' of European society weakened the very foundations and assumptions of liberalism. More conservatively inclined liberals in many countries, fearful of the mass democracy for which radical liberals hoped, began to be tempted by new, defensively minded, authoritarian redrawings of liberalism, involving a strengthening of the executive and restriction of the suffrage. Such tendencies, while visible throughout much of Europe, were most pronounced in turn-of-the-century Italy [7 *pp. 92–118*], in Austria-Hungary, and in Germany – especially following a dramatic socialist breakthrough in the general election of 1912 [10]. The heightening international rivalries and tensions of the time merely reinforced many conservatives' feelings that the interests of the nation and the state might be incompatible with democracy; even in Britain a preoccupation with the need for 'national efficiency' in the face of German and American competition led some in this direction [29].

Thus, although the decade before 1914 may have looked like the golden age of European liberalism, the truth is that much of Europe had actually reached a critical stage in its political development. Against the background of political 'massification', the emergence of organized labour and the left, and heightened international competition, liberal systems of government, most of them oligarchic in character, were increasingly faced with a difficult dilemma: whether to broaden their base and yield to more genuine democracy, or to respond to new situations, challenges and conflicts with authoritarian or other, entirely novel solutions.

CRITICS AND CRITIQUES OF LIBERALISM

During the quarter-century before 1914, much of Europe witnessed a cultural and, to a lesser extent, political revolt against the ethos, values and institutions of liberalism. The scale of this revolt must be kept in proportion, since it was largely confined to intellectual and educated circles and left most of the population untouched. Nevertheless it made significant inroads into the western and central European intelligentsia, achieved some erosion of previously liberal ranks, and had some success in undermining the ideological and political confidence of incumbent political systems. As such it played an important part in preparing the ground for fascist and other right-wing movements in the interwar years [33].

Europe between 1870 and 1914, notwithstanding periods of severe economic recession, witnessed unprecedented economic activity, development and enrichment. During this time, not only convinced liberals but also many conservative traditionalists and Marxist socialists accepted a view of the world and of human society that was essentially positivistic, rationalistic, materialistic and optimistic. For a vocal and growing minority, however, the European world of the 1890s and 1900s, and the value-system on which it rested, were unacceptably unspiritual and unheroic [*Doc. 1a*]. A variety of publicists, in a variety of ways, attracted a limited but – especially among the young – expanding audience to ideas that ran counter to prevailing orthodoxies. The French philosopher Henri Bergson, for example, insisted upon the importance of the *irrational* in human behaviour [4]; his compatriot Georges Sorel stressed the role of 'myth' as a spur to human activity, and violence as a means of pursuing those myths, notably in the sphere of social revolution [27; *Doc. 1b*]; and others like the German philosopher Friedrich Nietzsche [14] and the Italian poet Gabriele D'Annunzio [9 *pp. 166–86*] looked to individual male heroism to raise the West from mediocrity. The overall emphasis of such ideas was a stress upon the role of *will* in human affairs.

Other areas of intellectual activity, too, were seized on (often very selectively) by the cultural critics of turn-of-the-century liberal Europe. Sigmund Freud's development of psychoanalysis, for example, appeared to undermine that belief in the rationality of human behaviour on which liberal and democratic values were founded. Charles Darwin's evolutionary theory, having survived early controversy to become orthodoxy, during the later nineteenth century was (inaccurately) transmuted into 'social Darwinism', whereby conflict in human – and therefore political and international – relations was deemed to be inevitable and, indeed, healthy. The supposedly scientific study of race and the development of eugenics appeared to call into question ideas of human equality, betterment and fraternity, while another new 'science', also conducive to notions of inevitable conflict and particularly influential in Germany, was 'geopolitics', whereby international relations were understood in terms of countries' geographical positions, climate, natural and human resources, etc. The cumulative effect of such ideas was a confused challenge to belief in representative politics, tolerance and pluralism in public life, human betterment, and the rational, peaceful solution of social, political and international problems [33].

Most of the cultural criticism just referred to stopped short of detailed political criticism, much less the formulation of political alternatives to the *status quo* in the Europe of the early twentieth century. Other ideological assaults upon liberalism were more specifically political, taking issue with the very notion of government based upon electorates defined in terms of geographically drawn constituencies and contending opinions and interests. The Italian 'elitist' theorists Vilfredo Pareto and Gaetano Mosca scorned liberal democracy on the grounds that it was mediocre, corrupt and self-defeating; the modern world required the rule of new, authoritarian elites – though within political structures about which they were less than precise [23]. Especially within the European Catholic community there developed a vigorous critique of parliamentary liberalism based on the conviction that a superior form of representation and organization would be a 'corporative' one, a modern-day development of supposedly traditional institutions in which occupational interest – agriculture, industry, the intellectual world, the armed forces, etc. – would form the basis of social and economic organization and political representation [21]. Corporativist views of one kind or another were becoming widespread in pre-1914 Europe, variously held as a means of binding together capital, management and labour and thereby preventing class conflict; of making possible the more efficient ordering of modern, increasingly industrial, society; and of restoring a sense of identity to uprooted and alienated social groups.

The principal quest of most pre-1914 Catholic corporativists, it must be admitted, was a new approach to social and political representation that, far from being authoritarian, would if honestly applied deserve the label 'Christian democracy' [12]. Other Catholic – and non-Catholic – corporativists, however, were frank in wishing to *replace* liberal-parliamentary systems, which they viewed as intrinsically and irremediably flawed, with more authoritarian alternatives. This brand of corporativism was taken up in particular by 'integral nationalist' propagandists and organizations: for example the early twentieth-century Italian Nationalists; Charles Maurras and Action Française in France [17 *pp. 213–304*]; and Integralismo Lusitano in Portugal [18]. Italian Nationalist publicists like Enrico Corradini, Giuseppe Prezzolini and Giovanni Papini argued that a more authoritarian system would dispose of the compromise, indecisiveness and downright corruption of parliamentary government, permitting a youthful elite of educated nationalists and enterprising capitalists to develop Italy's economy and lead her in an international class war against the plutocratic powers, Britain and France [16 *pp. 97–164; Doc. 1c*].

The ideology and programme of Italian Nationalism displayed a converging of what many of liberalism's critics saw as the two dynamic ideologies and movements of the day: nationalism and socialism. Throughout much of Europe, intellectuals and publicists such as the Frenchman Maurice Barrès, who admired the vigour of both forces while rejecting orthodox, mainly Marxist, socialism, grappled with ways of harmonizing the two, of constructing a 'national' socialism that would bind the working class to the nation, and the rich and powerful, through the nation, to policies that would protect and benefit the lower classes [30]. The attempt took a bewildering variety of forms, some of which will be examined in the next section.

While critics of liberalism from what might loosely be termed the 'right' sought to unite society in the national interest, elements of the prewar left were undergoing an intellectual crisis of their own which was to play its part in sowing the seeds of fascism and giving it much of its distinctive outlook. While some supposedly revolutionary socialists accepted parliamentary liberalism as a necessary and perhaps lengthy stage *en route* to socialism, and others in doing so lost sight of the ultimate goal altogether, still others headed off in a very different direction. In Italy especially, 'revolutionary syndicalists' such as Arturo Labriola began to lose faith not only in the Italian Socialist *party* but also in the working class as an agent of revolution; believing that Italy needed more advanced capitalism before she could even think of socialism, and that the degenerate liberal system was holding back economic progress, they began to look for a 'national' rather than a 'class' revolution [25]. Similar tendencies were apparent within the left elsewhere, most notably in France [32].

While it is necessary to repeat that the currents just examined were all very much *minority* currents within the political and intellectual world of early twentieth-century Europe, their importance was far from negligible. It is now time to look more closely at what happened when they assumed organized political form.

THE 'NEW RIGHT', 1880–1914

With the development of more mass-based politics throughout much of Europe in the last quarter of the nineteenth century, there also emerged a motley of political organizations which, despite the considerable variety that they displayed, may reasonably be classified together as belonging to a 'new right'. What, we must nevertheless ask, placed them on the right, and what was it about them that was new? What, moreover, do they have to do with an understanding of fascism and the events of 1919–45?

The feature that best serves to identify these organizations as belonging on the political right was their rejection both of parliamentary liberalism and of the alternatives offered by the political left, whether reformists, revolutionary Marxists, or anarchists. What, broadly speaking, was 'new' was their embracing of new, popular forms and styles of politics. The new right may not have accepted parliamentary democracy, other than as a weapon to be exploited where possible, but it *did* leave behind traditional conservatism. Earlier forms of resistance to socio-economic, cultural and political change in the nineteenth century had sought to turn back or at least stop the course of history; movements such as French Legitimism, Spanish Carlism and their equivalents in Italy, Portugal and elsewhere had attempted – in all cases unsuccessfully – not merely to restore fallen dynasties and counter the ideological legacies of the French Revolution, but also to reverse or arrest industrialization and the transformation of agriculture and rural life by capitalism [5]. While 'new' right-wing movements – as fascism was to do later – often invoked a usually mythologized past, they also confronted the modern world with ideas and solutions that could not have been dreamed of before the late nineteenth century. Aggressive and 'integral' nationalism, imperialism, 'national socialism', biological anti-semitism and racism – these and other characteristic notions were themselves as much products, or by-products, of a turn-of-the-century environment as those other features that they deplored, combated, and sought to eliminate.

It is probably fair to say that almost every European country between the 1880s and the First World War produced examples of political move-ments, parties, clubs or societies espousing some or other combination of ultra-nationalist, authoritarian, anti-semitic and racist ideas. These took a bewildering variety of forms, and there is space here to do little more than offer some illustrative examples.

In France, authoritarian-nationalist organizations existed from the 1880s onwards, feeding upon a pervasive sense of national grievance following the defeat by Prussia and loss of Alsace-Lorraine in 1870–71. Leagues such as the Ligue des Patriotes of Paul Déroulède played an important part in the patriotic agitation of the 1880s which formed around the charismatic but shallow and indecisive General Boulanger: agitation that seemed, for a time, to threaten the very survival of the Third Republic. The Ligue des Patriotes' collaboration in the Boulangist affair with the left-wing Blanquists (follow-ers of Louis-Auguste Blanqui) offered a genuine foretaste of the kind of alliance that, in different circumstances after the First World War, was to nurture fascism [28]. The strength and fortunes of nationalist leagues like Déroulède's fluctuated wildly over the thirty years before the First World War, responding to the intensely polarized climate of the Dreyfus Affair around the turn of the century and the heightened national sensitivities of the years that followed [35]. By the early 1900s, the organizational leader-ship of the authoritarian right had been assumed by Charles Maurras and Action Française, an 'integral nationalist' and theoretically monarchist movement which, as well as playing the ideological and propagandistic role already referred to, also began to engage, through its youthful *camelots du roi* (king's newsvendors), in violence and intimidation of opponents [34].

Germany and Austria-Hungary, less democratic than France, produced nationalist organizations and agitation of rather different kinds. The domi-nant form in the German Empire was the special interest league: for instance the Agrarian League, the Navy League, the Pan-German League, and, perhaps most significant, the Imperial-German Mittelstand League. As well as pursuing their special interests, often at odds with the mainstream political parties, such organizations were generally authoritarian in outlook, invariably bitterly anti-socialist, and at the very least tinged with antisemitism. By the eve of the First World War, the German extra parlia-mentary right had been radicalized in a manner that, while making nothing inevitable, clearly had an influence on what followed [11]. In Austria, it was the Pan-Germans of Georg von Schönerer who introduced a new style of politics: raucous, socially radical, antisemitic and, through commitment to a greater Germany, hostile to the very survival of the Habsburg Empire. Although over time effectively marginalized by the Austrian establishment, the Pan-Germans' existence and campaigns illustrated the complex relationship of Austro-German nationalism in relation to the multi-national Habsburg Empire and a powerful and nationalistic Germany [6 *pp. 1–29*]. Right-wing radicalism of a different kind – loyally Austrian, ostensibly Catholic in inspiration, populist in style and embracing antisemitism – was represented in prewar Austria by the Christian Social Party, led by the demagogic mayor of Vienna, Karl Lueger [36]. One young Austrian who came to admire Lueger's political style was Adolf Hitler.

The emergence and outlook of the Italian Nationalist movement have already been noted. In 1910 its various elements – clubs, societies, press and individuals – came together to form the Italian Nationalist Association (ANI), which from this time onward represented a new brand of organized political rightism in Italy: elitist, authoritarian, and exalting Italy's supposed expansionist destiny in either the Adriatic and the eastern Mediterranean, north and east Africa, or both. Although the ANI remained very much a minority movement with only gradually increasing interest in building up popular support, its ideological force and its network of contacts and sympathizers within the Italian elite gave it considerable influence and leverage in the years before the First World War [8; *Doc. 1c*]. The same was true, in their respective countries, of Action Française [17; 34]; of the Portuguese nationalist movement Integralismo Lusitano [18]; and in Spain, for a time, of the 'Young Maurists'(Joven Mauristas) who attached themselves to the cause of the conservative leader Antonio Maura [3].

Many right-wing movements in the years before the First World War exhibited some sign of that 'national socialist' impulse referred to earlier, though there were few for which this was the main element. Action Française, chiefly through the activities of a future leader of early French fascism, Georges Valois, made a largely unsuccessful attempt to woo working-class support [20], while a right-wing trade union movement, Les Jaunes (The Yellows), registered rather greater success [22]. The Italian Nationalists, while making much of Italy's supposed 'proletarian' condition and status in the world, and advocating what they occasionally did explicitly term 'national socialism', did little actively to attract workers to their essentially elitist message; for that they would need a *rapprochement* with the revolutionary syndicalist left. Although its full fruition still lay some years in the future, the first serious sign of such a *rapprochement* came in 1915, when extreme rightists and dissident leftists collaborated in the campaigns to push Italy into the Great War. The Fasci de Azione Rivoluzionaria (Revolutionary Action Groups), formed by the interventionist left to agitate for Italy's entry into the war, were the first organizational incarnation of what, four years later, was to become Italian Fascism. One of their most vocal supporters was a former socialist, Benito Mussolini [13].

It was in Austria-Hungary that organized national socialism made most headway before 1914: specifically in German-speaking areas of Czech-dominated Bohemia. Here, German-speaking workers rallied in significant if not overwhelming numbers to a German Workers' Party, the progenitor of many of its kind, and one in particular [6 *pp. 32–9*].

If a quest for national socialism represented one variant within the pre-1914 'new right', another was antisemitism. Inspired by the explosion of antisemitic literature in the Europe of the late nineteenth and early twentieth centuries, openly antisemitic political parties existed at various times between the 1870s and the First World War in Germany, Austria-Hungary and Romania, without establishing any lasting hold; indeed, in Germany and Austria-Hungary their fortunes if anything declined in the years before 1914. This may have had as much to do, however, with the absorption of antisemitism by other, multi-issue right-wing parties, and even by those of the establishment, as with any real decline in the popularity of antisemitism itself [24; 15]. Elsewhere, the antisemitic pogroms of the Russian 'Black Hundreds' [26] and the antisemitic campaigns of Edouard Drumont in France testified to the ability of anti-Jewish agitation to mobilize elements of popular support [17 *pp. 65–116; Doc. 1d*].

In addition to ultra-nationalist, national socialist and antisemitic political parties and movements, prewar Europe also witnessed a proliferation of semi-political societies and organizations, especially aimed at young males, and which blended nationalism with other concerns and obsessions: a worship of physical strength and virility, the extolling of supposedly rural values and virtues, flirtation with mysticism, paganism and the occult, and of course contempt for the value-systems of liberalism, democracy and orthodox socialism. Although such organizations existed in many countries, it was in Germany and the German-speaking parts of the Habsburg Empire that their influence was greatest [31].

It is nevertheless vital to keep a sense of proportion about the existence of what some have termed a 'pre-fascist' climate in pre-1914 Europe. Awareness that such ideas, prejudices and impulses existed in most countries, and that in some they found their way into organized political movements, helps us to understand the fascism of the next generation. Had the intellectual, cultural and political climate of pre-First World War Europe not contained the elements briefly examined here, it is unlikely that fascism as we have come to know it would have emerged after 1918. *Nothing* that happened before 1914, however, made that emergence inevitable or even, in recognizable form, possible. For that – as Italian 'pre-fascists' dimly appreciated – a major convulsion was necessary. That convulsion was the First World War.

PART TWO ANALYSIS

CHAPTER THREE

INTERWAR EUROPE IN CRISIS

Without the kind of preconditions and precursors just examined, fascism, national socialism and other movements of the interwar European right would not have existed in anything like their actual form. Nevertheless it was the First World War and the new world which it created that truly forged fascism out of the primitive prewar ore. The war and the Versailles settlement of 1919 produced winners and losers, destroyed empires, created wholly new states, drastically redrew frontiers, altered the official nationality of whole populations, inflamed and wounded national and ethnic susceptibilities, and shaped the outlook of a generation of European males. In the economic sphere, postwar convulsion was followed in some countries by hyper-inflation, in many by agricultural depression, and then after 1929 by general depression and mass unemployment. These developments occurred, moreover, in the shadow of another event which totally transformed the political perceptions of all Europeans: the Bolshevik revolution of 1917 and the emergence of the Soviet Union as the world's first 'socialist' state. This was the volatile mixture with which the democracies of postwar Europe were compelled to deal – difficult enough for those with deep roots, and still more so for those striving to establish themselves.

It was this self-same mixture that produced fascism – in two senses. First, it provoked a set of intellectual responses which, while drawing on ideas current before 1914, were nevertheless truly of their time. In most parts of Europe sooner or later – and allowing for the important effects of imitation and would-be emulation – right-wing intellectuals and propagandists produced ideological packages which, in varying degrees, combined extreme nationalism; authoritarianism or what came to be known as totalitarianism; ideas of enforced social harmony in the cause of national unity and strength; and in their most visionary forms, notions of national, cultural or racial 'revolution'. Second, it inspired political activists across Europe to form organizations dedicated to the advancement of such ideas and the creation of new-style regimes based upon them. The Italian Fascist movement and party; the National Socialist German Workers' Party

(NSDAP); the Spanish Falange and Portuguese National Syndicalists; the British Union of Fascists; the Romanian Legion and the Hungarian Arrow Cross: these and literally hundreds more of their kind claimed to have the solution to their country's variant of Europe's interwar crisis. The majority found that their message fell on deaf ears; a significant minority exploited it to attract serious popular support; and a much smaller minority were able to use it as a springboard to power.

ECONOMIC TURBULENCE AND SOCIAL CONFLICT

While Marxist interpretations that once sought to explain the nature of fascism in purely socio-economic terms are less fashionable today, any attempted explanation that failed to take the socio-economic circumstances of interwar Europe into account would be of little use. As movements of opposition, fascism and national socialism proffered – among other things of course – solutions to the economic problems of the day, chiefly involving variants of corporativism and state direction of capitalism. In addition, fascism and other right-wing movements promised to eradicate social conflict by introducing, and if necessary imposing, a social order that would be more cohesive and harmonious: variants of what German National Socialism was to term *Volksgemeinschaft* (people's community). As for those who joined such movements (and the larger the movement the truer, probably, this was), they did so at least partly in response to socio-economic pressures. All this in turn needs to be seen within the framework of a wider right-wing response to social conflict and the threat – real, exaggerated or imagined – of 'bolshevism'.

Interwar Europe was battered by a succession of economic challenges and disasters, varying both in character and in social and geographical impact. With the coming of peace, industrialized or industrializing economies that had been transformed by the war were forced to make swift and painful adjustments. This was true not only of belligerent nations like Italy, Germany, France and Britain, whose economies had been distorted by the collapse of normal international trade and the demands of war production, but also of neutrals like Spain and Sweden whose industries (and agriculture), suppliers to both sides, had boomed unnaturally during the conflict, only to face a bleak reality immediately afterwards. Internal and international trade continued to be dislocated for some time after the war's end; millions of troops returned from the various battlefronts with high expectations of reward for their sacrifices and little tolerance of delay; workers who had stayed behind in protected industries found those industries contracting and their jobs threatened or disappearing; profiteers and middle-class speculators who had done well out of the war found themselves under attack.

In much of continental Europe immediate postwar problems gave way to a period, roughly from 1923 to 1925, of acute inflation – indeed in the German case hyper-inflation – which hammered savers and small investors, people on fixed incomes, and the many workers who lacked the trade union muscle to enable them to keep up with price rises. Although measures such as the introduction of the German Rentenmark, the 'Stabilization' in Austria, and the rescue (at a much reduced level) of the French franc caused things to settle down by the mid-1920s [47], many individuals never recovered. The boom of the mid-1920s that followed was short-lived; indeed, by the last third of the decade, much of rural continental Europe was entering what was to be a protracted agricultural depression, marked by collapsing agricultural produce prices, heightened landlord–tenant tensions, and rising rural unemployment. Then came the Great Depression of the 1930s. The collapse in international trade that followed the 1929 Wall Street Crash hit the more advanced industrial democracies, such as Germany and Great Britain, particularly hard, but sooner or later affected every national economy in Europe; indeed, some of those that took longer to show the effects of depression, for example France and Spain, also took longer to recover. And although the effects were uneven, particular economic sectors and individual regions of most countries experienced sharp contraction and rocketing unemployment [37].

The point of this rapid survey of interwar economic problems is not to suggest any direct, causal links between a particular set of problems and fascism. Rather it is to suggest that interwar Europe's unsettled economic climate was a major component of the complex context within which democratic systems struggled to take root or to survive, and out of which fascism emerged and sometimes prospered. The mere existence of democracies throughout most of Europe in the early 1920s and in some countries down into the 1930s allowed economic problems – inflation, industrial and agricultural depression, mass unemployment, etc. – to become matters for public discussion and, increasingly, a stick with which democracy's opponents could beat it. Lurching as it did from hyper-inflation to depression within well under a decade, European capitalism appeared to many contemporaries to be in crisis. Sections of the far left, for a time at least, viewed the traumas of contemporary capitalism as heralding its final collapse [38]. In contrast, the extreme right of almost every European nation offered, in effect, to *save* capitalism through the reordering of the socio-political environment within which it operated. Such a reordering, it may be suggested, would contain four principal elements: the binding and subordination of capitalism to a strong, national state; the reduction of that state's dependence upon international finance and trade; the suppression of the left, seen as 'internationalist', unpatriotic, and subversive; and the replacement of liberal-democracy with some form of authoritarian system – of which fascism was one.

The crushing of the left, and of the democracy which allowed the left free rein, was a crucial component of the extreme right's project, since the social climate of post-1919 Europe was inevitably affected by the repercussions of the Bolshevik revolution. However worrying the advancing left may have appeared to governments, elites, and much of the middle class of *prewar* Europe, this was nothing compared with the situation after 1919. Now, with most countries' industrial work-force vastly expanded during the war, a significant proportion of these workers unionized and an increasing proportion politicized, and the native left either threatening revolution or demanding far-reaching social reforms, a new actor had entered the stage. A great power – and one, moreover, that was already feared by many Westerners as semi-Asiatic – had been revolutionized itself, offered an example to socialists elsewhere, and (until the mid-1930s) made no secret of wishing to spread revolution across the entire continent. Given this changed climate, the social conflicts of interwar Europe inevitably assumed a very different tone from the lesser tensions of the prewar years. In the immediate postwar phase, either revolution or civil war between 'reds' and the right erupted in Germany, Hungary, Finland, the Baltic states and Poland, while conflicts that gave rise to serious fears of revolution occurred in other countries, notably Italy, Austria and Spain. For the whole of eastern Europe, from Finland south to Romania, the sheer physical proximity of the Soviet Union added a power-political dimension to social and ideological conflict.

From our point of view, perhaps the most important implication of the rash of social conflicts affecting postwar Europe was that among establishment groups and social elites they threw into question the capacity of the existing – and in several cases new – governmental and/or state apparatus to uphold the socio-economic *status quo* against the left. This feeling may have been all the greater where a substantial part of the left was openly revolutionary, as in Germany or Spain, but even where it merely pushed hard for social *reform* the reactions it was liable to provoke were not dissimilar. The German revolution of 1919 and the regional communist risings of 1923; the brief Soviet regime of Béla Kun, established in Hungary in 1919; the ambiguous activities between 1919 and 1922 of Italian 'maximalist' socialists, which created fears of revolution without ever seriously approaching it; and in both the early 1920s and the 1930s the militancy and growing strength of the Spanish socialist and anarchist left: such experiences, in the distinctive climate of the interwar years, fostered a 'red scare' mentality that affected many of the continent's rich, powerful and influential. Democracy was accordingly judged on its ability to control socialism and communism, suppress threats of revolution and, just as important, contain social-democratic pressures for reform. Where this ability was in doubt, the first instinct of many conservatives and right-wingers was to look towards a strengthening of the existing state, through the use of presidential or royal authority, the introduction of a military regime, or something similar. In some instances, however, the more radical alternative of a right-wing mass movement presented itself. What tended to distinguish such movements, and especially those deserving of the label 'fascist', in their attitude towards the left was violence and belief in a 'total' solution.

In order for a movement of the far right to exercise any appeal to defenders of the established order, it had of course to possess mass support. Economic difficulties and social conflicts played their part in generating such support where it existed, though not always in a direct way. Let us take just a few examples, from four countries where fascism emerged strongly: Italy, Germany, Romania and Hungary. The social base of Fascism in Italy, while varied, in the vital period of the movement's expansion (1921–22) rested substantially but not exclusively on what can broadly be termed middle-class elements, caught up in a predominantly rural social conflict between the temporarily dominant socialist and (to a lesser extent) Catholic peasant unions and those who were, or felt, displaced or threatened by them. The broad arc of the rural population from which Fascism drew its sustenance comprised larger landowners, lesser rural proprietors and tenant farmers (many of whom had prospered during the war), estate managers, etc., plus sections of the rural working class who, for one reason or another, were excluded from the benefits of socialist advances. Urban fascism embraced members of an emerging 'new' middle class (managerial staff, clerical workers, schoolteachers, and students) who, while hostile towards socialism, resented the closed 'liberal' elites then ruling Italy [46]. In Germany, while the effects of hyper-inflation unquestionably weakened the actual or potential loyalties of many members of the lower middle class towards Weimar democracy, it was the agricultural depression of the later 1920s that gave National Socialism its first major popular boost, chiefly among smallholders and tenant farmers [40]. As for the 1930s depression, unemployment drove more Germans leftwards into the Communist ranks than rightwards, Nazism recruiting proportionately more in almost every other sector of society than among the actual unemployed [42]. Although as their support expanded, the NSDAP and its linked organizations drew from all social classes, *proportionately* its hold on the lower middle class, urban and rural, was always crucial. Two other high-recruiting fascist movements, the Romanian Legion and the Hungarian Arrow Cross, drew support from very different social strata. The Legion was strong among students with poor employment prospects, sections of the urban lower middle class, and most important the vast Romanian peasantry [52]; the Arrow Cross, in a society where the left's activities were severely limited, attracted large-scale support among urban workers who, it may be suggested, might otherwise have been leftists [43].

Further examples, several of which will appear on later pages, would confirm this picture of fascist movements as drawing from a variety of social layers amid conditions of economic difficulty and social tension, the details depending very much on the particular setting. If few common, direct links can be discerned between economic conditions and the social bases of fascist movements, certain broad and important conclusions can be drawn. First, the economic turbulence of the interwar years made life for democracy difficult. Second, it encouraged the formulation and publicizing of alternative solutions to the apparent problems of capitalism and the accompanying challenges of communism and social democracy. Third, it persuaded large numbers of Europeans, ranging from monarchs to the poorest peasant, to place their faith in dictatorship, authoritarianism and sometimes fascism.

STATES, NATIONS AND PEOPLES

The half-century before 1914 had been marked in Europe by a coming together of more popular politics, intensified national and ethnic consciousness, and of course heightened international rivalries and tensions. Initially, at least, many Europeans had viewed the outbreak of war as a welcome release of tension that would resolve the situation in one way or another. Depending largely upon one's nationality and consequent point of view, a short and decisive conflict would, it was hoped, curb German ambitions in Europe or thwart attempts to 'encircle' Germany; it would reward French hopes of 'revanche' for the humiliation at German hands in 1870 or dash them once and for all; it would satisfy nationalist appetites in central and eastern Europe or definitively frustrate them; and so on.

The 'war to end war' certainly transformed Europe, but from the point of view of national feelings and international antagonisms it merely re-placed old problems with new ones. The convulsions which truly began with the Libyan and Balkan wars of 1912–13, continued through the First World War itself and the 1919 peace settlement, and also embraced the frontier struggles provoked by the Russian Revolution, did of course destroy four of the prewar empires whose ambitions, fears and rivalries – together with those of Britain, France and Italy – had helped tear Europe apart. Austria-Hungary and the Ottoman Empire were not only destroyed as *empires* but ceased to exist as states and historical actors; Germany and Russia, however, re-emerged in new incarnations which, in their very different ways, threatened the continent with renewed instability: Germany as a new, territorially truncated and vulnerable democratic republic, Russia as a revolutionized and revolutionary Soviet state with insecure western borders.

Germany's treatment at Versailles is a question of never-ending historiographical debate, the details of which are not our concern. All that needs to be said here is that the presence after 1919 of substantial German-speaking minorities in neighbouring states, the creation of a 'Polish Corridor' dividing East Prussia from the rest of Germany, the ban on union with a now totally ethnic-German Austria, and the general sense of grievance caused by reparations and the notion of Germany's 'war guilt' virtually ensured future trouble unless other factors – social, economic and political – proved extraordinarily conducive towards stable domestic politics and international peace. They did not. As early as 1920 Germany witnessed a foretaste of what was to come with the Kapp Putsch, an attempted seizure of power supported by paramilitary right-wing squads known as *Freikorps* (free corps). Although unsuccessful, the rising demonstrated the existence of intransigent right-wing elements and the potency of national grievance as a stimulus to anti-republican action in Germany [41 *pp. 67–74*].

'Revisionist' urges were also to affect the internal politics and international relations of two more of 1919's 'losers', the new Austrian Republic and what was officially the 'kingdom' of Hungary. Like the Germany of the Weimar Republic these were rumps of a former empire, overwhelmingly dominated by one ethnic group, and with populations many of whom found it hard to accept the new state of affairs. In both countries forms of fascism, the paramilitary groups collectively known as *Heimwehren* in Austria and so-called 'Szeged fascism' in Hungary, fed upon the sense of territorial loss and national humiliation, and on resentment against Slavs and Jews.

Another 'loser', subjectively if not officially, was Italy. Although actually on the winning side in the war, Italy was rewarded far less generously in 1919 than seemed fair to most Italian patriots, who embraced the myth of 'mutilated victory' as zealously as their German counterparts did those of the 'stab in the back' and the 'Versailles *diktat*'. The product, a new ultra-nationalist politics within an untried and shaky mass democracy, appeared as soon as the war itself ended. Its first dramatic expression was the seizure of the unredeemed port of Fiume by the poet-adventurer Gabriele D'Annunzio and a handful of war veterans [44]; a second, overshadowed at first by D'Annunzio's colourful exploits but later to overtake him, was the birth, in Milan in March 1919, of fascism.

The most obvious gainers from the re-drawing of the European map between 1912 and 1919 were the new or reborn nations carved (in most cases) out of the four vanished empires: Finland, Estonia, Latvia, Lithuania, Poland, Czechoslovakia, Yugoslavia and Albania. (Another new country, the Irish Free State, emerged out of an admittedly different process, though its birth might reasonably be regarded as the first stage in the dissolution of a fifth empire, that of Britain.) Their creation testified to the employment at Versailles of that principle of 'national self-determination' to which

President Woodrow Wilson was so attached. In practice, however, political realities, the desire to punish the 'guilty', and the intractable, kaleidoscopic complexities of eastern European ethnic distribution ensured that every new nation was born with ethnic minorities inside its borders, 'unredeemed' territory beyond them, or in some cases both. Now that most European states founded their legitimacy upon the nationality of their people, and in view of the continued currency of the 'national self-determination' idea, the salience of nationalist politics here, too, was guaranteed. A few examples, whose relationship with fascism will be explored in Chapter 4, will suffice to illustrate the point. Czechoslovakia and Yugoslavia, multi-ethnic states based on fragile notions of shared 'slavdom', were born with innate ethnic tensions, in both cases overlapping with religious ones, which threatened their very existence and encouraged extreme and conflicting interpretations of ethnicity and nationality. This was especially true among those peoples, Slovaks and Croats respectively, who rightly or wrongly felt themselves second-class citizens within the new state. No devisable set of frontiers could create an ethnically homogeneous, 'satisfied' Poland, or solve the minority problems of the Baltic states. Many Finns, celebrating their new nationhood, resented a long-established, culturally important Swedish minority and yearned to acquire more land in what was now Soviet-ruled Karelia.

Other, longer-established eastern European countries also gained from the demise of the Ottoman and Habsburg empires, but in ways that threw up new challenges. Greece and Romania (and to a much lesser extent Bulgaria, despite being on the losing side in the Second Balkan War and the First World War) emerged from the struggles of 1912–19 with greatly expanded frontiers and increased populations. Greece acquired extensive new territories in Epirus, Macedonia and Thrace, and then after 1922 was forced to try to absorb and assimilate over a million 'Asiatic' Greek refugees who arrived following Greece's disastrous Asia Minor campaign and defeat at the hands of a reborn Turkey. Romania vastly increased its area in 1919, chiefly through the acquisition of Transylvania at the expense of Austria-Hungary, gaining in the process large Hungarian and German minorities which were difficult to assimilate. The preoccupation of nationalistic Romanians with culturally 'Romanizing' the country's population also incorporated and aggravated an already virulent antisemitism, directed against Romania's substantial Jewish community [45].

Throughout most of eastern Europe, therefore, politics from the early 1920s became bound up with the need to assimilate new areas and populations, and to define and assert national identity and interests. Such priorities were seldom easy to harmonize with the 'head-counting' of parliamentary democracy – especially since that democracy was almost everywhere new and unfamiliar.

In western and northern Europe – from Portugal and Spain, through France and Switzerland, to Britain, the Benelux countries and Scandinavia (except for Finland) – the kind of conditions just discussed were mostly absent. Victory or neutrality in the war, together with national borders that were mostly well-established and secure, weakened even if it did not extinguish the ultra-nationalist 'edge' that characterized public life further east. Two partial exceptions need to be noted, however. In Spain the continued rise of 'minority' nationalism, notably in Catalonia and the Basque country, in theory at least threatened the country's integrity and perhaps even existence; not only was this supposed threat one of several preconditions for the establishment of military dictatorship between 1923 and 1930, but when mass democracy finally arrived in 1931, it was to help provoke an alternative *Spanish* (or Castilian) nationalism that in turn infused the Spanish version of fascism, Falangism [39]. In Belgium during the interwar period the delicate equilibrium between Flemings and Francophone Walloons on which the state was built, and which was tested by the differential impact of the 1930s depression, stimulated varieties of ultra-nationalism which, even if not actually threatening the country's unity, did present it with a serious challenge. Here too, as we shall see, fascism and its right-wing fellow-travellers were to feed on nationalist susceptibilities in a climate of popular politics and socio-economic difficulty [51].

To sum up: after 1919, for the first time throughout most of Europe, the advent of truly mass politics coincided with the general acceptance of ethnicity and nationality as the basis of the state. This occurred at a time when many states were new creations while others were affected by territorial or political transformation. Almost all had to grapple with new and provisional constitutional and/or political arrangements, some were aggrieved at their treatment in 1919, and many faced the possibility of left-wing revolution. It was therefore hardly surprising that a major ingredient of politics after 1919 should be a new, or renewed, populist nationalism.

DEMOCRACY IN DIFFICULTIES

During the generation before 1914, as we have seen, a fundamental question in European politics had been whether *liberal* systems of constitutional government, mostly still dominated by relatively narrow and privileged elites and some of them actually semi-authoritarian in character, could develop peacefully into mature *democracies*. After 1919 this question yielded to a new one, that of whether the mass democracies that suddenly were the norm in Europe could survive the challenges facing them. Could they, if new like the Weimar and Austrian republics, achieve the general acceptance that would give them legitimacy and the capacity for long-term survival? Could they, if longer established like the French Third Republic or

British liberal democracy, retain their vigour? And could they, regardless of age, deal effectively with the barrage of problems the postwar world threw at them? The majority, it transpired, could not, and in their failure to do so fascism had a part to play. In many cases it was as little more than a symptom of wider problems; in other cases it was also a direct or indirect agent of that failure; in a few, fascism as a regime was the *outcome*.

Although this could scarcely have been predicted much before the end of the war, Europe west of the Soviet Union entered the 1920s as at least superficially a democratic continent. Because – largely thanks to the late intervention of the United States – the First World War was won by democracies, with its chief casualties the more authoritarian central and eastern European empires, the early 1920s saw a fleeting 'vogue for democracy' throughout Europe which was not to be equalled until the end of the 1980s. All the new states of central and eastern Europe began their lives with liberal democratic constitutions and institutions, while several of those in the west broadened the suffrage or reformed their electoral system in the aftermath of the war. Germany resurfaced as a republic, with unprecedentedly democratic electoral and political structures; the new Austrian Republic was launched on its journey via an unlikely and quickly doomed coalition between the country's Socialists and the Catholic, right-wing Christian Social Party; Italy found itself wrestling not only with universal male suffrage but also with proportional representation and mass political parties; Britain gave votes to women; new-born Estonia was for a time perhaps the most formally democratic country in Europe.

It is self-evident that any new, would-be democratic regime must be, so to speak, 'on trial' for a considerable period during which its leaders seek to ensure its popular acquiescence and general legitimacy. By virtue of the very fact that democracies allow criticism and dissent, such regimes are clearly vulnerable to scrutiny and criticism extending beyond mere *issues* or the acceptability of a particular *government*, to embrace *the regime itself* and the principles upon which it is based. In all the countries of central and eastern Europe – that is, from Germany, Austria and Italy eastward – such acceptance and legitimacy proved elusive in the early postwar period, and indeed after. To the intrinsic difficulties of establishing a new juridic, constitutional and in many cases territorial order were added the socioeconomic problems already referred to, issues of national honour and identity, and the reality or threat of left-wing revolution. Economic, social and political issues quickly came to be considered in terms not simply of *how* a country's democratic institutions might tackle them but often of *whether* democracy was up to the task at all. Many clearly believed it was not, seeing it (rightly or wrongly) as characterized by hesitation and delay, talk in place of action, compromise rather than principle, deals in smoke-filled rooms, corruption and weakness. And, of course, once European democracies *began* to fall – Italy's in 1922, Spain's in 1923, Portugal's, Poland's and Lithuania's in 1926, Yugoslavia's in 1929 – authoritarian alternatives started to become increasingly fashionable, and the threat to those democracies that remained all the greater.

Lack of confidence in, and commitment to, democracy was understandably greatest where it had come suddenly at the end of the war, and especially where this was linked with defeat and/or national disappointment: such was the case with the Weimar Republic, the Austrian First Republic, the 'kingdom' of Hungary, and newly democratized Italy. Here and throughout much of eastern Europe – even where democracy had arrived with the achievement of independent nationhood – old 'liberal' or authoritarian elites retained much socio-economic power and underlying political influence, surrendering or agreeing to share open political power in 1918–20 reluctantly and without conviction. The officer corps of armies, high-level civil servants, captains of industry, financial magnates, rural estate-owners, church leaders, conservative politicians, and even monarchs: these were in many parts of Europe the forces which held the fate of democratic institutions in their hands. Their actions could be decisive: where, as in Finland, profoundly anti-leftist, conservative politicians and generals opted, at a crucial moment in 1932, to uphold democracy rather than help fascism overturn it, democracy survived. In many other instances, however, conservative interests acted not as the defenders of democracy but as its gravediggers.

Although in much of Europe conservatives of an authoritarian temper were perfectly capable of subverting and overthrowing democracy without assistance or competition from right-wing mass movements, these often did have to be taken into account. From the very start of the 1920s, and increasingly as the decade progressed, the European political stage began to witness the entry of new parties and movements which, while exploiting to the full the opportunities that liberal democracy and mass politics gave them, made no secret of their desire to replace democracy with some form of ultra-nationalist dictatorship. The first of these to win power was the Italian Fascist movement; hence most of those that followed, even if they did not formally assume the label 'fascist', drew clear inspiration from the Italian model and were regarded by their critics as belonging to the same family. For conservatives suspicious of, or downright hostile to, democracy, right-wing mass movements were often a source of some confusion: potential allies against the common enemies of liberalism and Marxism, yet worrying by virtue of their plebeian elements, raucous and sometimes violent behaviour, and often anti-establishment rhetoric. As for the actual supporters of democracy – genuine liberals, social democrats, progressive Catholics – they often, as in Italy between 1919 and 1922 and throughout much of the history of Weimar Germany, did it a disservice through (for example) their failure to co-operate in the face of its enemies [46; 49].

Although the novelty of the postwar situation may have been most glaring in central and eastern Europe, established institutions further west were challenged or questioned too. In Spain and Portugal, much as in Italy, liberal political systems faced a fast-changing political environment and the challenge of a broader-based politics than had existed before the war. Spain's disintegrating liberal political system, under critical assault from all sides, came close to collapse in 1917, by the early 1920s was plainly living on borrowed time, and succumbed to a military *coup d'état* in September 1923 [48 *pp. 187–207*]. Portugal's desperately unstable and financially chaotic First Republic, founded only in 1910, was similarly overturned by the military in May 1926 [53]. Even Britain and France, along with Italy the chief European 'victors' of 1914–18, found their existing political systems under strain, though this was more evident amid the depression of the 1930s than during the 1920s [50]. Nevertheless it is both clear and unsurprising that, roughly speaking, those liberal democracies already established or evolving smoothly before 1914 proved most resilient after 1919: Britain, France, Switzerland, the Benelux countries and the countries of Scandinavia.

The problems of the 1920s proved sufficient to undermine democracy throughout much of Europe, and in several countries brought about either its overthrow, as in Italy, Spain and Portugal, or its weakening in favour of a kind of semi-authoritarianism, as in Poland, Lithuania and Yugoslavia. The 1930s brought a 'second wave' of assaults on the democracies that remained – and on the one new democracy, established in 1931 against the general European trend: the Spanish Second Republic. The onset of agricultural depression in the late 1920s and then of general depression following the Wall Street Crash in 1929 contributed massively to the paralysis, subversion and eventual overthrow of democracy in Germany, Austria and Spain, and gave rise to problems that threatened its stability and even survival elsewhere. By this time, of course, 'fascism' and dictatorship had become more than mere *alternatives* to democracy: as well as being suggested cures for the supposed shortcomings of democracy, they themselves had become one of its major problems.

CHAPTER FOUR

FASCIST AND RIGHT-WING MOVEMENTS, 1919–1939

In Chapters 2 and 3, it has been suggested that many of the *ideas* now associated with fascism were born in response to the problems of pre-1914 'liberal' Europe and, appropriately developed and refined, given a new relevance in the very different Europe forged by the First World War, the Versailles settlement, and the Russian Revolution. The Europe of 1890–1914, however, for reasons that have been explored, had seen neither truly formidable mass movements of the far right nor, with unimportant exceptions, dictatorships of the kinds that proliferated in the 1920s and 1930s. This chapter examines the emergence of fascist and right-wing *movements* between the two world wars, their successes and failures, and considers the place of *fascism* within the wider spectrum of the European interwar anti-democratic right.

THE ITALIAN MODEL: THE FASCIST MOVEMENT AND PARTY, 1919–1925

Fascism, in the form of a political movement named the Fasci di Combattimento (Combat Groups), was born in Milan in March 1919. In its early form it was the product of the prewar intellectual ferment on both the right and the left of the Italian political spectrum, of the political fissures created by Italy's interventionist crisis in 1914–15, and most of all of the wartime experience itself. During the war, the apostate socialist Mussolini, in his newspaper *Il Popolo d'Italia*, had conceived of a postwar revolution made by the 'productive forces' of a society hitherto dominated by parasitism. More particularly, it would be a revolution of the 'trenchocracy': that generation of mainly young (and of course male) Italians whose experiences in battle, or even as mere supporters of the war-effort, had instilled in them a respect for heroism and comradeship, and filled them with contempt for both the old, liberal political order and the materialistic alternative offered by the orthodox, mainly Marxist, left [110].

Most of the hundred-odd Italians who met to found the new movement were veterans of the war, or the interventionist struggles, or both. Many, like Mussolini himself, were former militants of the left, still revolutionaries in their own minds, or, like the Futurists of Filippo Marinetti, apostles of cultural revolt. Their new movement was launched as a self-consciously radical affair; its early pronouncements, while not conventionally socialist, called for measures scarcely less radical than those advocated by all but the most left-wing of the Italian Socialist Party – a republic, land reform, the confiscation of war profits, etc. [*Doc. 2a*]. Without question, the few thousands of Italians, mostly in Milan and the urban north, who joined the *fasci* during 1919 thought in terms of a radical, patriotic alternative to orthodox socialism. This early version of Fascism was a dismal failure, however; at the general election in November 1919 the Fascists were humiliated, above all in their 'stronghold', Milan, where they won a mere 5,000 votes out of some 275,000 cast; worse, the victors there were their deadly rivals, the Socialists [99].

During the winter of 1919–20 Fascism struggled to survive. It did so in part thanks to the support of wealthy Milanese businessmen who recognized its potential as an *anti*-socialist, rather than an alternative socialist, movement, and then, as 1920 wore on, to a marked change of direction. During 1920–21, Fascism emerged as a virulently anti-leftist movement, albeit one with radical pretensions of its own. The shift was most marked in the countryside of Italy's most conflictive postwar regions, Emilia-Romagna and Tuscany. Here, Socialist unions and co-operatives and Catholic peasant leagues had assumed considerable power, with socialism in particular threatening the position of the large landowning *agrari* and the status of a rural middle class consisting of leaseholders, estate managers, richer peasants and technocrats. It was in the cities and large towns of these regions (Bologna, Ferrara, Florence, etc.) that urban Fascists formed the armed 'squads' which then undertook punitive expeditions into the countryside, destroying physically the installations and organizations of the rural left, and inflicting violence and personal humiliation upon its militants [62].

Between the later part of 1920 and the March on Rome in late October 1922, Fascism developed into a mass movement several hundred thousand strong. Although weak throughout much of southern Italy (the southeastern region of Puglia being a notable exception [103]), it was vigorous across much of the north and centre, especially in regions where social conflict had been acute both before and after the war. Its sociological core was without question the lower middle class, both urban and rural. It was not, however, simply a question, as Marxists argued both at the time and later, of a lower middle class threatened with 'proletarianization' amid the economic uncertainties of postwar Italy; just as important was a desire for betterment, or for social and political power consonant with better education and fatter wallets, of all of which the decrepit liberal system seemed to many Italians to deprive them. Fascism continued to appeal for working-class support, both urban and rural, at the very time it was destroying working-class organizations. Initially unsuccessful, it began to recruit some workers as its strength increased: some resentful of the monopolistic activities of the Socialists, many more desperate for the protection and job opportunities once offered by their own unions but now available only via the Fascists' alternatives. Truly spontaneous working-class support, however, was unimpressive [54].

The Fascist movement, once it adopted a militant anti-socialist strategy, grew so fast that neither its structure nor its programme was anything like clear. Although from the start Mussolini occupied the position of overall leader, for much of the time initiative remained at provincial or even local level, and much of the real day-to-day power was exercised by local bosses or *Ras*: Italo Balbo of Ferrara, Roberto Farinacci of Cremona, Dino Grandi and Leandro Arpinati of Bologna, etc. Quite what Fascism meant to those who freely committed themselves to its rank and file was not always evident, even to them. For many, certainly, there was little more to it than anti-socialism, a sense of male comradeship, and a taste for physical violence. Others, more thoughtful, did nurse ideas of a 'revolution' that would crush the left, sweep away a 'decadent' liberal regime, and introduce a system characterized by classlessness and decisive leadership. Many of those whose journey to Fascism had begun on the left hoped for a radical, if 'national', revolution which would control and direct capital, harnessing the energies of labour in a programme of economic modernization that now replaced socialism at the head of their wish-list [25].

Thousands of rank-and-file Fascists certainly shared with Mussolini an emotional radicalism from which much of their movement's distinctive character was derived, and which boiled down to two closely connected elements: resentment of the rich, powerful and privileged who upheld and sheltered behind the existing liberal regime, together with rejection of the alternative radicalism offered by the Socialist left, with its class analysis, economic determinism and unforgivable lack of patriotism. Fascists were often critical of the way capitalism worked, especially on a financial level, but seldom of capitalism itself; rejecting the Socialists' negative view of private property, they had no alternative *but* to accept a broadly capitalist view of economy and society. Other pillars of the established order, for example the monarchy, the aristocracy and the Catholic Church, began as targets of Fascist vitriol, only to become less so as the possibility of power became real and it became necessary to confront the question of how it might actually be achieved [100].

During the course of 1921, Fascism firmly assumed a position on the right of the conventional political spectrum. In March, Mussolini committed his movement to a conservative electoral alliance with liberal forces; the outcome was a group of thirty-five Fascist deputies who, on entering the Chamber of Deputies, took their seats on the extreme right. In November, Fascism became for the first time a formal political *party*, the Partito Nazionale Fascista (PNF), with a programme very different from that of 1919: one that, for example, accepted the previously rejected monarchy. What was becoming clear was that even if Fascism nursed revolutionary dreams of what to do with power, its leaders recognized that power was unlikely to be won *against* the forces of the Italian establishment [66 *pp. 18–37*; *Doc. 7a*].

And so it proved. Fortunately for Mussolini and Fascism, much of that establishment decided during 1922 that Fascism deserved the governmental role that Mussolini was now demanding – indeed, that a brief administering of Fascist 'muscle' might be just the thing that Italian politics and society needed. Although the manner of Fascism's achievement of power was ambiguous, involving a large measure of pseudo-revolutionary rhetoric and sheer bluster, symbolized by the essentially celebratory 'March on Rome' itself, the crucial element was the acquiescence of so many liberal politicians, the military leadership and the king, Victor Emmanuel III. At the end of October 1922 Mussolini was prime minister of a coalition government, soon to be voted emergency powers.

At this stage, it is doubtful if anyone in Italy had much idea as to what a Mussolini-led future would hold. The conservative forces who had allowed him to assume the premiership, and who until it was too late retained but shrank from using the power to unseat him, tended to see Fascism as a temporary phenomenon, at its best a youthful, vigorous force that would inject 'health' into a sick system, complete its emasculation of labour and the organized left, and then be either discarded or, in timeworn Italian fashion, 'transformed' within a reinvigorated, perhaps rather more authoritarian, liberal system. Among those beguiled by this 'normalization' scenario were many of the liberal politicians and local political potentates whose bumbling failure to adjust to the new, popular, postwar politics had done so much to vacate 'political space' for Fascism [64 *pp. 41–57*].

If, in retrospect, Italian establishment figures appear to have been naïve in their relations with Fascism, two things must be acknowledged in partial extenuation: first, that the movement's explosive rise and achievement of power were utterly novel phenomena, for dealing with which no obvious lessons were available from the recent history of either Italy or any other European country (something that cannot be said of German conservatives' similar but far more serious misjudgement a decade later); and, secondly, that not even the Italian Fascists themselves knew at this stage where Fascism was heading. The movement between 1922 and 1925 was actually a complex and fluid coalition, within which it is possible to identify at least six significant strands: (i) the former *squadristi* and their leaders, the *Ras*, who, while often vague about the ultimate purpose of Fascism, generally sought a 'revolutionary' takeover of political power by themselves and the mainly lower-middle-class interests they crudely represented; (ii) what might be termed the Fascist 'left': mostly renegade anarchists or revolutionary syndicalists such as Michele Bianchi and Edmondo Rossoni, who hoped Fascism would introduce a 'national syndicalist' regime capable of arousing and channelling popular enthusiasm and energy; (iii) intellectuals, middle-class professionals and 'technocrats' such as Giuseppe Bottai, who wished to put aside violence and use Fascism as an elitist vehicle for the modernization of Italy; (iv) the Nationalists, who threw in their lot with Fascism in 1923, determined to guide it on a statist, pro-capitalist, and imperialist course; (v) conservative bandwagon jumpers, among them many southern large landowners and professionals, who chiefly sought to protect the socio-economic *status quo*, preferably through at least partial 'normalization' but if necessary via outright authoritarianism; and (vi) a small but determined clique of 'clerico-fascists', refugees from the right wing of the Popular Party who wished to inject Fascism with a Catholic spirit and reunite Church and state within an authoritarian Italy [94].

Whatever remained uncertain, what quickly did become clear was Mussolini's determination to hang on to power by whatever means proved most advantageous. And if he initially hesitated to pursue a full-scale political revolution, the dynamics of events and of the movement he led eventually propelled him in that direction. Between October 1922 and the end of 1924 Mussolini walked a tightrope between an establishment suspicious of Fascist maximalism, eager in theory for eventual 'normalization' yet fearful of what over-hasty normalization might bring; and an expanding, hard-to-control Fascist party most of whose leading figures wanted some kind of 'second wave', some kind of 'Fascist revolution' [86]. During the winter of 1922–23 Mussolini formally unified the unruly squads into a national Fascist militia, the MSVN (Voluntary Militia for National Security), and established a Fascist Grand Council to govern the PNF, thereby going some way towards creating a more disciplined party and hinting at a future one-party state. The privileging of Fascism was further enhanced in July 1923 with the passing of the Acerbo electoral law, whereby a party or alliance winning a bare plurality of votes would be presented with two-thirds of the seats in parliament; at the ensuing general election in April 1924, the official, Fascist-led list won 66 per cent of the votes and returned 374 out of 535 parliamentary seats. Although results in Milan and Turin demonstrated stubbornly surviving left-wing loyalties despite all that Fascism had done to eradicate them, there and more particularly in the south, where once-liberal electoral managers now rigged the polls in Fascism's favour, liberalism was visibly crumbling as Fascism advanced.

Fascism's electoral triumph ignited a crisis that threatened its fall, but instead ended with Italy's becoming the dictatorship for which many Fascists yearned. When parliament reconvened, opposition deputies loudly criticized the *squadrista* violence and intimidation that had accompanied the elections. In June 1924 one of Fascism's most vociferous parliamentary critics, the independent socialist deputy Giacomo Matteotti, was murdered by Fascist thugs. When, two months later, Matteotti's body was discovered and the murderers exposed, Mussolini's moral if not actual guilt was clear. Amid a rising tide of anti-Fascist feeling, most socialist, Catholic, democratic and, eventually, liberal opposition deputies abandoned parliament in protest: the so-called 'Aventine secession'. Had the king demanded Mussolini's resignation at this point, the panic-stricken premier would probably have surrendered. As in 1922, however, the king and his conservative supporters preferred Fascism to any immediately available alternative – partly from fear of a left-wing revival, partly perhaps from fear of orchestrated violence from Fascism itself, and partly out of hope of reasserting their influence over Mussolini at this moment of weakness. The opposition was thus rendered impotent and Mussolini survived as prime minister. Now, however, he faced virtual mutiny in his own ranks. The former *Ras*, now known as 'Consuls', insisted that the crisis demonstrated the need, not for concessions to the opposition, but for its permanent suppression. In December 1924 they collectively demanded that Mussolini either move towards the implementation of the 'Fascist revolution' of which the March on Rome had been only the first stage, or step down as leader of Fascism. This was a challenge that Mussolini could not face down, and on 3 January 1925 he announced to the complaisant rump of the Italian parliament that a new age of dictatorship was about to dawn.

The history of the Italian Fascist movement and party between 1919 and the start of 1925 demonstrates that Fascism, while by 1922 a numerically powerful movement with genuinely spontaneous sources that has to be understood in its own terms, could neither win nor retain power save with the acquiescence of established, essentially conservative, forces: the Crown, the Vatican and the Catholic Church, the armed forces, big landowners, and substantial sectors of heavy industry and banking. The character of the Fascist *regime*, which will be examined later, would inevitably be affected by the developing relationship between the Fascist *movement* itself and these established interests.

In any case, and to complicate matters further, the Fascist movement as we have seen comprised not one strand but many, their members united chiefly by shared contempt for the liberal political *status quo* and its personnel, antagonism towards the Marxist left and its 'materialistic' notions, and a passionate nationalism. Which of these strands would assert themselves most successfully within the new regime introduced in January 1925 was by no means self-evident at the start.

THE GERMAN VARIANT: THE NSDAP, 1919–1933

As the Italian Fascist movement was moving remarkably swiftly to power and then to the construction of a new kind of state, in Germany a movement similar in some ways but quite distinct in others was pursuing power via its own, very different paths. German National Socialism as a *movement*, like Italian Fascism, was the product of the war and the postwar climate, but drew its ideological sustenance – arguably more substantial than that of Mussolini's movement – from the radical nationalism, 'German socialism', and racial antisemitism of the prewar era.

The German Workers' Party (DAP) was founded in Munich early in 1919, just one of over seventy such organizations formed in the febrile political atmosphere of post-Armistice Germany. In all probability the DAP, created by a journalist, Karl Harrer, and a railway toolmaker, Anton Drexler, would like many of these groups have been consigned to historical insignificance had it not been joined in September 1919 by an obscure Austrian corporal, Adolf Hitler. In 1919 Hitler, unlike the former high-profile socialist Mussolini in 1919, was a political unknown. Having fought for Germany in the war with modest distinction, he was now beginning to establish himself in the reactionary climate of postwar Munich as an effective ultra-nationalist speaker. Ordered by the Bavarian military authorities to investigate and report on the DAP's activities and outlook, Hitler was unimpressed by the party as it stood but grasped its potential as a vehicle for his own political dream of helping to resurrect a fallen Germany. Once in the DAP Hitler soon became its star, thanks to a carefully practised and rapidly maturing oratorical skill. As the party expanded in and around Munich, Hitler's influence within it grew also. During 1920 he was instrumental in changing its name to the National Socialist German Workers' Party (NSDAP), and played a leading role in drafting the 'Twenty-Five Points' which formed, and were to remain, its basic (though much ignored and contradicted) programme [*Doc. 2b*]. In 1921, driving out or marginalizing the DAP's founders and early leaders, he became the NSDAP's chairman and undisputed leader. By 1923 the party's ranks numbered well over 50,000, mostly youthful, ultra-nationalist war veterans and members of the lower middle class. A notable degree of mainly passive sympathy was also forthcoming from elements of Bavaria's deeply conservative social, political and military establishment, deliberately wooed by Hitler. Although beginning to extend its activities into other regions, the party was still by 1923 predominantly Munich-based [59].

As yet Hitler saw himself, not so much as the future saviour and *Führer* (leader) of Germany, as the 'drummer' for a movement of national revival more likely to be headed by a respected military figure. The party's strategy at this stage, in so far as it can be said to have had one, was conspiratorial and insurrectionary – in keeping with the volatile and violent socio-political climate of Germany between 1918 and 1923. In November 1923 Hitler accordingly led his party into an apparent attempt to emulate Mussolini's March on Rome, the ill-fated Munich 'Beer-Hall Putsch' [73]. The *putsch* was easily crushed; abandoned by the Bavarian elites for whose support he had hoped, Hitler was arrested, tried by a largely sympathetic court, found guilty of treason, and jailed. During his absurdly brief imprisonment, Hitler occupied his time writing his political statement, *Mein Kampf* (My Struggle), and holding court to admirers both within and outside the party [77].

The 1923 *putsch* represents the end of the first phase in the NSDAP's history, and in what later became immortalized as the *Kampfzeit*, the 'period of struggle'. Hitler's imprisonment and the ineffectual interim leadership of the racial ideologist Alfred Rosenberg temporarily extinguished the NSDAP as a significant force. Rather as with Italian Fascism following its near-collapse at the end of 1919, however, Hitler's early release from prison was followed in 1925 by a re-foundation of the party and a pronounced shift of direction. Although throughout the later 1920s the NSDAP may have struggled electorally, organizationally and tactically it was so transformed as to be able to grasp the opportunities presented after 1929 by renewed economic and political crisis. During this period the party (i) became for the first time truly *national*; (ii) abandoned the failed insurrectionary road to power in favour of an electoral one; (iii) replaced a mainly urban recruitment and electoral strategy with a broader-based appeal which met with particular success in rural and small-town Germany; (iv) assumed the organizational shape which carried it into the 1930s and, indeed, into power; (v) developed unprecedentedly sophisticated propaganda techniques; (vi) absorbed most of its closest rivals to become the dominant force on the far right of German politics; and, crucially, (vii) fell squarely and irreversibly under the spell and control of Hitler, whose personality cult as Führer now became central to the NSDAP's message and popular appeal. Party membership rose during this period from around 50,000 in 1926 (somewhat less than before the Munich *putsch*), to over 100,000 in 1928, and 175,000 in 1929. By the latter year, the movement's main paramilitary body, the Sturmabteilung (SA), numbered around 100,000 [79].

This organizational transformation might still have counted for little had the economic improvement and consequent political stabilization of the mid-1920s lasted into the next decade. Beyond its actual membership the party's appeal remained limited: at the May 1928 general election, the NSDAP polled only 810,000 votes (2.6 per cent) nationwide, returning a mere dozen deputies to the Reichstag; even though in some depressed, mainly rural, areas such as Schleswig-Holstein its showing was much stronger [111], there was little sign that within two years it would be a truly national force.

This situation was transformed by an agricultural recession which began to bite seriously during 1928, the general economic depression which hit Germany quickly and hard in the wake of the Wall Street Crash of October 1929, and the deep crisis of government and state into which the country then sank. For almost three years from March 1930, as businesses collapsed and unemployment rocketed, parliamentary government was effectively suspended as successive chancellors – Bruning of the Catholic Zentrum (Centre Party), another conservative Catholic, Papen, and an army general, Schleicher – governed by decree according to Article 48 of the Weimar constitution. At the general election of September 1930, unnecessarily called by Bruning, the Nazi vote shot up to 18.3 per cent. On the back of this success, and against the background of continuing depression and political crisis, the Nazi advance accelerated. At the presidential election of February 1932, Hitler, running (after much hesitation) against the aged, conservative-nationalist president, Hindenburg, polled over 11 million votes (30.1 per cent) in the first round and well over 13 million (36.8 per cent) in the run-off round a month later. This figure closely foreshadowed the NSDAP vote (over 8 million: 36 per cent) in the Prussian Landtag elections of April 1932, and its success in the general election of July 1932, when it obtained 13,745,000 votes (37.3 per cent) and returned 230 deputies, making it the largest party in the Reichstag. Hitler's electoral strategy, adopted following the 1923 fiasco and so unsuccessful for so long, was finally bearing sensational fruit [75; 60].

Electoral success, however, did not guarantee political power for a party openly committed to destroying the parliamentary system – especially when, at another general election in November 1932, the NSDAP's fortunes went into reverse, the loss of 2 million votes and thirty Reichstag seats indicating that Nazism's advance was not after all irresistible. While what remained of Weimar democracy may now have been doomed and an authoritarian outcome of some kind inevitable, a Nazi takeover certainly was not. What made it possible were the machinations of conservative politicians and generals, and the complaisance of influential economic interests that Hitler had been courting since 1930 [*Doc. 7b*]. Even when, at the end of January 1933, Hitler was given the chancellorship in a mainly conservative government, these groups mostly considered they had, in Papen's words, 'hired' him. Even more than the Italian establishment figures who had wrongly assumed they could use and then discard Mussolini, the German elites who opened the way to Hitler and the Nazis gravely misunderstood and underestimated the force with which they were flirting [113; 90]. It is now time to look at that force more closely.

In its DAP days, and later as illustrated by the Twenty-Five Points, the NSDAP shared with Italian Fascism something of an 'alternative socialist' outlook, following its early economic ideologue, Gottfried Feder, in concen-

trating its assaults on finance capital, large companies (which it threatened
to nationalize) and unearned income. This raucous social radicalism, which
clearly distinguished Nazism from the conservative rightists of the German
Nationalist Party (DNVP), remained an important strand within Nazism
down to 1933 and beyond. For some Nazis, notably the Strasser brothers,
Otto and Gregor, and for many members of the movement's main paramilitary arm, the SA, it was central to National Socialism's existence, a
means of contesting and overcoming the left's grip on the working class.
Nor was Nazism's appeal to sections of the working class remotely a
failure. Though its inroads were very modest before 1930, and largely confined to the membership of the SA, after 1930 working-class party membership and voting support were far from negligible; since the working class
was of course much the most numerous class, even a relatively low proportion of working-class membership and support produced significant
numbers of working-class adherents and voters. Proportionately speaking,
however, Nazism was more successful in appealing to the working class in
smaller Protestant communities than in big cities, industrial areas, and
Catholic regions. It won relatively few converts from the established forces
of Social Democracy, Communism, and Catholic trade unionism and – despite what many believed – was much less successful than the Communists in
appealing to the millions of unemployed after 1929 [42; 98].

From its Bavarian beginnings onwards, the NSDAP was consistently
more successful, proportionately speaking, in attracting the support and
votes of lower-middle-class and, during the late 1920s, peasant Germans.
From its re-launching in 1925, the party's principal emphasis shifted from
that of 'alternative socialism' to one of 'people's community' (*Volksgemeinschaft*), and from 1926 concentration upon the cities was replaced by
attempts at seeking support from every kind of community and all layers of
society. This reflected both the way party support was naturally evolving,
and also the increasing influence of a leader who, unlike some of his subordinates, had no prewar roots in 'German socialism' and who, far from
feeling any affinity with the working class, actually nursed a fear of it that
betrayed his petit-bourgeois, status-conscious origins. For reasons both
ideological (his belief in a 'people's community' rather than a society based
on class) and tactical (his increasing desire to woo the middle class and
employers in particular), Hitler gave little encouragement to those Nazis
who wished to develop a powerful Nazi trade union movement; the dispersed and unthreatening NSBO (Nazi Factory Cell Organization) was as
much as he would permit [109].

Middle-class support, in its widest possible sense, was another matter.
Even during Weimar's stable years in the mid-1920s, middle-class political
parties such as the right-liberal DVP (German People's Party) and the more
authentically liberal DDP (German Democratic Party) were starting to lose

support to special-interest parties; with the onset of crisis after 1929, both of these political sectors saw their electoral support shrink, ultimately to the Nazis' benefit. While parties with firm ideological foundations – the Socialists, the Catholics and the Communists, the last of whom advanced strongly during the depression – were able to hold on to most of their electoral support, the collapse of the Protestant and 'liberal' centre and right parties was intimately linked to the sudden and rapid rise of a party that successfully preached certainty, patriotism, unity and 'people's community' where others merely defended special interests [40]. The NSDAP's success among the young was particularly dramatic; its stress on pseudo-military comradeship, male bonding, and – for many – exhilarating violence against the Marxist enemy possessed an appeal to middle-class and unaligned working-class youth. Between 1930 and 1933, 40 per cent of new party members were under thirty. By the end of 1932, party membership stood at 450,000 and that of the SA at 400,000. If Nazism at the start of 1933 was far from an irresistible force, it is easy to see its fascination for conservatives and reactionaries keen to destroy both Weimar and the German left and to erect an authoritarian regime according to their own tastes. What is less credible, especially in the light of the Italian lesson now available to them, is how they can have believed Hitler and Nazism were 'for hire'.

By the time Nazism entered the German government, with its leader as chancellor, in January 1933, Hitler's leadership of the NSDAP was utterly secure, and the place of his leadership central to the party's ideology. It is therefore appropriate to conclude this section with a brief discussion of the Führer's own ideas and goals. Most of these were given expression in *Mein Kampf* – not, admittedly, a detailed *plan* of action, but a revealing blueprint for much of what was to be essayed between 1933 and 1945.

Hitler's ideas brought together, in a highly distinctive fashion, prewar pan-Germanism, virulent antisemitism, biological racism, crude social Darwinism, German-centred 'geopolitics', and – the last major ingredient to be added – obsessive anti-Marxism. Focused and projected by an individual utterly sure of his own rightness, wisdom and destiny, and possessed of an extraordinary will and power of persuasion, this toxic cocktail became the central ideology of the Nazi regime. In practical terms it involved the imposition of unity upon a fragmented society, the replacement of a 'decadent' democratic culture by a new, Germanic one, the abandonment of the humiliating provisions of Versailles, the incorporation of all Germans within a single Reich, the 'colonization' of easterly territory required as German 'living space', the destruction of Soviet Communism, and the ending – by means that remained unspecific – of the alleged power of world Jewry [77; 80 *pp. 16–36*].

To a greater or lesser extent, the great majority of Nazi *activists* embraced this package and the programme it implied, even if many perhaps reflected little upon its deeper and longer-term implications. How many of the millions who merely *voted* for the NSDAP did likewise is another matter. Tempted into voting Nazi by the failings of other parties and the effectiveness of propaganda which often concentrated on local issues, a generalized patriotism, and the vote-winning figure of Hitler, much of this electorate must have had little idea of what it was letting itself, and the wider world, in for.

That Hitler's ideology and programme differed considerably from those of Italian Fascism is undeniable, yet liberal and left-wing contemporaries were surely correct to see the two movements as members, however different, of the same family. In a purely negative sense, both sought to suppress liberal pluralism and all forms of 'anti-national' leftism. More positively – from their own point of view, that is – both sought to create a new kind of state based on an enforced social unity and a supposedly new kind of national or racial consciousness, the goal being an escape from an alleged condition of national decadence into a new age of national expansionism. In these two cases, at least, onlookers who believed and argued that 'fascism means war' were absolutely right.

THE FASCIST CONTAGION

German National Socialism, even if affected by the success of Italian Fascism, was very much an autonomous creation which might well have been much the same even if Mussolini's movement had never existed or had failed to achieve power. Elsewhere in Europe, while fascist and national socialist movements drew on their own indigenous traditions and experiences, the element of imitativeness was more – and increasingly – pronounced. An important shift of emphasis, often ignored by writers on fascism, nevertheless needs to be noted here. Broadly speaking, as time passed the emphasis altered from attempting to emulate fascism as a *movement* of combat, anti-socialism, cultural revolt, and even a kind of revolution, to drawing inspiration from the supposed achievements of Fascism as a *regime*, as a system of authority – a more conservative appeal, it might be argued, and one, certainly, that appealed to many authoritarian conservatives. Within this shift, moreover, can be observed another, as Italian Fascism's position as chief exemplar was usurped after 1933 by Nazism and the Third Reich.

What was it that fascists outside Italy and Germany believed they were embracing? The answer varies, depending upon whether we are discussing intellectual, or at least educated and 'thinking', fascists, or other activists less disposed towards theoretical reflection. There can be no escaping the fact that for a significant number of European interwar intellectuals, fascism – as they saw it – had something to offer. Although the details differed, such people as the Englishman Wyndham Lewis, the Frenchman Drieu La Rochelle or the Spaniard Giménez Caballero looked to fascism as a vigorous, youthful, romantic and national revolt against the materialistic, utilitarian, socialistic spirit of the age [74]. Others, observing the institutionalization of Italian Fascism in the late 1920s and the suppression of the Nazi 'left' in 1934, were attracted less by the disorderly excitement of fascism in opposition than by the apparent order, unity, discipline and state direction represented by Fascism and/or Nazism in power. For their part, rank-and-file European fascists were drawn to a cause which, allowing for local variations, combined a strident and chauvinistic nationalism, bitter anti-leftism, resentment of and contempt for the established political order, a new and exciting 'style' of political behaviour and rhetoric, and a general willingness to be more extreme than both rivals and enemies.

Here it is necessary to state the obvious: that in the 1920s especially, those Europeans intrigued by and attracted to fascism could have no sense of its destiny, and in particular of what would happen when 'fascism' came to be equated with, and all but devoured by, its German variant. With this in mind, let us now examine some specific examples of the fascist contagion.

FASCISM IN CENTRAL AND EASTERN EUROPE

The emergence of fascist and extreme right-wing movements in interwar central and eastern Europe, from Finland in the north down to the Balkans, can best be understood in terms of three factors: first, the ambitious re-drawing of the international map which took place at the end of the First World War, giving rise to a complex tissue of irredentism and ethnic tensions; second, the more or less simultaneous and widespread experience of left-wing revolution or near revolution, exacerbated in several countries by the physical proximity of the Soviet Union; and third, the intrinsic difficulty of establishing a new, liberal democratic political system, or adapting an existing and highly imperfect one, to transformed circumstances. When, especially with the onset of the post-1929 depression, acute economic problems collided with these fundamental difficulties, circumstances were propitious for the emergence and growth of fascist and far-right movements, as well as for the subversion of democracy by conservative elite forces: monarchies, army officers, bureaucracies, etc. With the exceptions of Czechoslovakia and Finland, the democracies established in eastern Europe during the period 1918–21 failed to survive challenges from the political right. However – and we must never lose sight of this fact – in every case of liberal-democratic failure in this vast region it was *not* a fascist movement that overturned democracy but a conservative-authoritarian right, which, however fascist-tinged it may sometimes have been, often found itself at odds with the unruliness and radicalism of fascism proper. Closer attention will be paid to these relationships and tensions in discussing fascist and right-wing regimes later; for now, let us look more closely at the fascist and national socialist movements which burgeoned there in more or less frank imitation of their Italian and German models.

The successor states: Austria, Hungary and Czechoslovakia

In its collapse and dissolution, the Habsburg Empire, as well as contributing substantial tracts of territory to other established or newly emerging states (Galicia to Poland, Transylvania to Romania, Croatia, Slovenia and Bosnia to Yugoslavia), produced wholly from within itself three new nations: Austria, Hungary and Czechoslovakia. As the formerly dominant powers within the Austro-Hungarian 'Dual Monarchy' created in 1867, Austria and Hungary entered the 1920s defeated and shrunken, discouraging ground for new democracies. Czechoslovakia, on the other hand, gained from the empire's defeat the freedom for which the Czechs, particularly, had previously struggled in vain.

The Austria of the First Republic (1919–38) provides a striking example of a country affected by a broad range of right-wing activity: authoritarian-conservative Catholicism; an authoritarian veterans' movement tending towards 'Italianate' fascism; and unbridled fascism in the form of Austrian Nazism. All of these attracted the epithet 'fascist' from their critics and opponents at the time, and determining precisely what did and what did not constitute Austrian fascism has much preoccupied historians and social scientists ever since.

The dominant political force in Austria down to 1938, as it had been in prewar German-speaking Austria, was the Catholic, conservative Christian Social Party. The party's popular base lay in rural and small-town Austria, and among the Viennese middle class formerly mobilized by mayor Karl Lueger, with powerful support coming from the business community and the Catholic Church. Like other interwar European Catholic parties, the Christian Social Party was divided between a genuinely Christian-democratic wing, which until 1920 attempted to co-operate with the Austrian Socialists in giving the new regime a firm foundation, and a right wing whose commitment to parliamentary democracy was never wholehearted and diminished as time passed. Following a Socialist general strike in 1927, and in an atmosphere of heightening social tension and political paralysis, the right of the party gradually seized the initiative and itself became more openly authoritarian in outlook and intentions. With the onset of depression this process accelerated until, after 1933, a Christian Social-led government under Engelbert Dollfuss suspended parliament and set about replacing the democratic republic with an authoritarian, corporate state (see Chapter 5). The party thus provides us with a good example of those growing authoritarian tendencies within European political Catholicism which were also evident in the German Zentrum and, as we shall soon see, in Poland, Lithuania, Spain and elsewhere.

The right-wing Christian Socials' subversion of Austrian democracy received conditional co-operation from an important independent far-right force, the *Heimwehr* (pl. *Heimwehren*) (Home Guard). This was originally a loose confederation of paramilitary organizations, born in the immediate postwar days of struggle against 'reds' and South Slavs, and drawing much of their support from the provincial peasantry and lower middle class. Inspired and patronized by Mussolini, the Heimwehr adopted in 1930 what amounted to a fascist programme (the Korneuburg Oath) based on fusing ideas selected from Italian Fascism with those of the homegrown corporativist theoretician and publicist Othmar Spann [83; *Doc. 3a*]. As authoritarianism began to be imposed upon Austria in 1933–34, the Heimwehr's leaders, notably Prince Ernst Rüdiger von Stahremberg, continuously demanded the installation of what they termed 'Austro-Fascism'. As with many another fascist movement confronting an authoritarian regime of essentially conservative character, the Heimwehr's relationship was an uneasy and unstable one which climaxed in October 1936 with the organization's forced dissolution. Even so, during the previous couple of years much of the Heimwehr's vigour had been absorbed by, and continued to affect, the regime [69].

If the Heimwehr tended to admire Italian Fascism and operate in *de facto* alliance with the Christian Social Party, the third major force of the interwar Austrian right, national socialism, represented something very different. Like German National Socialism but more directly, the Austrian version had its organizational origins in the 'German Workers' movement of prewar Austria and Bohemia. Through the 1920s it was a minor player in Austrian life, and suffered internal conflicts among factions favouring, respectively, (i) an 'Austrian' national socialism which stressed a 'socialist' appeal to the working class; (ii) a harmonizing of national socialism with Catholicism; and (iii) an openly 'German' national socialism closer in spirit and goals to the German party. By the 1930s, with the rapid rise of the German NSDAP, not only had this last tendency emerged dominant but the party had begun to expand appreciably, notably at first among frustrated members of a minority pan-German movement that had survived the First World War and naturally continued to yearn for union with Germany. Unlike the ambivalent Heimwehr, the Austrian Nazis nursed pan-German goals that were explicitly incompatible not only with Austrian democracy but equally with the 'Christian corporative' state established in 1933–34, and following an unsuccessful rising in July 1934 the party was outlawed. During the next four years the Austrian NSDAP nevertheless continued to grow, winning over (among others) former socialists following the party's suppression in 1934 and radical members of the Heimwehr, especially after its dissolution in 1936. Even so, as things stood in 1938, by no stretch of the imagination could Austrian Nazism have won power by its own strength and efforts in the face of conservative forces for whom the 'Christian corporative' state provided all they wished [6 *pp. 189–210, 293–315*]. For that it needed the intervention of Hitler and German Nazism.

The various Hungarian fascist and national socialist movements of the 1920s and 1930s operated within a political environment that was unique in Europe. The semi-authoritarian, semi-pluralist regime of the 'regent' Admiral Miklós Horthy (see Chapter 5) represented the interests of Hungary's dominant classes and interests, and marginalized the organized left. In this situation, political and social radicalism found its most powerful expression and outlets on the far right, taking two main forms: so-called 'Szeged fascism' (Szeged being the southeastern town from which had been launched the 1919 'reconquest' of Hungary from Béla Kun's communist regime) and national socialism. The latter in turn was divided between organizations inspired by German Nazism and others more enterprisingly offering an indigenous national socialism eventually labelled 'Hungarism'.

'Szeged fascism' emerged early in interwar Hungary, superimposing an admiration for the Italian movement and early Fascist regime upon a homegrown mixture of anti-communism, contempt both for Habsburg legitimism and for the residual liberalism of the Horthy regime, antisemitism, and a militaristic revisionism regarding the postwar peace settlement. Szeged fascism was not a single organization, far less a mass movement, so much as a network of individuals and groups seeking not so much to overthrow the incumbent system as to nudge it in a more openly authoritarian and generally extreme direction. Such wider support as it possessed was chiefly among middle- and lower-ranking army officers and in Hungary's inflated, under-worked and under-paid bureaucracy. Its ambiguous relationship with the Horthyist establishment, roughly paralleling that of the Austrian Heimwehr with the Christian Socials, was exemplified by its most representative figure, Gyula Gömbös. Gömbös ('Gömbölini' to his detractors) helped found and then led a movement of 'Racial Defence' during the 1920s, but rejoined the government party in 1928. In 1932 he got his big chance when, in the depths of the depression, Horthy responded to right-wing and business pressure by appointing him prime minister. Although, as we shall see, Gömbös's death in 1936 cut short his attempt to 'fascistize' the Horthy regime from within, it seems unlikely that through him, and by this route, Szeged fascism would have triumphed [71].

As well as nursing a bitter, negative antisemitism, many Szeged fascists embraced a vague notion of Hungarian, Magyar or, as it was frequently termed, 'Turanian' (roughly 'Turkic') racism. This, together with a degree of social radicalism which seldom seriously gripped the mainly well-heeled or at least socially snobbish Szeged fascists, characterized the various forms of Hungarian national socialism that emerged in the 1930s. Of these (and there were many, mostly insignificant), two deserve particular attention: the Hungarian National Socialist Workers' Party or Scythe Cross movement, founded in 1931 by Zoltán Böszörmény and suppressed by the regime in 1936; and the Arrow Cross Party–Hungarist Movement of Ferenc Szálasi which rose to dominate the far right during the late 1930s [65].

Böszörmény and the Scythe Cross attempted, with some success, to attract and mobilize the deprived peasants of eastern Hungary behind a quasi-millennarian programme of land reform: hence its ruthless crushing at the hands of what was, after all, in part a landlords' regime. The Arrow Cross proved harder to extinguish. The ethnically mixed Szálasi, until 1935 an army officer, developed an authentically fascist, or national socialist, vision of a Hungarian-dominated 'Carpathian-Danubian Great Fatherland' which would collaborate with Fascist Italy and Nazi Germany in saving Christian civilization. A corporative system of 'national capitalism' would reform and reunite society so as to make this vision achievable. Between 1937 and 1939, despite Szálasi's being imprisoned by the regime for two years after 1938, Hungarian national socialism, led by the Arrow Cross, attracted a six-figure membership and, at the 1939 general election (the most democratic in Hungary's history), a vote variously calculated at between 25 and 45 per cent, but in any event almost certainly the best fascist or national socialist electoral showing outside Germany in any (more or less) free election [96].

Alone in central Europe, interwar Czechoslovakia may be regarded as representing a success for liberal democracy – a success which its eventual fate at the hands of Nazi Germany must not be allowed to obscure. Despite the presence of a large German minority and tensions between Czechs and Slovaks, there is little reason to believe that, without direct German intervention, the country's democracy would have succumbed during the 1930s to any kind of authoritarian, much less fascist, alternative.

Unalloyed fascism in Czechoslovakia flourished only among its German minority: a fifth of the country's population concentrated along its northern and western edges. Here, building on the prewar foundations of the Bohemian German Workers' Party, a German National Socialist Workers' Party (DNSAP) emerged in the 1920s, only to be suppressed by the government in 1933; in the meantime it paralleled the experience of the Austrian Nazi Party by assuming increasing similarity to the German party. The same trajectory was undergone by the force that superseded the DNSAP: Konrad Henlein's Sudeten German Party, which by 1935 had become the majority force among Czechoslovakia's Germans. With the country's dismemberment following the Munich agreement in September 1938, Henlein's party was simply swallowed whole by the NSDAP [88].

The Czechs themselves – urbanized, educated, culturally liberal, receptive to democracy, and instinctively resistant to German example – proved as immune to the appeal of fascism, and all kinds of authoritarianism, as any people in interwar Europe. Two small parties, the National Fascist Community (NOF) of General Rudolf Gajda and the Czech National Camp or *Vlajka*, attracted little popular support. The NOF, which took Mussolini's Italy as its model, was anti-German, anti-Nazi, anti-Soviet and antisemitic, its few thousand military and middle-class adherents dreaming of a vast pan-Slavic federation. When the Germans entered Prague in March 1939, the party was immediately proscribed. The pro-Nazi *Vlajka* was even less numerically or politically significant [118].

The political and social climate in the Slovak east of Czechoslovakia proved more conducive to fascist-tinged authoritarianism than that in the Czech districts of the west, for two main reasons: first, widespread Slovak resentment of Czech political and economic dominance within the new state; and, second, the strength within mainly Catholic Slovakia of a Catholic populist movement, the Slovak People's Party, which – as with so many Catholic parties in interwar Europe – succumbed over time to anti-democratic ideas. By the mid-1930s the militant, and indeed paramilitary, strand of the party was emerging as, at the very least, strongly influenced by fascism [78]. The dismemberment of Czechoslovakia and Hitler's establishment of an 'independent' Slovakia was to give the Slovak proponents of what has sometimes been termed 'clerical fascism' the gift of that power which would surely otherwise have escaped them.

Romania and the Balkans

Sooner or later during the interwar period, each of the Balkan countries – Romania, Yugoslavia, Albania, Bulgaria and Greece – witnessed the replacement of the local version of parliamentary democracy by some kind of authoritarian regime. With a single exception the sheer strength of conservative forces in this region, and their willingness to resort to authoritarianism, meant that major fascist or even fascist-influenced movements failed to appear. The exception was Romania, where a highly idiosyncratic form of fascism operated as a radical alternative to 'establishment' authoritarianism – and paid the price for doing so.

Romanian fascism, in the form of the Romanian Legion or Legionary Movement, also often referred to by the name of its militia, the Iron Guard (Gard de Fer), ranks as one of the most important, interesting and, in terms of mass support, successful fascist movements *anywhere* in interwar Europe. The Legion was born in 1927 as the Legion of the Archangel Michael, when its youthful founder, Corneliu Zelea Codreanu, broke away from the main existing party of Romanian antisemitic nationalism, A.C.

Cuza's League for National Christian Defence (LANC). Under the genuinely charismatic leadership of the young, handsome, mystically inclined Codreanu, the Legion was originally a student-based organization, dedicated to ethnically and culturally 'Roman-izing' the reshaped Romanian state and operating mainly via conspiracy and armed terror [116]. During the mid- and late 1930s, however, the movement acquired a much broader popular base; exploiting the weakness of the Romanian left and the negligence and corruption of other political parties, Legionaries literally 'went to the people' and deliberately built up a vast following, notably among peasants and sections of the urban skilled working class. By 1937, despite heavy official harassment, the Legion's membership was around 200,000 and its electoral vote (as the political party Totul Pentru Ţara, or All for the Father- land) 800,000 (25 per cent). Although different from most indisputably fascist movements in its religious – in this case Orthodox – devotion, the Legion laid great stress on another characteristically fascist notion, that of a 'new man', together with a violent antisemitism, a determination to purify Romania's allegedly decadent, Westernized society, politics and culture, and cults of personality, sacrifice, and death by 'martyrdom' [57; *Doc. 4*].

By 1938 the Legion found itself at odds, not only with Romania's officially liberal, though in practice increasingly repressive political regime, but also with the powerful social forces and interest groups which lay behind it. For them, and not least for the king, Carol II, if Romanian liberal parliamentarism was unable to restrain the radical right, more convention- ally authoritarian alternatives would have to be attempted. In 1938, the king assumed political control himself, inaugurated a fascist-tinged dic- tatorship, and outlawed the Legion; in murdering Codreanu and other Legionary leaders, the king's security forces appeared to have crushed it altogether. However, by boosting the Legion's cult of martyrdom they merely ensured that a cause that seemed dead would later return to haunt the king, his allies, and Romania as a whole.

That neither Greece nor Bulgaria produced a significant fascist or far- right mass movement during the 1920s and 1930s may at first sight seem surprising. Greece, having emerged victorious from the Balkan Wars and the First World War, suffered in 1922 a humiliating military defeat in Asia Minor at the hands of a renascent Turkey. At a stroke, Greece's leaders and intellectuals were forced to abandon the historic 'Great Idea' of a vast and powerful Greece surrounding the Aegean and incorporating Constantinople. This trauma, together with the desperate social problems associated with absorbing over a million refugees from Turkey, Bulgaria and the Soviet Union, and bitter, recriminatory political differences between the liberal followers of Eleftherios Venizelos and their conservative, sometimes monar- chist opponents, might seem likely material for the forging of a Greek popular fascist movement. Yet no such thing emerged. Rather, during the politically unstable mid-1920s, and again when the depression hit Greece in the 1930s, it was a case of conservative and right-wing politicians and army officers becoming attracted to the firm government and orderly society which they observed first in Italy and later in Germany, and looking to achieve similar results via different means. Two dictatorships were the outcome, those of General Pangalos (1925–26) [61 *p. 108*] and, far more important, General Ioannis Metaxas (1936–41); the latter will be considered later (see Chapter 5).

What inhibited any possible growth of popular fascism in Greece was the country's low level of industrialization, its comparatively equitable rural society, and the consequent absence of the kinds and levels of conflict which helped generate fascist support in Italy and elsewhere. All this was even more true of Bulgaria. As a loser in both the Second Balkan War (1913) and the First World War, Bulgaria was affected by a sense of national grievance which, with different socio-economic ingredients, might have provided a fascist movement or movements with manpower. Instead, from the mid-1920s to the mid-1930s a number of small fascist and national socialist groups came and went, of which only the *Ratnitsi* (Warriors) attracted even a modicum of popular support. As in Greece, what was more important was the appeal of a loosely fascism-inspired authoritarianism within the army and governing elite, making it possible to introduce an authoritarian regime under the Crown in 1934 [63 *pp. 119–29*].

Sociologically speaking the new state of Yugoslavia, too, was a mainly peasant society with a low level of social and ideological conflict. What undermined the country's hesitant democracy and encouraged the emergence of at least one significant fascist-style movement was something largely absent from the ethnically quite homogeneous nations of Greece and Bulgaria: that ethnic diversity that over half-a-century later was to rip Yugoslavia apart. Between the wars there proliferated in Yugoslavia a bewildering number of nationalist clubs, associations and movements: Serb, Slovene, Croat and Muslim. These were mostly non-fascist, although some did gravitate towards a fascist position.

Since the 'Kingdom of the Serbs, Croats and Slovenes' possessed a Serb monarchy and in other ways too was Serb-dominated, it is unsurprising that fascist-influenced nationalist movements should chiefly espouse one of two causes: either 'Yugoslav' nationalism that was Serb in all but name and viewed Yugoslavia as effectively Greater Serbia; or other nationalisms, chiefly Croat, which (as with Slovak nationalism in Czechoslovakia) threatened the dismemberment of the state itself. *Zbor* (Convention), founded in 1935, was the chief exponent of a 'Yugoslav' (i.e. Serb) nationalism that was authoritarian, corporativist, religiously Orthodox, stylistically fascist, and, by its very nature, inimical to the nationalism of the Croats. The movement's popular impact was nevertheless limited. In Croatia, the *Ustaša* (Uprising) movement, formed in 1929 by the lawyer Ante Pavelić, was a rather weightier affair: not so much as a mass movement (most of its activity lying in the spheres of conspiracy and subversion, and its maximum prewar membership reaching perhaps 40,000 out of a Croat population of 2.9 million) but through its dissemination of a brand of Croat nationalism whose anti-Serb, antisemitic and authoritarian character was to cast a long – and still not fully extinguished – shadow. As with many an interwar fascist or fascist-influenced movement, it was the coming of war in Europe that was to guarantee a place in history to a movement that might otherwise have soon been forgotten [67].

In the Yugoslavia of the 1930s Zbor, the Ustaša, and other far-right groups were operating within a political climate that was itself at least partly authoritarian, following the introduction of a 'royal dictatorship' by King Alexander in 1929. As will by now be clear, the 'establishment dictatorship' was a generalized eastern European phenomenon about which more will need to be said later. Albania, desperately backward and tribalized, and where no fascist movement arose, will be discussed at that point.

Finland, Poland and the Baltic states

These five countries of northeastern Europe, all new or re-emergent states in 1919–20, were inevitably affected by the proximity of the Soviet Union and later by that of a reviving Germany with strong cultural influence in the Baltic region. Their politics were also decisively shaped by the communism of their great eastern neighbour and the struggles between communists and 'Whites' that accompanied their birth. Although Finland – which, probably crucially, before the war had enjoyed considerable autonomy and a parliamentary system within the Russian Empire – managed to emulate Norway, Sweden and Denmark by surviving the interwar period as a parliamentary democracy, it was at one point touch and go. Poland, Latvia, Lithuania and Estonia all succumbed for much of the period to conservative authoritarian regimes that, like those further south, found themselves faced, and often at odds, with more radical rightists and outright fascists.

Much of the intellectual and ideological climate for Finnish radical nationalism and fascism was created in the 1920s by the Academic Karelia Society, a group of academics, intellectuals and literati who advocated anti-communism and anti-Sovietism, authoritarian government, the elimination of non-Finnish (chiefly Swedish) influences from Finnish life and culture, and the ultimate creation (how was never clear) of a Greater Finland extending eastward as far as the Urals. Other relevant and important currents in Finnish public life were a strong distaste for democracy within the German-influenced army officer corps, widespread and aggressive anti-communism born of the 1917–18 civil war, and a deeply conservative Lutheranism.

Finnish fascism proper, however, began to emerge in 1929 in the shape of Lapua, an anti-communist, staunchly Lutheran, authoritarian mass movement of farmers and small-town bourgeois, based chiefly in southwestern Finland. Exploiting the agricultural depression, Lapua prospered for three years, but in 1932 overreached itself in an attempted and unsuccessful coup. The outcome was a rallying of democratic forces under the leadership of the reassuringly conservative president Swinhufvud. Compared with what was to occur in 1934 further south in Estonia and Latvia, this outcome testifies to the deeper roots and greater resilience of parliamentarism in Finland. Lapua was proscribed, but resurfaced in 1933 as the People's Patriotic Movement (IKL), a more or less unambiguously fascist party that attracted 8 per cent of the national vote in 1936, but declined thereafter [114].

The three 'Baltic states' – Estonia, Latvia and Lithuania – and Poland all between the wars witnessed the emergence of radical right-wing movements that enjoyed complex and sometimes troubled relations with authoritarian regimes established to replace or 'revise' the parliamentarism introduced in 1919–20. The Estonian and Latvian experiences, however, fall broadly into one category, and those of Lithuania and Poland into another.

The Estonian extreme right was far more numerically powerful than its Latvian (and Lithuanian) counterparts, sharing both the 'anti-red', anti-Russian origins and outlook of the Finnish interwar extreme right. It was less clearly fascist in character, however, than either Lapua or elements in the other Baltic states; its principal expression, the paramilitary Estonian Vaps (Veterans' League), advocated authoritarianism and an 'Estonia for the Estonians' policy, but showed little interest in other aspects of the Italian-style fascism vaguely admired by many of its activists [92]. This was very different from the Latvian Perkonkrust (Thunder Cross), founded in 1933 after a host of previous far-right parties had made negligible impact. The Thunder Cross, as its name suggests, was an authentically fascist movement which sought to cleanse Latvia ethnically of its various minorities and establish a racially pure, morally reborn order. If anything, and despite its hostility towards Latvia's German minority, the Thunder Cross modelled itself more on German Nazism than on Italian Fascism. Like the Romanian Legion it was strong among students, but rapidly achieved a much broader social base [76 *pp. 51–2*].

By 1934, the Estonian Veterans' League was emerging as the country's most popular political force, and the Latvian Thunder Cross as at least a potential challenger for power. During that year, however, the two movements shared a common experience of suppression at the hands of newly established 'emergency' regimes which – in response partly to the perceived threat of 'fascism' and partly to the wider problems of the depression – sought to replace shaky democracies with more authoritarian, if far from fascist, alternatives. The comparison with Finland, already made, is a telling one: here, in order that fascism be overcome and conservatives appeased, democratic institutions were deemed to require a degree of constitutional 'strengthening' that actually went a long way towards undermining them.

Whereas in Estonia and Latvia democracy survived well into the 1930s and the far right was a victim of its eventual disappearance, in Lithuania and Poland a shift towards authoritarianism occurred in the mid-1920s, with the extreme right then evolving in conditions that veered between the congenial and the semi-clandestine.

Lithuanian radical rightism and fascism were born in the nationalist Lietuviu Tautininku Sajunga (LTS: Lithuanian National Union), led by a former professor of history and philology, Augustinas Voldemaras. Following a *coup d'état* in 1926 and the replacement of Lithuanian democracy by the conservative authoritarian regime of Antanas Smetona, Voldemaras served for three years as prime minister. Within the LTS the most extreme *tautininkai* (nationalists), chiefly army officers, from 1927 formed a government-sponsored secret organization, Gelezinis Vilkas (Iron Wolf). Iron Wolf's programme was frankly fascist, dedicated to repressing the country's Russian, Polish and Jewish minorities, recovering from Poland the historic Lithuanian capital of Vilnius, and recreating the 'Greater Lithuania' of the past. From 1929, however, Smetona distanced himself and his regime from the more radical LTS. Voldemaras was ejected from the premiership in 1929, and the increasingly troublesome Iron Wolf, with whom the ousted premier was closely linked, dissolved in 1934. The mainstream LTS nevertheless continued to play an important role within Smetona's regime until its wartime collapse in 1940 [89].

Poland provides an example of a country with, from 1926, increasingly authoritarian institutions which nevertheless witnessed a large measure of fascist-style activity. The regime of General Piłsudski, which following a coup in 1926 'revised' Poland's democracy in a more 'controlled', if not wholly authoritarian and certainly not fascist, direction, gave way during the 1930s, and especially after Piłsudski's death in 1935, to a more openly authoritarian system. Against this background, a succession of movements appeared that were ultra-nationalist, staunchly Catholic, xenophobic and antisemitic, and strongly influenced in their authoritarianism by Italian Fascism. The native source of these movements, which itself displayed all of these characteristics, was the National Democratic Party (NDP), strongest among the middle class of western Poland and hostile both to the democracy established in 1921 and to Piłsudski's still semi-liberal regime. During the late 1920s the NDP gave birth to the autonomous, youth-dominated Camp of Great Poland (OWP), to its more radical, nazified successor the National Radical Camp (ONR), and finally to an unambiguously fascist youth movement, Falanga, inspired by and named after the

Spanish fascist movement Falange Española (see pp. 55–6). The first two of these acquired, or at any rate claimed, a genuine mass membership, and largely for that reason were suppressed by the authorities. Falanga was less successful, not least because from 1935 the regime of the 'Colonels' who succeeded Piłsudski itself moved sharply to the right and began to construct an 'establishment' authoritarian regime comparable with (though by no means identical to) others in central and eastern Europe [117].

FASCISM AND CATHOLICISM IN SPAIN AND PORTUGAL

The rapid rise of the Fascist movement in Italy, and more particularly the establishment of a Fascist regime, inevitably made a significant impression upon Italy's fellow Latin, southern European nations, Spain and Portugal. In the early 1920s both Iberian countries were in a state of political crisis. In Spain the liberal system originally established in the 1870s appeared paralysed in the face of challenges from advocates of wider democracy, regionalist forces, and an emergent workers' movement. The Portuguese Republic, founded in 1910, was if anything even more plagued by political instability and in addition by financial mismanagement and corruption. And since both countries succumbed to a right-wing, authoritarian takeover – Spain in September 1923 and Portugal in May 1926 – the influence of fascism would seem to be clear. The dictatorships of General Primo de Rivera in Spain (1923–30), established as a result of the 1923 coup, and of António Salazar in Portugal, which emerged more gradually following that of 1926, will be examined more closely in Chapter 5. Suffice it to say here that, while the installation of an anti-liberal, anti-leftist, authoritarian regime in Italy provided numerous Spanish and Portuguese rightists with example and inspiration, and while many enthusiastically embraced what they considered to be fascist ideas, at no time in the 1920s did an actual fascist *movement* of any significance appear in either country. Why was this?

In the early 1920s Spain (notably industrial Catalonia and rural Andalusia) was affected by social conflict bitter and extensive enough to suggest comparisons with the conditions in northern and central Italy that helped generate fascism. Spain's wartime neutrality, however, ensured the absence both of that sense of national grievance which nurtured fascism in Italy, Germany, Austria and Hungary, and of those war veterans who provided it with vital support. Most Spaniards had by now reconciled themselves to the irreversible loss of overseas empire, and the ruling elites' attempts to establish a new empire in Morocco were widely unpopular. Spanish nationalism was largely introspective, conservatively Catholic in inspiration and flavour, preoccupied with national cohesion rather than national aggrandizement, and lacking the middle-class assertiveness characteristic of Italian Fascism [58]. Where a version of this last ingredient did exist was in

Catalonia and to a lesser extent the Basque country, but Catalan and Basque nationalism were by definition antithetical to a putative Spanish fascism and, moreover, increasingly democratic in outlook and demands. As for fascism's possible appeal to 'Castilian' conservatives as an imposer of order, discipline and authority, Spaniards had two alternatives that both Italians and Germans lacked: first, a nakedly 'political' army which, if the need arose, could be relied upon to 'save Spain' from politicians or revolutionaries, and, secondly, a Catholic Church able and willing to inject ideological cement both into the political right generally and into a possible authoritarian regime [95 *pp. 3–29*; 81].

The Portuguese case was very similar in important ways, if different in others. Portugal, unlike Spain, *had* participated in the First World War, fighting alongside Britain and France following a divisive and bruising intervention/neutrality debate. Although Portugal's wartime experience had been a painful one, the country emerged on the winning side with its previously vulnerable overseas empire intact and internationally guaranteed, and therefore with no lasting sense of national trauma. The early 1920s were years of serious political and social troubles as they were elsewhere, yet Portuguese society was still insufficiently developed to generate the kind of social conflict that might in turn have fed a significant movement of fascist type. And in any case, here too, as in Spain, social and political Catholicism and an interventionist army helped reassure conservative elements who might otherwise have found fascism attractive. When, after 1922, 'fascism' *did* begin to attract a significant number of right-wing intellectuals, businessmen, politicians and army officers, it was by virtue more of the 'order' it appeared to promise than of its supposedly more novel and revolutionary qualities [53].

Not until the 1930s did unambiguously fascist movements emerge in the Iberian countries, and then in utterly divergent circumstances. In Spain the collapse of the Primo de Rivera dictatorship in January 1930 was followed in April 1931 by that of the monarchy and its replacement of the democratic Second Republic. Amid the political turmoil and social polarization which followed, fascism began to have some appeal. The two most important movements, the Juntas de Ofensiva Nacional-Sindicalista (JONS), founded in 1931 by Ramiro Ledesma and Onésimo Redondo, and Falange Española, founded in 1933 by Primo de Rivera's son José Antonio, merged in 1934 to form Falange Española de las JONS. All these organizations adopted a characteristically 'fascist' posture: rhetorically, they attacked the established right as well as the left, while accepting financial and tactical assistance from rightist organizations (and from Mussolini) and engaging in violence only against militants of the left; and they sought to attract support from all social classes, advocating a corporativist organization of society and polity and a vaguely stated imperialism [93].

Spanish fascism was nevertheless utterly unsuccessful in attracting mass support; as late as the general election of February 1936 the Falange suffered a débâcle, winning only around 40,000 votes nationwide. Perhaps the principal reason was that the 'space' which Spanish fascism sought to fill was occupied by existing Catholic and monarchist parties. These comprised the devoutly Catholic, traditionalist Carlists; the restorationist Renovación Española, which itself displayed increasingly fascist characteristics and in 1934–36 injected these into a wider right-wing alliance, the Bloque Nacional (National Bloc) [*Doc. 3b*]; and the Catholic-conservative CEDA (Spanish Confederation of Autonomous Rightist Organizations). The CEDA was a major force between 1933 and 1936, and briefly promised to achieve by peaceful means the authoritarian exit from republican democracy which Falangism also offered. The CEDA's electoral defeat in February 1936 brought about that party's collapse, and a sudden influx of its former members – especially from its youth wing, the JAP (Popular Action Youth) – into the Falange. After the start of the Spanish Civil War in July 1936, this growth accelerated dramatically within the rebel Nationalist zone, as not only Catholic rightists but also frightened members of republican and left-wing organizations sought refuge within a movement which at this time would accept anyone. The wartime Falange found itself effectively leaderless, however, thanks to the Republicans' execution of José Antonio Primo de Rivera. In April 1937 the leader of insurgent, Nationalist Spain, General Francisco Franco, forcibly merged the Falange with organizations of the Catholic and monarchist right to form the single party of his regime, Falange Española Tradicionalista y de las JONS [70; *Doc. 7c*]. The nature of the Franco regime and its relationship with 'fascism' will be considered in the next chapter.

Whereas an authentically fascist movement emerged in Spain as a product of a more 'open' political system, in Portugal it appeared as an expression of frustration with an essentially conservative dictatorship, that of Salazar. In the early 1930s, as Salazar's 'New State' was taking shape, radical right-wing elements came together under the leadership of a former Integralist, Rolão Preto, to form the blue-shirted National-Syndicalist movement. Attracting the support of some Integralists, renegade former left-wing activists, students and members of the urban lower middle class, National Syndicalism sought to shift the stuffy Salazar regime in a more 'revolutionary' direction or, failing that, to overturn it. Salazar was disinclined to be shifted, and in 1934 ruthlessly crushed the movement and exiled its leader. Analytically speaking, the chief significance of National Syndicalism is in helping us to draw a line between an authoritarian regime of the right, often regarded as 'fascist', and the more self-consciously radical outlook of the fascist right proper [72].

UNSUCCESSFUL FASCISM IN THE ESTABLISHED DEMOCRACIES OF NORTHWESTERN EUROPE

In the countries of northwestern Europe – France, Switzerland, Britain, Ireland, Belgium, the Netherlands, and Scandinavia (Norway, Sweden, Denmark and Iceland; Finland as we have seen was a very different case) – interwar fascist and national socialist parties, as well as other movements and parties of the authoritarian right, were on the whole numerically weak and never seriously threatened to achieve political success. There would seem to be three main reasons for this: relatively stable political systems that had been well established before 1914 and possessed the capacity for peaceful evolution in line with changing circumstances; the weakness of the revolutionary left; and the absence of any pervading sense of national crisis.

France

Despite a significant 'fascist scare' in the mid-1930s, France was never seriously threatened by fascism or by other forms of right-wing authoritarianism, until militarily crushed by Nazi Germany in 1940. The France that emerged from the First World War possessed a well-established constitutional framework and political system; the Third Republic may not have been loved by the French but the 'Republican idea' was widely and for the most part zealously embraced. The Republic was, moreover, at least temporarily strengthened by France's wartime sacrifices and ultimate triumph. France's victory, unlike Italy's, was not 'mutilated' but sanctified by the recovery of Alsace-Lorraine and the extension of an already vast overseas empire; between 1919 and 1940, national psychology was security-minded and defensive. And while adjustment to peacetime conditions was not easy, postwar France suffered few of the social convulsions affecting Italy, much less Germany. In the mid-1920s, when hyper-inflation along German lines threatened, the conservative Poincaré government saved the franc at a reduced but respectable level, thereby preventing a collapse of fixed incomes and savings and possible middle-class alienation from the Republic. In the 1930s, although France was eventually hit by the depression, it was belatedly and less acutely than Germany, or even than Great Britain. Nor was there a plausible threat from the revolutionary left such as helped generate support for fascism in Italy and elsewhere.

These conditions help explain why, for most of the interwar period, France was infertile ground as far as any possibility of mass fascism was concerned. Nevertheless with 'fascism' very much in the European air, there was enough raw material to encourage the appearance of fascist intellectual critiques and organizations, the latter mostly on a relatively small scale, and the wider infection of right-wing politics by fascist styles and examples. Parliamentary politics, especially by the 1930s, were unstable and increasingly beset by financial scandals. Germany, while defeated in the war, was visibly recovering by the mid-1920s, while a demographically sluggish France remained in undignified diplomatic subordination to Britain. Critics of 'decadence' and devotees of authoritarian solutions thus had plenty to criticize.

As we have already seen, the France of the prewar Third Republic, for all that republicanism and liberalism had become firmly established, had witnessed the emergence of radical-nationalist dissent via publicists such as Barrès, the vigorous authoritarian monarchism of Maurras and Action Française, a strand of cultural antisemitism, and periodic outbursts of 'street' and league politics of (at the very least) implicitly authoritarian character. Along with Italy, France had also been the scene of some of the more thoughtful attempts to bring together elements of left and right in a 'third way'. The explosion on to the European political scene of Mussolini and Italian Fascism, which possessed a not dissimilar set of intellectual and political forebears, accordingly evoked considerable interest on the French intellectual and political fringes. Indeed, one of the most remarkable features of French fascism before 1940 was the strength of its appeal to such intellectuals as Pierre Drieu La Rochelle, Maurice Brasillach and, in the more directly political sphere, Marcel Déat, when its wider appeal was, as we shall see, so limited [104; 112].

In the 1920s, the most significant expressions of a fascist or *fascisant* assault on the French political establishment were the Faisceau (Fascio) and the Jeunesses Patriotes (Patriot Youth) [106]. The first, as its name suggests, was unambiguously fascist. The creation of Georges Valois (an assumed name), a militant of Action Française who had flirted with elements of the syndicalist left before 1914, the Faisceau espoused corporatism, producti-vism and a belief in a new elite, all of course within a framework of nation-alism and authoritarianism [*Doc. 5*]. Valois attempted a cross-class appeal, actively wooing left-wing and working-class support; his movement, which at its peak attracted perhaps 30–40,000 adherents, nevertheless remained predominantly middle-class. As the movement languished amid the pros-perity of the late 1920s, Valois grew disillusioned – not just with his own failure but also with the reality of Italian Fascism in power, which he saw destroying syndicalist radicalism in favour of a conservative statism [68]. Dissolving the movement in 1929, Valois commenced a leftward trajectory which was to lead to a role in the wartime resistance and death, in 1945, in Belsen. The banner of self-proclaimed fascism was, however, taken up in the 1930s by a former Faisceau militant, Marcel Bucard, who in 1933 founded the Francistes in open but utterly unsuccessful imitation of Italian Fascism.

The Jeunesses Patriotes of Pierre Taittinger, founded in 1924, were inspired by Italian Fascism's 'mass' nature and anti-communist activism, but displayed none of the self-conscious social and cultural radicalism of the PNF or the Faisceau. Rather, in a country where organized conservative politics were weak, the Jeunesses Patriotes, most of whose support came from middle-class youths and nationalistic ex-servicemen, represented a kind of conservative populism. From a peak of around (so Taittinger claimed) 100,000 in the late 1920s, the movement's support declined during the early 1930s even as it showed signs of increasingly explicit authoritarianism [105].

Two further rightist movements at least partly inspired by selective interpretation of Italian Fascism's successes, and which moved rather closer to outright fascism themselves, were Colonel François de la Roque's Croix de Feu (Fiery Cross), founded in 1927, and the Solidarité Française (French Solidarity) of perfumier François Coty, established in 1933. The latter, explicitly authoritarian and more antisemitic than most of its competitors, flowered briefly for a year or so, but failed to survive the death of its founder in 1934. The Croix de Feu was far more successful and enduring; it was, indeed, numerically the most successful of all the far-right movements of interwar France. From fundamentally conservative, patriotic origins not very different from those of the Jeunesses Patriotes, the Croix de Feu in the 1930s began to show clear signs of social radicalism and a 'third way' approach to the achievement of social unity which brought it some way closer to the fascism of which its critics accused it [107].

During 1933–34 these movements, together with Action Française, temporarily converged to attack a Republic afflicted by political scandal and instability. What the French left interpreted as a 'fascist threat', chiefly manifest in the Parisian riots of 6 February 1934, was in reality neither strictly fascist nor a truly serious threat, and had the effect of rallying the Republic's supporters and making possible the left–centre coalition, the Popular Front, elected in May 1936.

Ironically, the election of a left-wing government, with Communist support, raised a (largely illusory) 'red scare' which strengthened the French right through a process of reaction. Most of the aforementioned right-wing organizations, it is true, declined or disappeared after February 1934, especially once the Popular Front government transformed the climate for right-wing activism by banning political leagues and uniforms. Some right-wing extremists went over to conspiracy and terrorism in the clandestine Cagoule, others adopted a Hitlerian 'political' strategy with considerable success. Popular support for two rightist parties in particular grew dramatically in the late 1930s. One of these was the Parti Social Français (PSF), a revamped version of the old Croix de Feu, which after 1936 developed into the most powerful organized party of the right in the history of the Third Republic. The PSF certainly contained 'fascistizing' elements and tendencies, while remaining ambivalent as to its intentions regarding republican democracy. Its relationship with 'fascism' consequently remains unclear and disputed. Very different was the Parti Populaire Français of former Communist Jacques Doriot, the increasingly fascist tone of which was inescapable [55]. Relations between the two mass parties of the late-1930s French right were poor, but it seems likely that had another general election followed that of 1930 their combined impact would have been considerable [108]. The election was never to take place, however, and events after September 1939 were to give an unforeseeable but violent twist to the history of the French right.

Britain and Ireland

Britain during the 1920s witnessed the appearance of several extreme right-wing groups clearly inspired by Italian Fascism, or at least by what their members perceived or imagined Fascism to be. Organizations such as the British Fascisti, later the British Fascists, were nevertheless little more than authoritarian, strike-breaking fringes of the Conservative Party, solidly middle-class in composition, with little of the early radicalism or iconoclasm characteristic of the Italian version. They demonstrate the tendency of European 'fascists' and rightists to treat 'fascism' very selectively, borrowing at will from whichever characteristics or supposed characteristics of foreign examples they supposed relevant to their own situation. Although the antisemitic Imperial Fascist League of Arnold Leese, with its explicitly racist ideology, was an exception, none of these movements possessed much more than curiosity value within the British political world of the 1920s [56].

With the 1929 crash and subsequent depression, however, a potentially more serious manifestation of British fascism appeared. The depression seemed to expose chronic and worsening economic problems, as well as the inability of Britain's constitution, political system and politicians to deal with them. The British Union of Fascists (BUF), founded in 1932 out of the wreckage of the short-lived New Party, began as an attempt to transform Britain's institutions in a more authoritarian, corporativist direction, in order to guarantee political decisiveness and economic efficiency. The BUF's founder and leader, Sir Oswald Mosley, a former Conservative MP and more recently a rising figure in the Labour Party, was a charismatic minor aristocrat with a genuine if paternalistic concern for the unemployed. Like many European fascist intellectuals (as which he certainly qualifies), Mosley was at one and the same time obsessed with contemporary 'decadence' and convinced that fascism was *the* 'modern movement' [102; *Doc. 6*]. Like many fascist movements, the BUF initially recruited dissident leftists as well as right-wing authoritarians; like Italian Fascism, it swiftly moved from a position of 'alternative leftism' to one of militant and violent *anti*-leftism and, very soon, antisemitism. Violence and antisemitism attracted significant support in big cities – the East End of London [85], Manchester, Leeds – but alienated many more people, among them wealthy potential supporters such as Lord Rothermere, proprietor of the *Daily Mail*. Although tens of thousands of Britons passed through the BUF during the 1932–39 period, membership at any one time was never more than 50,000, electoral success was meagre, and fascism never remotely threatened to overturn the established political order [97].

In retrospect it is not difficult to see why British fascism failed so utterly in the 1920s and 1930s. Quite apart from the shortcomings of Mosley himself – a fine orator and a genuinely intelligent man, but with a defective tactical (and, indeed, moral) sense and little true understanding of ordinary British people – interwar Britain was simply not propitious territory for fascism. A victor in the war, Britain was plagued by few of the postwar national or ethnic traumas that affected much of central, southern and eastern Europe; her constitutional and political systems, whatever their deficiencies, were not novelties or undergoing stressful transformation; and, notwithstanding the emergence of a powerful Labour Party and such episodes as the General Strike of 1926, there existed no *credible* threat of 'bolshevism' such as helped lubricate the wheels of fascism and right-wing authoritarianism elsewhere. The British political party system proved capable of accommodating the various social components of the electorate and, in the crisis of 1931, the National Government succeeded in rallying the mass of the population behind it. The depression, while causing acute suffering to the industrial working class, affected the middle class much less, and in any case was past its worst by the time the BUF came on the scene. By the late 1930s the BUF, significantly now renamed the British Union of Fascists and National Socialists and basing what remained of its appeal on a mixture of antisemitism and opposition to the looming war with Germany, had become even more marginal to everyday British politics.

The newly created Irish Free State was the only 'new' state in post-1919 western Europe. With its poor, largely peasant society, recently militarized culture, disputed borders, and irredentist claims on the northern 'Six Counties', Ireland might appear ideal breeding ground for fascism. Such was not the case, however. Despite the psychological completeness of the Free State's break with Westminster, parliamentary institutions were from the start firmly established under the presidency of the devoutly Catholic, deeply conservative Eamonn De Valera. Social conflict was largely absent and socio-cultural cohesion guaranteed by a powerful, traditionalist Catholic Church. In this climate, the attraction of a few intellectuals towards continental authoritarianism or outright fascism met with little wider response. General Eoin O'Duffy's Blue Shirts, an authoritarian, corporativist and pro-fascist fringe group founded as the Army Comrades' Association in 1932, could not compete with the Catholic conservatism of the Fine Gael party, into which it was largely absorbed in 1935. After leading an Irish volunteer battalion on the Nationalist side in the Spanish Civil War, O'Duffy left politics in 1937 and the last vestiges of the Blue Shirt movement disappeared [87].

Belgium and the Netherlands

Although in the mid-1930s fascist and related movements achieved some modest support in Belgium and the Netherlands, taking the interwar period as a whole these countries too are striking for their relative immunity from fascism and authoritarianism. Both entered the 1920s as stable constitutional monarchies with substantial overseas empires, possessed well-established and little criticized parliamentary systems, and largely lacked the kind of intellectual and cultural traditions that helped nourish fascism elsewhere. The Netherlands had been neutral in the First World War and was little affected by the national/ethnic turmoil so prevalent elsewhere; Belgium, as the stage of so much fighting and a modest territorial gainer at the peace settlement, was as defensively minded as France. In both countries the postwar left emerged as social-democratic rather than revolutionary, rendering any suggestion of a 'red scare' implausible.

The interwar Netherlands resembled Britain in its lack of the kind of authoritarian but non-fascist movements that were so plentiful in pre-1933 Germany, France and elsewhere. Thus, like the BUF, the Dutch fascist organizations that emerged in the 1930s did so out of a political and organizational vacuum and were even more mimetic of foreign examples. Although tending to adopt the labels of nearby 'national socialism', they were actually more enthused by an Italian Fascism which by now presented itself as a regime rather than a movement or a set of cultural and intellectual values. Only one movement merits individual mention: the National Socialist Movement (NSB), founded in 1931 and led by a civil servant, Anton Mussert. The NSB was unambiguously fascist in 'style' but at first rejected antisemitism; advocating a corporativist economic system, it was able amid the depths of the depression to win almost 8 per cent of the vote at provincial elections in 1935. This proved to be the movement's peak, for economic recovery and the resolution of the democratic parties sent it into reverse. As with the BUF, the NSB's contraction during the late 1930s was paralleled by intensifying extremism, especially on racial matters [91]. Only a miracle could arrest the movement's decline, and for that miracle Mussert, like so many European fascists, was dependent on a fascist far more successful than himself: Adolf Hitler.

The prospects of fascist and authoritarian movements in Belgium were always likely to be inhibited, not only by factors already mentioned but also by the country's linguistic division between the Flemish north and west and the Walloon (French-speaking) east and south. Generally speaking, of the numerous, mostly tiny, rightist movements which emerged in interwar Belgium, those with French roots tended to take an 'all Belgian' national-istic approach, while Flemish-based organizations either were preoccupied with autonomy for Flemish-speaking Belgium or sought a fundamental re-casting of frontiers in that region of Europe. Three movements, all (like their Dutch fascist counterparts) founded in the 1930s, deserve particular mention: the VNV (Flemish National Federation), Christus Rex (Christ the King) or 'Rex', and Verdinaso.

The first two of these, the former led by a Flemish schoolteacher, Staf de Clercq, and the latter by a genuinely charismatic young publisher, Léon Degrelle, are of interest because both arose upon solidly Catholic found-ations yet evolved in a clearly fascist direction. The more successful was Rex, founded in 1935 when young authoritarian Catholics broke away from the main, Christian Democratic, Catholic party. Under Degrelle's genuinely inspiring leadership, Rexism attracted 11.5 per cent of the vote and elected twenty-one deputies at the general election of 1936, only to go into reverse when the triumphalist Degrelle tried to take on the political establishment and lost. As with the BUF and the NSB, a symbiotic process of growing extremism and spiralling decline characterized Rexism's experi-ence during the late 1930s [115].

Rexism and, to a lesser extent, the VNV achieved what little they did by exploiting the alleged shortcomings of parliamentary democracy during a time of depression. What they lacked, along with fascist movements in other territorially 'satisfied' countries like Britain, France and Scandinavia, was an expansionist grand design such as characterized Italian Fascism, German National Socialism, and some of the eastern European movements considered earlier. The third movement, Verdinaso, did possess such a design: 'Verdinaso' was actually an acronym standing for 'Federation of Low Countries National-Solidarists', and the movement, led by Joris van Severen, advocated the uniting of Belgium, the Netherlands, Luxembourg and large tracts of eastern France in a reborn medieval Burgundy. Quite how such a redrawing of the European map was to be achieved was never clear: certainly not by a movement that never recruited more than 5,000 supporters [101].

Scandinavia

Like the Netherlands, the Scandinavian countries – Norway, Sweden, Denmark and Iceland – had all been neutral in the First World War and remained largely detached from the convulsions which followed it else-where. Although Norway had only separated from Sweden in 1905, and whilst in the latter the prewar extension of the suffrage had lagged somewhat behind the western European norm, all were internally stable constitutional monarchies with relatively equitable societies, a high level of ethnic homogeneity, and undisputed boundaries. (Denmark acquired the predominantly Danish-speaking, former German territory of northern Sleswig by plebiscite in 1920.) Most of the sources of fascist ideas and appeal were therefore absent.

All these countries were nevertheless affected by the agricultural depression which began in the late 1920s and by the wider slump of the 1930s, and in all of them conservative groups were sufficiently alarmed by the emergence of organized labour and the political left to flirt occasionally with authoritarian ideas. Semi-authoritarian leagues, youth movements, and special-interest (especially farmers') organizations accordingly proliferated, without ever seriously threatening to overturn democracy or even develop into full-blown fascist movements [82]. In the 1930s, sensitivity to a common 'Germanic' culture gave national socialism some appeal to a minority of Scandinavian intellectuals and young people, even if for most Danes – as for the majority of Dutch – actually sharing a border with a renascent Germany lessened rather than enhanced any attraction a native nazism might otherwise have exercised. Parties such as the Norwegian Nasjonal Samling (National Unity) of Vidkun Quisling and the Danish Nazi DNSAP (Danish National Socialist Workers' Party) of Frits Clausen were nevertheless mere fringe groups in the interwar period, and it was only the transformed and artificial climate of wartime German occupation which gave some of them opportunities for growth, influence, and even a taste of power; significantly, Swedish neutrality during the Second World War ensured that its fascists remained marginalized [84].

CHAPTER FIVE

FASCIST AND RIGHT-WING REGIMES

Of the many right-wing dictatorships that emerged in Europe between 1919 and 1945, some, especially after 1940, were explicitly fascist or national socialist in orientation; others, without concealing their debt to Italian and German examples, claimed to be neither. In this chapter, the Italian Fascist dictatorship and the Nazi Third Reich will be examined *as fascist regimes*: that is, as exemplifying the outcome of a fascist/national socialist acquisition of power. Other European dictatorships – in the Iberian peninsula and in central and eastern Europe – will then be considered in terms of their relationship with 'fascism'. As with *movements*, so with *regimes* it is the Italian case that provides us with a starting point and a model against which to examine other dictatorships of the political right, the Third Reich included. It was, after all, not only the first of its kind, but also, for obvious reasons, the most unambiguously and explicitly 'fascist'.

THE CLASSIC CASE: FASCIST ITALY, 1925–1943

In contrast to the uncertainties of the 1922–25 period, Mussolini's declaration of a dictatorship in January 1925 was followed by decisive moves towards the elimination of opposition and the establishment of a new kind of regime. By the end of the 1920s, many of its essential features were in place. Fascist propaganda, increasingly suffused by the leadership cult surrounding the *Duce* (Leader), Mussolini, proclaimed the regime to be revolutionary, 'totalitarian' and corporative. Fascism, it declared and continued to declare throughout its life, was recreating Italy in an entirely new spirit, and raising the country to a position of international greatness. It is in the light of these claims that Fascism needs to be judged.

The Italian Fascist regime was the first proudly to don the label 'totalitarian', thereby elevating into something supposedly positive a description initially hurled at it by its critics. This is an important issue for anyone studying Fascism, for two main reasons. First, the equation of Fascism (and Communism) with totalitarianism was later offered by political scientists as a way of understanding, and linking, the two (see below, pp. 100–1); second, since many of the officially non-fascist authoritarian regimes of interwar Europe, and especially those of Catholic ideological inspiration, also repudiated totalitarianism [*Doc. 12b*], this ought to be a way of differentiating one kind of dictatorship from another.

The original 'architects' appointed by Mussolini to design the institutions of the Fascist regime were chiefly former Nationalists, notably Alfredo Rocco. This was significant, for the Nationalists believed in strengthening the structures and organs of the existing state rather than permitting its absorption by either the Fascist Party, as desired by many former *squadristi*, or the Fascist syndical organizations, as desired by elements of the Fascist 'left'. As a result, during the mid and later 1920s a system was constructed in which the role of the Fascist Party, for all its importance and pervasiveness, was neither a policy-forming nor a decision-making one [133], while 'left-Fascist' syndicalism was crushed in favour of an unthreatening corporativism. Although the political powers of Mussolini as Duce and 'Head of the Government' were all but unlimited, his constitutional position remained ultimately subordinate to the Crown: a sharp contrast, as we shall see, to the position of Hitler. Rival political parties and free trade unions were outlawed, and dictatorship reinforced by an elaborate apparatus of censorship, propaganda, special laws and police powers. Within a structure that in itself was certainly *authoritarian*, totalitarianism would actually be achieved through the activity of the Fascist *movement*, participation in the various elements and activities of which would circumscribe each individual's area of privacy and inject the Italian population with new values and a new, patriotic, disciplined, warrior mentality. At the same time the state would ensure that sectional interests – the Church and Catholicism, the armed forces, big business and agriculture – would be subordinated to collective, national needs. The outcome would be a nation united, resolute and efficient in the pursuit of its interests and destiny [*Doc. 11a*].

Fascism had something like eighteen years (1925–43) to realize this vision – long enough, that is, to be judged according to its achievements. On the surface revolutionary change and totalitarianism may have appeared realities, especially to foreign observers either, according to their outlook, over-impressed by uniforms, salutes and ostentatious hyper-activity or understandably concerned at limitations on individual and collective freedom. In truth, however, the limits to totalitarianism and 'fascistization' were substantial.

Most serious was the survival and potential independence of the Crown. This constitutional anomaly, a compromise necessary for Fascism to win and retain conservative support, was irritating to many committed Fascists and increasingly to Mussolini, not least as a focus for moderate and conservative loyalties and potential opposition [158]. The monarchy's continued existence hindered in its turn the full 'fascistization' of other important institutions, notably the civil service, the officer corps of the armed forces, and the academic world, most of whose members were neither sincerely converted to Fascism nor purged and replaced by Fascist zealots. Dutiful obedience to a Fascist regime blessed by the Crown was one thing in such circles, Fascist enthusiasm quite another [127]. With the Vatican and the Catholic Church, the regime compromised explicitly in the Lateran Accords of 1929. Mussolini thereby bought temporary security at the cost of longer-term vulnerability. The subsequent relationship was never an easy one; the agreement, far from marginalizing the Church, recognized the importance of its role, drew demarcation lines between Church and state, and actually prepared the ground on which Italian Catholicism was able to prepare itself for a post-Fascist future [152]. Most important of all, perhaps, it confirmed and reinforced Catholicism as a public and private world immune to 'fascistization'.

With the economic establishment Fascism reached an early accommodation that thereafter showed little serious sign of being threatened by the dreams of Fascist radicals. Unlike in the case of bolshevism, with which it was at first much compared and later much contrasted, Fascism's achievement of power was unaccompanied by social revolution. On the contrary, it was the defence of existing (and threatened) socio-economic relationships, especially in rural Italy, that was the key to Fascism's success in 1921–22. By this time even those Fascists (like Mussolini himself) with left-wing pasts had repudiated class conflict and proletarian revolution in favour of class collaboration and a 'national revolution' of 'producers'. While rejecting the abolition of private property and abandoning early flirtations with ideas of 'worker control', Fascist corporativists, and syndicalists like Rossoni, nevertheless nursed a hotchpotch of ideas involving the subjection of private capital to the national interest. Some kind of 'corporate state' was to be the means of achieving this. For Rossoni and Fascist syndicalists down to 1928 this meant taking workers' interests seriously via a powerful Fascist trade-union organization; for ex-Nationalists and for Fascist 'technocrats' like Bottai, minister for corporations from 1929–1932, it meant something very different: namely, organizing the component elements of each economic sector within a state-directed 'corporation' for the purposes of discipline, efficiency and production [25].

Although the corporate state was perhaps Fascism's most prized innovation and certainly one of the aspects of Fascism (along with punctual trains) most admired abroad [156; *Doc. 8a*], its actual development was stuttering and piecemeal. Its structural origins lay in the Palazzo Chigi and Palazzo Vidoni agreements, successive steps towards regulating employer–worker relations during 1923–25. Even this early it was clear that employers were enjoying greater freedom than workers; with the 1927 Labour

Charter and the breaking up ('*sbloccamento*') of Rossoni's Fascist Confederation of Workers' Syndicates in 1928, the balance within the Fascist regime shifted decisively in favour of a 'top-downwards' form of corporativism over 'bottom upwards' syndicalism, and accordingly in favour of employers over workers. While the Fascist unions were devoured by the corporative structure, the employers' umbrella organization, Confindustria, retained its independence as yet another of those sectional autonomies that inhibited the achievement of totalitarian goals [155].

During the years that followed, Bottai and other Fascist enthusiasts for a corporate state found that even their version was difficult to make a working reality. During the early 1930s, a National Council for Corporations was established and corporations introduced for the various sections of the economy. As late as 1939 the ghost of the old Chamber of Deputies was finally replaced by a Chamber of Fasces and Corporations, via which corporativism was supposed to become the basis of a new system of representation. But for all the trumpeting of the corporate state's achievements, these were actually few. The corporativist structure was overmanned with Fascist bureaucrats, its provisions easily squashed, manipulated or evaded by Confindustria, and genuine workers excluded from its proceedings [100]. Like the Fascist Party itself, it was marginal to serious policy-formation and decision-making.

What increasingly counted during the 1930s was not corporativism but intervention by the *real* state. There can be no denying that, under Fascism and especially during the 1930s in response to the depression, state intervention in the Italian economy greatly increased – so much so that it has been interpreted by some historians as evidence of a deliberately interventionist and developmental policy [135]. On balance, however, and without understating the importance of what by 1940 was a massive state sector, this seems to have been a matter of expediency rather than ideology or evidence of the regime's 'radicalization'.

If the Italy of Mussolini was to be truly 'Fascist' and 'totalitarian', then 'Fascism' would have to penetrate deeply into Italian society and culture, extinguishing traditional and liberal culture and values; this, rather than a redistribution of wealth or a reordering of the social structure, would *be* the 'Fascist revolution'. The Fascist regime went to great lengths to achieve this goal. The controlled press, the new medium of radio, and novel artistic styles in posters, etc., were employed to *persuade* Italians that a revolution was indeed happening; uniforms, parades, salutes, and the ubiquitous cult of the Duce created a feeling of excitement and dynamism; large sections of the population were drawn into Fascist organizations, notably the young through the Fascist Youth and student bodies and workers through the Dopolavoro ('After Work') cultural and recreational organization [128; 143; 129]. Fascism unquestionably did much to stimulate 'acceptable' forms of high and popular culture, notably via the plastic arts (painting, sculpture and most notably architecture), the cinema, and sport. Alternative political messages, meanwhile, were silenced: by censorship, police surveillance, and the persecution of active anti-Fascists, many of whom were jailed, internally 'exiled' to remote corners of Italy, or driven abroad [130].

How successful was this attempt to 'revolutionize' Italy? One school of Italian scholars, following in the wake of the late Renzo De Felice, holds that Fascism did indeed penetrate both Italy's high culture and its wider society. It was this, they further suggest, that helped make possible by the early 1930s a 'consensus' behind Mussolini's regime – a consensus that was then, later in the 1930s, squandered by Fascist 'radicalization' (for example the unpopular adoption of racial policies) and Mussolini's alliance with Hitler [126]. Most historians, however, continue to believe that Fascism was never more than surface-deep. Italians may have joined the Dopolavoro or the Fascist Youth, and even enjoyed the activities they had to offer; they may have admired Mussolini, rejoiced at the conquest of Ethiopia, and celebrated Italy's sporting achievements under Fascism; but the great majority never remotely internalized Fascist values as a whole.

Since these values were nothing if not martial, the ultimate test of 'fascistization', and indeed of Italian Fascism itself, was war. From the start, Fascism and a fascination with war were inseparably linked. The defining characteristic of early Fascism was its militants' identification with interventionism and the subsequent war-effort, and their determination to rectify the supposed slight of 'mutilated victory'. Soon, Fascism repudiated the ethos of the League of Nations, and by the 1930s the regime had assumed a position in which Italy's ability to make war and achieve territorial conquest was its chief purpose. Even domestic policies were pursued for military reasons and articulated in pseudo-military terms – the 'Battle for Births', the 'Battle for Grain' – while Mussolini's speeches and Fascist propaganda resounded with martial images. And Fascism, it might be suggested, *needed* violent outlets: to maintain and channel the aggressiveness that had been crucial to its rise, to excite young Fascists, to prevent the movement and the regime from becoming 'middle-aged'.

Fascism failed the test of war dismally. Despite the triumphant conquest of Ethiopia in 1935–36, the signs were visible during Italy's intervention in Spain in 1936–38 that the country was ill-prepared, economically, militarily, and indeed psychologically, for modern warfare on any scale [142]. Italy's poor military performance in north and east Africa in 1940–43, and the widespread defeatism apparent by the latter year, confirmed the worst. Italy's wartime experience not only tells us much about the shortcomings of a supposedly totalitarian regime in preparing the country's economy, armed forces, and popular spirit for war; it also carries lessons concerning both the continued strength of pre-Fascist interests and institutions when it came to a major crisis, and the extent of Fascism's penetration of Italian society and culture. In the summer of 1943, with Allied forces in Sicily, Mussolini was effectively overthrown by 'moderate' opportunists in his own Grand Council, working with conservative military figures and the monarchy. With remarkable smoothness, power reverted to the king and his military supporters; Mussolini was detained and imprisoned; and in September Italy surrendered to the Allies [157; *Doc. 14a*].

The death of the 1922–43 Fascist regime demonstrated that the continuing constitutional role of the king was no fiction. The old Italian establishment of Crown, army and bureaucracy, now joined by the Church, when they could bring themselves to work together against Mussolini, proved more powerful than an apparently well-established, supposedly totalitarian dictatorship. Complaisant throughout two decades towards a Fascist regime they could have prevented from ever existing, and could have toppled in 1924, they now revealed the extent of its hollowness. For the monarchy, however, it was to prove too late, for in 1946, tainted by too long an association with Fascism, it was overturned by plebiscite.

With Mussolini gone and the powers of Crown and military restored, Fascism throughout southern Italy simply dissolved. In so far as it survived another year in central Italy and almost two in the north, it was largely owing to direct German occupation and the installation there of a puppet fascist regime, the Italian Social Republic (see below, pp. 91–2). Although some Fascist zealots were determined to fight on, as the Allies moved northwards thousands of office-holders abandoned their party uniforms as cynically as many had donned them, while the mass of the population watched Fascism die with no apparent regret [131].

The nature of Fascism's defeat and death lends support to the view that its revolution was ultimately a superficial one. The possibility of anything more profound and far-reaching was inhibited throughout by its early and continuing compromises with established interests, restrained by Mussolini's own preference for state over party, and perhaps vitiated by an intrinsic lack of ideological drive. Italian Fascism unquestionably created a dictatorship with a completely new *style*, one that envisaged a new kind of state, a transformed national culture, and a new kind of 'man'. It devised and introduced novel institutions, and through its inventiveness in the spheres of propaganda, presentation and political choreography *did* change the surface appearance of urban Italy in ways that persuaded many at home and abroad that a profound revolution was indeed afoot. The practical shortcomings of Fascism, in terms both of the revolutionizing of Italian state, society and culture, and – by its own reckoning no less important – the creation of a new national mentality, masculine, ruthless and warlike, nevertheless indicate that this was predominantly a revolution of appearances and illusions rather than of substance. And although over the course of two decades significant economic and social changes did take place in Italy, it is difficult to feel that these were changes consciously and deliberately effected by Fascism, rather than independent of, or even in spite of, Fascism.

THE EXTREME CASE: THE THIRD REICH, 1933–1945

In discussing the Third Reich *as a fascist regime*, it is necessary to examine the relationship between, on the one hand, Nazism's ideology and mass support, and, on the other, the structure of power and pursuit of policy within the regime. In particular, and given the thrust of the foregoing discussion of Fascist Italy, we must consider how far Hitler and Nazism escaped from the accommodation with conservative forces which had made possible their accession to power. In addition, of course, we must reflect upon the distinctiveness of Nazism in the context of 'fascism' as a whole.

When Hitler became chancellor in January 1933, there was one important sense in which Nazism's position resembled that of Italian Fascism a decade earlier. Hitler's initial government, like Mussolini's, was a coalition, with his party in a small minority. This reflected the non-revolutionary way in which power had been won, and the collusion of established interests and their political representatives. In other ways, however, Hitler's situation differed sharply from Mussolini's. Whereas Fascism's rise between 1919 and 1922 had been meteoric, the NSDAP had behind it thirteen years of struggle and gradual, if accelerating, growth. Highly visible and potentially threatening to its opponents, Nazism was a formidable force, with a party of 850,000 adherents and a violent paramilitary wing, the SA, of 450,000. In wider terms, even if Nazism at this stage could command the support of less than a third of the electorate, this remained a significant popular base on which a governing party could hope to build. And crucially, whereas Mussolini assumed the premiership with no clear strategy for a full seizure of power, proceeded cautiously, and took well over two years to establish a dictatorship, Hitler pressed ahead unhesitatingly. After an intimidated Reichstag granted his government emergency powers under the Weimar constitution, new elections, held in March 1933 in an atmosphere of SA coercion, gave the NSDAP a narrow overall Reichstag majority. During the following months, regional governments were swept aside, while all other political parties and trade unions either were banned or prudently went into voluntary liquidation. Well before the end of 1933 Nazism's 'seizure of power' (*Machtergreifung*) was effectively complete [59]. Hitler's personal supremacy was sealed in 1934 when President Hindenburg's death enabled him to abolish the office of president. Hitler – in sharp contrast to Mussolini – was now constitutionally unchallengeable as Führer and chancellor. On 30 June 1934, on the so-called 'Night of the Long Knives', he moved decisively and bloodily against relics of the conservative right, notably

Schleicher, and more importantly against the most radical and undisciplined elements in his own paramilitary wing, the SA. The principal agent of Hitler's taming of the SA was his elite guard, the Schutzstaffel (SS), the relentless rise of which began at this point.

The seizure of power was accompanied and followed by a process euphemistically labelled 'co-ordination' (*Gleichschaltung*), of which in twenty years Fascist Italy experienced no real equivalent. 'Co-ordination' involved the creation of Nazi administrative organisms alongside or replacing those of the existing state. The process was an uneven one, but over the course of what was, after all, a mere twelve years, the traditional German state yielded before the pressures of the party, and later of the SS, Nazism's most dynamic and fanatical element. That this happened was deliberate, even if the details were anything but carefully planned. In Germany, as in Italy, the party–state relationship reflected both official ideology and the leader's personal preferences. Italian Fascism's failure to sweep aside existing state institutions reflected Mussolini's Nationalist-inspired philosophical idealization of the 'ethical state', and his consequent view of the Fascist Party as the state's servant; Hitler, in comparison, shared many of his followers' contempt for the traditional German state and was committed to a national-racial revolution effected through a revolutionary party. The result was a Nazi, and after 1939 an SS, takeover, which while never total went far beyond anything even attempted, much less achieved, in Italy. Of course, as the ranks of the party and its affiliated organizations swelled, many (as in Italy) joined who were opportunists rather than ideological zealots – but the overall radical drive of Nazi bosses and activists was seldom in doubt [79].

The actual *structure* of power in the Third Reich presents two striking features. The first is the incarnation of the 'leadership principle' (*Führerprinzip*) in the person of Hitler himself; the second is the confusing distribution of authority, responsibility and power at every other level. After 1934, the Führer's official power was unlimited [*Doc. 11b*]. 'Charismatic' rather than strictly constitutional in origin, it drew sustenance from a lavish and grotesque 'Hitler myth' supported by the unceasing efforts of Goebbels's propaganda ministry [141]. This did not, however, mean that Hitler stood atop a tightly structured, efficiently operating pyramid of authority such as foreign contemporaries often believed existed. On the contrary, so dispersed and overlapping was much administrative activity and decision-making within the Third Reich, certainly until well into the Second World War, that some have described the system as one of 'polyocracy' [124]; indeed it has even been suggested that for all his theoretical power Hitler was actually a 'weak dictator' in terms of his ability to direct policy [146].

The former suggestion appears largely justified, although the imperatives of war after 1942 belatedly brought about more effective centralization and a superficially more rational structure of authority. Hitler's personal position, however, cannot be readily described in terms of 'weakness'. Access to the Führer was the crucial condition of personal power within the Third Reich's upper echelons, and Hitler's favour the key to the rising and falling fortunes of Nazi bosses and *Gauleiters* (regional party leaders). At lower levels what counted was the ability to demonstrate that one was 'working towards' the Führer: that is, fulfilling what were known or believed to be the Führer's wishes [80]. As for the overlapping spheres of responsibility, and the related rivalries among Nazi hierarchs such as Goering, Goebbels, Himmler, Bormann and the rest, these had their attractions for Hitler in two respects. Ideologically, the 'system' was consistent with his social-Darwinist belief in the benefits of a 'winner'-producing struggle; pragmatically, it enhanced his leading subordinates' need for his support against rivals and hence the security of his own position. The crucial point is not that Hitler oversaw or determined everything that happened in the Third Reich, but that he decided what he wished to decide in areas that particularly interested him: notably foreign policy and, after 1939, the conduct of war.

The issue of power is vital in any understanding of fascism. The question nevertheless remains: what, in the Third Reich, was the ultimate *purpose* of power? Like Mussolini but more so, Hitler was uninterested in power and its trappings for their own sake. Power was there to be used: in this case, for the regeneration of a decadent Germany, the creation of a racially homogeneous 'people's community', the creation of a racial empire well beyond Germany's existing borders, and the destruction of 'bolshevism'. Whether or not Hitler also envisaged from the start the physical elimination of Jewry and ultimate world domination remains in dispute [136]; suffice it to say that nothing in his outlook was inconsistent with either goal, while the virulence of his anti-semitism and his fervent social Darwinism made both perfectly logical. As for other Nazi leaders, most combined enthusiastic commitment to the broader Nazi project with the nursing of their own personal ambitions and, sometimes, ideological hobby-horses. For Himmler, as head of the SS, this meant pushing Nazi racial policies to the limit and, through the ever-increasing power of the SS itself, truly revolutionizing Germany and its dominions; for Robert Ley, head of the vast German Labour Front (DAF), it meant building up his organization and winning the working class for National Socialism; for Martin Bormann, eventual head of the party chancellery, it meant controlling access to Hitler and concentrating in his own hands the power that resulted; for Goering, it meant developing the Luftwaffe and the industrial complex he headed after 1936; and so on. None of this personal empire-building was inconsistent with Hitler's vision, though whether it was consistent with its successful realization is quite another matter.

In largely replacing the old German state apparatus with a new, albeit 'polyocratic' one, Nazism went well beyond anything achieved by Italian

Fascism and also dashed the hopes of those conservative politicians, bur- eaucrats, generals and businessmen who believed Nazism was 'for hire'. Whereas Italian Fascism never fully escaped the compromises which en- abled it to win and retain power, Nazism proved itself unique among fascist movements in its ability to transcend its pragmatic alliances. Business, impressed by economic recovery, construction and rearmament projects, and the weakening of labour, adjusted more or less comfortably to a regime which spared it even the notional shackles of an Italian-style corporativism. Elsewhere, just as the distinction between party and state became blurred, so the regime increasingly encroached upon other interests such as in Italy retained most or all of their autonomy. Most notably, while their Italian counterparts remained very incompletely 'fascistized', the German armed forces, after a slow beginning, became after 1938 – and especially with the onset of war – increasingly 'nazified' as a result of rapid expansion and selective promotions. As the war progressed, they also became exposed to the challenge of the rival armed SS. Although some conservative officers attempted to resist both processes, they were unsuccessful; the attempt to kill Hitler in the 1944 'bomb plot' was their last, desperate throw [148].

In eliminating, weakening or incorporating established 'interests', then, Nazism came closer to accomplishing totalitarian goals than did Italian Fascism. Whether the vision of a 'people's community' attuned to Nazi values can be said to have been achieved is nevertheless doubtful. The Third Reich's own propaganda, together with the effects of contemporary cinema newsreels, subsequent television documentaries, and the seemingly unstopp- able 'Hitler' publishing industry, have done much to create the picture of an omnipresent Nazism and a German population either convinced of Nazism's message or cowed into total submission by the regime's repressive apparatus of Gestapo, special courts, concentration camps, etc. That Nazism penetrated further into German society than Fascism did into that of Italy cannot be seriously disputed. This was due in part to the greater effective- ness of Nazi propaganda and takeover of education, in part to the famil- iarity (admittedly in milder and more abstract forms) of much of its content, and in part to the greater concreteness and accessibility of Nazi ideology compared with the intellectual abstractions of Italian Fascism. During the Second World War especially, significant numbers of young Germans absorbed much of Nazism's radical message.

It is nevertheless easy to exaggerate the extent and profundity of Germany's 'nazification', and to confuse acceptance with enthusiasm. Three ingredients gave Nazism much of whatever acceptance it did win among the population at large: the perceived successes of the regime's early years, in appearing to pull Germany out of the depression and restore its place in the world; a generalized patriotism to which Nazi propaganda was well attuned; and personal regard for Hitler, which to the very end vastly exceeded popular attachment to the Nazi party, its other potentates, and its overall radical programme. Hundreds of thousands of Germans grabbed the job security and fringe benefits offered by the DAF and its leisure organization, Strength Through Joy (KdF), took what suited them from bodies like the Hitler Youth, admired the Führer, but retained a healthy scepticism towards Nazism as a whole. Despite the weight of Nazi repression, and the virtual impossibility of *political* resistance, other forms of resistance did exist: for example worker absenteeism [145], alternative youth cultures to that of the Hitler Youth [151 *pp. 145–74*], and a widespread rejection by German women of the 'Children, Church and Kitchen' role that Nazism tried to force upon them [159]. Although the Protestant churches' organizational and intellectual autonomy was eroded by Nazism, German Catholicism achieved some success both in withstanding ideological subversion by Nazism and in obstructing the application of some of the regime's more radical policies in the areas of eugenics (selective breeding) and euthanasia [125]. However, if 'nazification' had its limits, it must be acknowledged that twelve years is a short time, especially in relation to a Reich that was supposed to last a thousand. Nazification went a long way in that short time, and would certainly have gone further in a victorious Germany dominated by the SS.

For Hitler, the creation of a 'people's community' was inseparable from the pursuit of foreign policy; on the one hand, the support of a united people was essential to the success of policies that involved the likelihood if not the certainty of war; on the other, the acquisition of 'living space' (*lebensraum*) and colonies would provide the rewards that would help sustain that unity in the future. Hitler's bloodless diplomatic successes in the years before the outbreak of a European war, notably the 1936 remilitarization of the Rhineland, the 1938 Anschluss with Austria, and the annexation later that year of the Sudetenland, were immensely popular. The large-scale war unleashed in 1939 was another matter, but while few Germans may have wanted (or welcomed) it, the ideological and psychological inseparability of Nazism and war meant that some such conflict could not have been long postponed. Like Italian Fascism, Nazism embraced notions of 'healthy' struggle between nations or, in this case, races, together with an obsession with male physicality of which war was the ultimate test. While it is hard to prove, it is reasonable to suggest that, psychologically speaking, Nazism *needed* war. In a more strictly ideological sense, Nazism's belief in 'autarky' (economic self-sufficiency) made conquest, occupation and resettlement of vast non-German territories in the east necessary. Nazi racism and social Darwinism provided justification for the subjection, exploitation, relocation or, as it turned out, elimination of other peoples. None of this is to suggest that Hitler – and the broad direction of Nazi foreign policy was always his – had a precise master-plan or timetable, so much as a *vision* and an acceptance (to say the least) that sooner or later major wars, above all with the Soviet Union, would be needed to realize it. Although many Germans, especially conservative ones, subscribed to the territorial goals accomplished up to the start of 1939, Nazism's vastly more ambitious aims were of a completely different order. Their existence, and the zeal with which they were pursued, differentiated Nazism not merely from the German conservative right but also from Italian Fascism, whose expansionist dreams were neither as resolutely pursued nor remotely realizable. In the event Nazi aims proved, like those of Italian Fascism, self-defeating. It would nevertheless be rash to conclude that, as with Italy, Nazi Germany's eventual defeat was inevitable and thus exposes weaknesses in Nazism itself. Any of several possible contingencies, which cannot be explored here, might have produced a German victory, with inconceivable consequences – including for the study of fascism.

Nazism at its most extreme – and therefore fascism at its most extreme – reached its logical, whether or not inevitable, destination in what we now know as the Holocaust: the mass murder, by shooting or gassing, of over 6 million Jews, gypsies and others the Nazi racial code deemed 'sub-human'. This is not the place to discuss such issues, important as they are, as *when* a decision to proceed to a 'final solution' of exterminating European Jewry was taken, or the degree and nature of Hitler's personal involvement in it [144]. In a book on *fascism*, what is important is the connection between *Nazism* and the Holocaust. What, we need to ask, was it about *Nazism* that made the Holocaust possible?

In the first place, Nazi ideology, to which all Nazi activists adhered and which a substantial minority of the German population at least accepted, was explicitly anti-humanistic, placing very different values upon different kinds of life. It privileged the strong over the weak, the whole over the malformed, the healthy over the sick. With respect to race it regarded 'Aryan' lives as more important than non-Aryan ones, reinforcing this preference with all manner of pseudo-scientific 'evidence'. It specifically de-humanized and demonized Jews as biologically inferior to 'Aryans' and allegedly responsible for worldwide financial manipulation, bolshevism, and cultural corruption. Furthermore it esteemed such personal qualities as intolerance, individual ruthlessness, and unquestioning obedience to hierarchical superiors. The outcome was a value-system within which the adoption and implementation of racial extermination programmes would be subject to no moral or ethical constraints.

Secondly, Nazism's 'polyocratic' system of government and administration, blessed by Hitler himself, fostered, over time, a competitive radicalization among the bosses and bodies who strove to interpret the Führer's will. Under the pressures of war, following the German invasion of the Soviet Union in 1941, one consequence of this climate was a generalized lurch towards 'solving' the supposed 'Jewish problem' in a manner that would truly be 'final'. Even if it is true, as is nowadays widely argued, that the racial extermination programme was the consequence of problems and pressures created by the war in the east, rather than the outcome of longer-laid plans, the essential nature of the link between Nazism and the Holocaust remains unchanged. The war in the east created conditions of conquest, occupation and logistical chaos in which strongly held Nazi ideas on race and morality fused together; wholesale racial extermination thus became possible and, in the twisted minds of Nazi bosses like Himmler and Heydrich, necessary and desirable. That war was itself the product of Hitler's obsession with the need for German 'living space' and with the destruction of Soviet communism. In a wider sense it derived from Nazism's characteristically 'fascist' conviction that war was the best and healthiest way of achieving national (and in this case racial) goals. The Holocaust, and the war that made it possible, were natural outgrowths of Nazism itself.

AUTHORITARIAN REGIMES IN INTERWAR EUROPE

With the exception of Fascist Italy and the Third Reich, none of the numerous anti-democratic regimes established in Europe between the world wars would be regarded as 'fascist' by most present-day authorities on fascism. Many of these other regimes were nevertheless strongly influenced by Italian Fascism and/or German National Socialism, and most were 'fascist' in the minds of those they arrested, imprisoned, exiled and otherwise harassed.

Spain and Portugal

Of all the right-wing dictatorships established in Europe between 1919 and 1945, the two longest-lasting were in the Iberian peninsula. Both were founded during the heyday of European fascism and were therefore commonly seen as fascist, but both endured for long after that heyday had passed. The Portuguese Estado Novo (New State) of António Oliveira Salazar, introduced during the early 1930s following the military overthrow of the Portuguese parliamentary republic in May 1926, survived the death of its creator in 1969 only to be toppled by the revolution of April 1974. The dictatorship of Francisco Franco in Spain took shape within the Nationalist zone during the Spanish Civil War of 1936–39 and was dismantled from within only following Franco's death in November 1975. It is important to remember, however, that twentieth-century Spain had experienced another significant dictatorship a decade before Franco's: that of General Miguel Primo de Rivera (1923–30).

For reasons already explored, none of these three regimes came into existence as the product of a fascist movement, strictly defined. As we have seen, neither Spain nor Portugal spawned significant movements of clearly fascist character in the 1920s, but both did so in the 1930s: the JONS and the Falange in the Spain of the Second Republic (1931–36) and the National Syndicalists in Portugal *after* the inauguration of Salazar's New State. In addition, important elite groups in both countries, while holding back from totally embracing the radicalism that many would regard as inseparable from true fascism, were nevertheless strongly influenced by selected aspects of the Italian Fascist *regime*. In Portugal these included the members of Integralismo Lusitano and many younger army officers, while in Spain a leaning towards 'fascism from above' was evident, first among prominent supporters of the Primo de Rivera dictatorship and later, under the 1931–36 Republic, within organizations such as Renovación Española. The relationship of the Primo de Rivera, Salazar and Franco regimes with Iberian fascism, and with the general phenomenon of 'fascism', is therefore a particularly interesting one.

Primo de Rivera, a bonhomous army officer of broadly conventional views, led the peaceful military overthrow of the Spanish parliamentary regime in September 1923. In doing so he had the acquiescence (if not indeed outright support) of King Alfonso XIII – who was soon publicly to refer to the dictator as 'My Mussolini' – and most of Spain's socio-economic, military and religious elite. The dictator's principal bugbears were the parties and politicians of a parliamentary system he regarded as 'bankrupt', and who had signally failed to 'regenerate' Spain following its humiliation in the Spanish-American War of 1898; in addition he deplored and suppressed 'divisive' forces such as Catalan nationalism and the anarcho-syndicalist labour movement, the CNT. Primo de Rivera initially saw his regime as a temporary, cleansing 'parenthesis' in Spanish political life rather than a new beginning, but as with the possibility of 'normalization' in the Italy of the early 1920s this limited vision soon yielded to another, more ambitious one. Early popularity and successes, facilitated by the boom conditions of the mid-1920s, combined with the blandishments of advisers dazzled by Mussolini's supposed achievements to persuade the dictator to attempt a full-scale institutionalization of his regime. This involved, among other things, the creation of a single state party, Unión Patriótica, and the beginnings of a corporate state: a process that has been referred to as 'fascism from above' [121].

Only by the loosest of definitions could Primo de Rivera himself, a conservative paternalist in outlook, be termed a fascist. Moreover his regime, relatively mild towards its critics, willing to collaborate in social policy with elements of the Spanish Socialist movement, and largely bereft of stress upon the 'new', lacked several features that many would consider inseparable from fascism. Primo's lack of a mass base or a plausible equivalent of Italian *squadrismo* proved crucial to his fate, for when in the late 1920s the Spanish establishment turned against him, he, unlike Mussolini in 1924, had nothing with which to threaten it. Significantly, it was the withdrawal of support by his fellow senior generals and then by the king that forced his resignation: a foretaste, after a fashion, of what was to happen to Mussolini in 1943.

It would nevertheless be too hasty to dismiss the Primo de Rivera dictatorship as having nothing to do with fascism. Without the Fascist takeover in Italy and the wider climate it inaugurated, Primo might never have taken power in the first place; and certainly without the example of Fascist Italy his regime would have been unlikely to assume the semi-fascist form that it did. The dictatorship served not only as the focus for right-wing nostalgia once the new democracy of the 1930s turned sour, but also as a 'school' for fascist and fellow-travelling theorists and propagandists who would do much to undermine that democracy and lay the ideological foundations for another dictatorship, that of Francisco Franco [122]. Franco himself, a favourite, protégé and devotee of Primo de Rivera, appears to have learned at least three important lessons from his predecessor's fate: never to resign, not to be constitutionally bound to a monarch, and not to be soft on enemies and critics [153].

By the time that Primo de Rivera fell from power, thereby precipitating the fall of the Spanish monarchy and the arrival of the democratic Second Republic in 1931, a dictatorship of a different kind was under construction in neighbouring Portugal. In May 1926, in circumstances broadly resembling those in Spain three years earlier, a military coup overthrew the ailing Portuguese parliamentary republic introduced in 1910. Unlike Primo de Rivera, however, Portugal's military rulers showed little taste for entrenching their authority, and during the 1926–30 period they allowed power to fall into the hands of their chosen finance minister, António Oliveira Salazar.

A professor of economics at Coimbra University until drawn into government after 1926, Salazar was a devout Catholic of humble, peasant origins and profoundly conservative temper. During the late 1920s, as miracle-working finance minister under the military regime of General Carmona, Salazar made himself the quiet hero of Portugal's conservative establishment and swiftly emerged as the government's most powerful figure. From 1930 onwards he was effectively Portugal's dictator, and in 1932, as prime minister for the first time, he set about erecting the authoritarian Estado Novo.

Salazar's own ideological inspiration was social-Catholic rather than fascist or national socialist; order, traditional hierarchies and social stability, rather than dynamism, 'revolution', or anything truly 'new', were his guiding principles. His suppression in 1934 of Portugal's authentic fascists, Rolão Preto's National Syndicalists, showed clearly where he drew the ideological line. Yet while the raucousness, unruliness, violent discourse and totalitarian enthusiasms of National Syndicalism and most foreign fascist movements were uncongenial to Salazar, like many other European conservatives he was nevertheless appreciative of the order and discipline which Mussolini and Fascism seemed to have introduced to Italy. The Estado Novo, constructed in a fellow Latin country at a time when Italian Fascism, after a decade of power, stood at the peak of its reputation, inevitably assumed some 'fascist' aspects. These included its espousal of corporativism, its repressiveness and use of an elaborate police apparatus, and its introduction during the 1930s of fascist-inspired institutions: an official party, União Nacional (into which many ex-National Syndicalists were absorbed), a paramilitary organization, the Portuguese Legion, and a youth movement, the Moçidade. It even constructed a somewhat paradoxical personality cult around the private, retiring Salazar himself, albeit one inevitably very different from those of Mussolini and Hitler.

The chief differences between Salazarism and Italian Fascism lay in areas upon which the latter placed great stress without, it might be argued by way of qualification, actually achieving as much as was hoped and claimed: the rhetorical challenging of the established social order, a course which for Salazar had absolutely no appeal; the creation of a vast, complex and (in some areas) powerful single party apparatus, which (quite deliberately) União Nacional never remotely approached; the forging of a new elite, which had no place in Salazar's cautious thinking; the pursuit of totalitarianism, to which Salazar's Catholicism made him fundamentally hostile; and the cult of youth, violence, virility and 'heroism', all of which were alien to his way of thinking. Although during the late 1930s and the early years of the Second World War some of Salazar's governing circle were more attracted to such notions than he was, they made little headway against the resistance of the dictator. And while both regimes were imperialist, the implications of Portugal's *defence* of its African and Asiatic empire were quite different from those of Italian Fascist expansionism [72; *Docs 8b, 12b*].

The most superficially 'fascist' years of the Salazar regime were those during which Franco's dictatorship was emerging in Spain: the years, that is, of the Spanish Civil War (1936–39). The war was the product of a rebellion against the Spanish Republic's democratically elected Popular Front government. The insurgents were elements of the Spanish armed forces, supported by a variety of right-wing parties: the Catholics of the now disintegrating CEDA, the authoritarian, fascist-influenced 'Alfonsine' monarchists of Renovación Española, the ultra-traditionalist Carlists, and – both last and least before the war began – the openly fascist Falange.

Francisco Franco became unchallenged leader of insurgent, now Nationalist, Spain in October 1936, and thereafter forged within his continuously expanding zone an authoritarian regime with outwardly fascist (i.e. Falangist) overtones. Franco's 'unification' decree of April 1937 merged all the political forces of Nationalist Spain into a single party under his personal leadership, with the cumbersome title Falange Española Tradicionalista y de las Juntas de Ofensiva Nacional-Sindicalista – later known simply (if somewhat misleadingly) as the Falange or merely the 'Movement' (*Movimiento*). To this were added, by the end of the Civil War in April 1939, the principal elements of a regime that, like Salazar's, was to last long beyond the end of the Second World War.

In the circumstances of the late 1930s and the 1940s, Franco's regime was considered to be 'fascist' not only (as was natural) by its enemies and victims but also by more detached observers and even by some of its adherents, notably 'old shirt' Falangists who had joined the original Falange before the Civil War. Franco's military victory was, after all, won with the indispensable military help of Fascist Italy and Nazi Germany, while throughout the 1940s and beyond he repressed the left and other enemies no less strenuously – and far more bloodily – than Mussolini. During the early years of the Second World War especially, Falangist propaganda and media control gave the regime an appearance, and Spain a politico-cultural atmosphere, that were ostentatiously 'fascist'. While Spain never directly entered the war on the Axis side, Franco's and the regime's pro-Axis stance was undisguised, and the regime sent a division of Falangist 'volunteers', the Blue Division, to fight alongside Germany on the Russian front.

Even in the early 1940s, however, the Falange's position within Franco's regime was less strong than superficial appearances suggested. From the very end of the Civil War, Falangist radicals found their 'revolutionary' and totalitarian dreams thwarted by the conservative military, economic and clerical interests with whom the Caudillo (Leader) himself was far more in tune [*Doc. 10a*]. Once an Axis defeat began to loom, Franco scraped away his regime's Falangist veneer to reveal a species of authoritarianism inspired not so much by the Falange's style of fascism as by the 'national Catholicism' that had actually dominated the prewar Spanish right. This demonstrates not only the underlying conservatism of Franco's regime, but also how far the Caudillo's relationship with his single party – and it *was* his – differed from that of Mussolini with the PNF. For Mussolini, Fascism and its institutions, however limited their scope of operations and achievements, were important realities, and the regime was self-evidently a *Fascist* regime. For Franco the Falange was merely his instrument, however vital, and the regime never remotely Falangist in its essential character [150].

Of course, it is possible to argue that the dictatorships of Salazar and, more plausibly, Franco were *objectively* as 'fascist' as that of Mussolini.

The Italian Fascist regime, it might be suggested, was actually less 'fascist' than it appeared, while all three regimes represented broadly similar sets of compromises among a variety of rightist factions and established interests, and a broadly comparable set of experiences for the mass of the population. It is the latter that explains and surely justifies the use of the term 'fascism' by many of those who lived, and also in many cases suffered, under Salazar and Franco. In the case of the Franco regime, and bearing in mind the fluidity of the Italian Fascist regime itself, it is probably reasonable to suggest that the 1940s represented a 'fascist phase' that then gave way to something more conventionally authoritarian. In relation to the Salazar regime, however, the verdict must be that the 'fascist' label has more emotional than analytical validity.

Central and eastern Europe

The many dictatorships and authoritarian regimes established in central and eastern Europe between the two world wars took a variety of forms, from what has been called 'authoritarian democracy' in the Baltic states of Estonia and Latvia, to more fascist-tinged systems in Lithuania and Poland, a Catholic-corporativist authoritarian regime in pre-Anschluss Austria, a conservative-authoritarian 'regency' in Hungary, and a variety of 'royal dictatorships' in the Balkans. While all these regimes attracted the designation of 'fascism' from their opponents, nowhere in central and eastern Europe did a fascist or national socialist movement, strictly defined, win sole power before the start of the Second World War.

The authoritarian regimes of constitutional presidents Konstantin Päts in Estonia and Karlis Ulmanis in Latvia were both introduced in 1934 and extinguished, along with the states themselves, following the Hitler–Stalin pact in 1940. Neither was by any serious reckoning fascist; indeed, in both cases, authoritarianism was adopted as a means of restraining extremes of both left and far right, the latter being represented by, respectively, the radical-rightist Estonian Veterans' League and the nazi-style Latvian Thunder Cross, both of which were now dissolved. The Päts and Ulmanis regimes reflect the problems which political extremism of any and all kinds presented to new and still provisional democracies lacking the firmer foundations and consequent resilience evident further west, or even as it turned out in Finland. In Estonia and Latvia, previously moderate politicians concluded that a degree of authoritarianism was necessary in order to prevent something far worse. Both Päts and Ulmanis ruled by decree with the help of bureaucracy, army and a paramilitary 'defence league', but also retained a degree of pluralism and steered clear of even the superficial 'fascistization' adopted by other dictatorships further south [92; 76].

1. Mussolini looks up to Hitler. The Führer's visit to the Duce, 1938.

2. 'International Facscism'. Franco's allies – German, Italian and Portuguese – in the Spanish Civil War (1937).

3. The Left against fascism: Spanish Socialist poster from the Civil War, 1936–39.

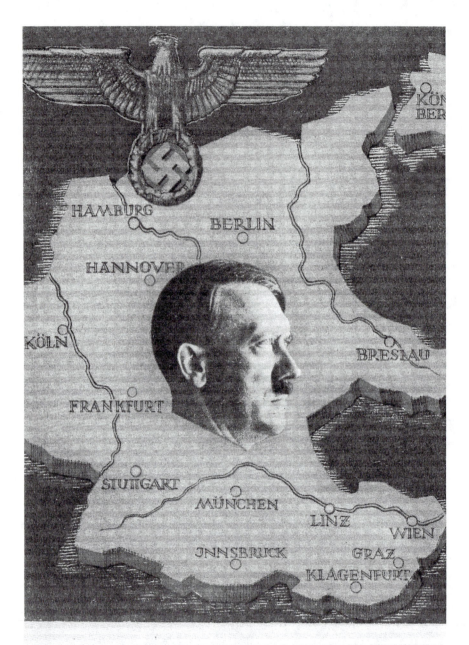

13·MÄRZ 1938
EIN VOLK EIN REICH
EIN FÜHRER

4. After the Anschluss: Hitler as the focus of a greater Germany (1938).

5. Wartime fascism and the 'Anti-Bolshevist Crusade' (1941).

6. Nazism in the 'Time of Struggle': Hitler and supporters (*c.* 1930).

Las primeras galopadas.

7. First steps as a fascist. Spanish Falangist Propaganda, 1938.

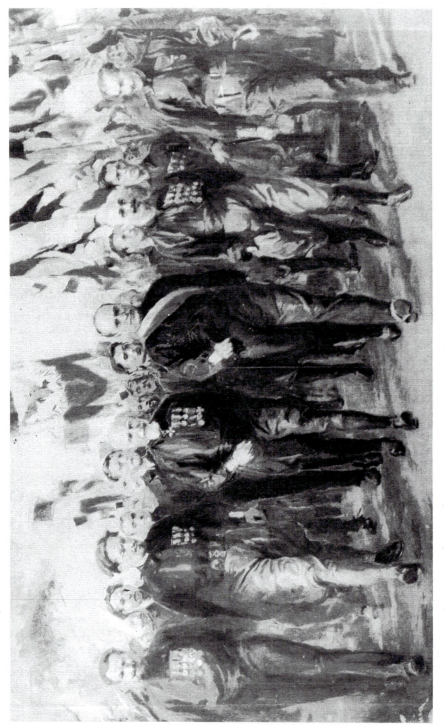

8. Italian fascist mythmaking: The march on Rome as it never was (1922).

Developments in Lithuania and Poland differed markedly from those in Estonia and Latvia. Here, parliamentary democracy collapsed much earlier, in the 1920s, while the resulting authoritarian regimes lived with radical rightist and fascist groups in a complex relationship that fluctuated between partnership and confrontation. The regime of Antanas Smetona, established in Lithuania following the coup of 1926, was an unambiguously rightist response not only to chronic political instability but also to the sudden intrusion of a left-wing government with radical intentions and a pro-Soviet posture. Smetona adopted the right-wing nationalist LTS or Tautininkai as his official party, but found himself frequently at loggerheads with its more extreme elements, notably the followers of Augustinas Voldemaras (prime minister 1926–29) and the secret Iron Wolf organization. From 1934, with the now rebellious Voldemaras jailed and Iron Wolf banned, Smetona's personal power stood unchallenged. During the late 1930s, with the LTS mainstream still active within the regime and Smetona influenced by Catholic corporativism, Lithuania was moving decisively towards a dictatorship of what might be termed the 'fascism from above' variety [89].

Much the same was true in Poland, where following the death of Piłsudski and the introduction of a new constitution in 1935, the country was subjected to a brand of Catholic corporativist authoritarianism ideologically related to the regimes of Salazar and Dollfuss (see below) and channelled through an emerging single party, the Camp of National Unity (OZN). The explicitly fascist Falanga was for a time a partner in this enterprise, but was later dropped: a relationship not unlike that between the Portuguese Estado Novo and Preto's National Syndicalists. Although Poland did not produce a single leader of the standing of Lithuania's Smetona, being led during this period by what amounted to a junta of right-wing army officers, politicians and bureaucrats, it shared with its neighbour in the late 1930s a lurch towards ever more institutionalized and fascist-influenced authoritarianism [119]. The attraction of authoritarianism for both countries' governing elites was enhanced by, ironically, their mutual antagonism and, more important, the nearness of, and possible threat from, their powerful German and Soviet neighbours.

The two principal 'successor states' of the defunct Habsburg Empire, Austria and Hungary, offer interesting examples of states with authoritarian regimes enjoying complex relationships with 'fascism' and 'national socialism'.

It was in 1933, shortly after Hitler's takeover in Germany, that the leader of Austria's dominant Christian Social Party, Engelbert Dollfuss, exploited a parliamentary impasse to suspend parliament and launch the transformation of the Austrian Republic into a new, authoritarian regime. The process, uncertain at first, accelerated in 1934 with the physical crushing of Austria's Socialists in February and the publication of a new constitution in May. The regime of Dollfuss and (following his murder by

Nazis in July 1934) his successor Kurt Schuschnigg was inspired by social-Catholic principles and the ideas of the Heimwehr's intellectual hero, Othmar Spann. It was intended to be corporativist, based on seven occupational 'estates'; a single political organization, the Fatherland Front, would parallel but remain separate from (and subordinate to) the state. Rather like the contemporary regimes in fellow-Catholic Poland (for which it represented something of a model), Lithuania and Portugal, the Dollfuss–Schuschnigg regime assumed more of a fascist appearance as time passed. Like those regimes, it demonstrated that Catholic authoritarianism, while not strictly fascist in inspiration, could draw sustenance from the fascist 'climate' of the 1930s and construct regimes which, on a day-to-day basis, seemed to many of their subjects little different from what they understood by 'fascism'. Nevertheless, like other Catholic corporativist regimes its attempts to carry though its programme were half-hearted and never approached completion. For the restless Heimwehr, which while partially accommodated within the Fatherland Front continued to demand full-scale 'Austro-fascism' and in 1936 found their organization dissolved, and for the Italians who initially propped up the regime, it was a half-hearted affair [*Doc. 12a*].

What truly sets the Dollfuss–Schuschnigg regime apart in any discussion of fascism, however, is its consistently tense relationship with the growing threat of Austrian nazism. Dollfuss's assassination by Austrian nazis during an unsuccessful nazi *putsch* in July 1934 highlights the incompatibility between a Christian Social–Heimwehr regime and nazism. The former, despite some nostalgia for the Habsburg past and occasional irredentist stirrings, did broadly accept Austria's independent albeit truncated existence; Austro-nazism was a latter-day, more extreme pan-Germanism, anxious for Anschluss with National Socialist Germany and Austria's disappearance as a separate state. Compared with a regime which was always an elite, 'top-downwards' affair, Austrian nazism's mass base – especially after the suppression of the socialists, some of whose support shifted the nazis' way – was more *active*, more socially heterogeneous, and in every sense more radical in its ambitions. With the international climate moving after 1935 in Hitler's favour, the 'regime of estates' could not survive the combination of massive German pressure, growing internal nazi subversion, and international failure of nerve [154]. By March 1938 Anschluss was a reality and Austria part of the Third Reich.

It has been plausibly suggested that the Dollfuss–Schuschnigg regime in Austria, resting as it did on the military, police, bureaucracy, Catholic Church and social elites, actually resembled not so much contemporary fascism as those authoritarian phases into which the nineteenth-century Habsburgs had periodically retreated when faced with social and ethnic challenges [6 *p. 145*]. Much the same might be said of the Hungarian regime of Admiral Horthy, imposed in 1920 following the military over-throw in 1919 of the short-lived communist regime which itself had replaced a brief stab at liberal democracy. From then until 1944 Horthy ruled Hungary as 'regent' (for the absent but increasingly irrelevant Habsburgs) with the support, and in the interests, of army, bureaucracy, aristocracy and gentry. Although superficially 'liberal' and parliamentary and always falling some way short of outright dictatorship, the regime's political structures and behaviour were in practice hangovers from the prewar era. Horthy's constitutional powers were vast and unchallengeable, the franchise was narrowly restricted until the late 1930s, and dubious electoral practices were employed throughout. From 1921 onwards, power and patronage were monopolized by the governmental Party of Unity. With the organized left's activities closely circumscribed while Szeged fascists and the various national socialist groups proliferated, the Horthy regime was under-standably considered 'fascist' by its enemies and critics, yet in no meaning-ful sense can the term be accepted by historians or political scientists. Twice, under the premierships of the leader of Szeged fascism, Gyula Gömbös (1932–36) and Béla Imrédy (1938–39), the regime threatened to develop in a clearly fascist direction, but on each occasion it was Horthy's essential conservatism that prevailed. Although before his early death in 1936 Gömbös did go some way towards injecting greater authoritarianism and dynamism into the regime, his achievements fell far short of his rhetoric and, such as they were, died with him; when it came to the test, the 'gentle-men fascists' of the Szeged school were unable to sweep aside Horthyist conservatism [147].

Given time, the 'new wave' of 1930s Hungarian national socialism might have presented the Horthy regime with a sterner test. Whether, with-out the transforming effects of war, Szálasi and the Arrow Cross movement in particular would have seriously challenged the control of Hungary's conservative establishment we shall never know; it seems possible but also likely (to judge from events elsewhere) that the challenge would have been absorbed or overcome. How the Horthy regime and Hungary's undisguised fascists and national socialists fared with the onset of war we shall consider shortly.

From Romania south to Greece, the dominant pattern during the 1920s and 1930s was for troubled and flawed democracies to give way to dicta-torships based on the country's reigning monarchy and its bureaucratic and military allies, some of which then exhibited selected external character-istics of fascism.

The least fascist even in appearance were the royal dictatorships of King Zog of Albania and King Boris III of Bulgaria. In backward and still tribal Albania, a short-lived, chaotic and violent 'democratic' interlude ended in December 1924 with the seizure of power by a former tribal chieftain, Ahmed Zogu. Assuming the role of monarch in 1928, King Zog governed Albania as a would-be 'enlightened', modernizing despot, until removed when his erstwhile protector, Italy, occupied Albania in March 1939 [139]. Boris III's personal regime was introduced in 1935, following the overthrow of Bulgaria's deeply troubled democracy in 1934 by military elements linked with a fascist-influenced, elitist pressure group, Zveno (Link). Having rid themselves of this group, Boris and his circle of supporters governed down to 1940 in a spirit of non-doctrinaire, improvisatory authoritarianism. His regime embraced no fascist or even *fascisant* ideas, introduced no significant new institutions, and comfortably kept at bay the country's two main (though still weakly) fascist and far-right movements, the Ratnitsi and Dr Alexander Tsankov's National Social Movement [63 *pp. 119–29*].

A third Balkan royal dictatorship, that inaugurated in 1929 by King Alexander of Yugoslavia, again had little that was truly fascist about it. Harking back in spirit to nineteenth-century Serbian absolute monarchy, and concentrating power in the hands of the Crown and its bureaucratic and military allies, it stressed order, centralism, anti-communism and of course monarchy. Although a new constitution in 1931 softened the regime's dictatorial features, Yugoslavia's system of government remained a semi-authoritarian one down to the German invasion in 1941. Far-right, fascist and national-socialist groups proliferated, though most of them were small and uninfluential. Between 1935 and 1938, under the premiership of Milan Stojadinović, some attempt was made to 'fascistize' the regime, complete with a leadership cult, uniforms, state trade unions, etc. The attempt was nevertheless unconvincing and its external trappings, according to one historian, 'operetta like' [67 *p. 130*].

The two most interesting dictatorships established in the southeastern Europe of the 1930s were those in Romania, where popular fascism in the distinctive form of the Legion or Iron Guard was genuinely strong, and Greece, where it was to all intents and purposes non-existent.

King Carol II of Romania introduced his version of the southeast European royal dictatorship in 1938, following general elections in which, in the face of the electoral manipulation and falsification typical of 'liberal' Romania, the Legion *officially* won 16.5 per cent of the nationwide vote (the true percentage must certainly have been higher), with still greater success in regions where it was particularly strong. Given the Legion's social radicalism, scorn for the country's 'Westernized' ruling class, and willingness to use violence against its enemies, the establishment of the Carolist dictatorship represents the clearest case of an authoritarian regime of the right, with obvious fascist inspirations and embellishments, created in order to deflect or destroy a genuine, radical, fascist threat; it is as if Victor Emmanuel III had established his own dictatorship in 1922 to keep out

Mussolini. Carol and his ruling clique introduced a fascist-style youth movement, a single party, and an ambitious national economic plan. Most important, however, the new regime attempted in 1938 to destroy the Legion, murdering its charismatic 'Captain' Codreanu and other leading Legionaries, driving others into exile (mostly in Germany), and going some way towards disarticulating the movement's organization. The Legion was certainly never to be the same again, but any thoughts of its death were soon shown to be premature. When, with the onset of war in Europe, the Legion re-emerged as a major force, the king's response was to attempt to incorporate it within a reconstructed, would-be totalitarian, Carolist dictatorship. The attempt foundered when Carol's forced surrender of Romanian territory to the Soviet Union (Bessarabia) and Hungary (most of Transylvania) led to his regime's collapse and his own abdication. Power was assumed by a conservative-authoritarian dictator, Marshal Ion Antonescu [52; 116; 147].

It was certainly not fear of the fascist right that brought about the imposition of an authoritarian regime in the Greece of 1936. The pretexts for King George II's appointment of General Ioannis Metaxas as prime minister and leader of a quickly established 'regime of 4 August' were a supposed communist threat and the alleged inability of parliamentary politicians to achieve stable government in the face of it. In reality the threat from Greece's admittedly growing but still weak Communist Party was illusory, while the politicians were on the point of solving a serious but temporary political crisis when the king and Metaxas stepped in. For Metaxas, longtime critic of parliamentary democracy and leader of a chronically feeble right-wing party, the king's gift of power – for such it was – represented an opportunity that was unlikely to come to him in any other way. For five years, until his death in 1941, Metaxas presided over a dictatorship which openly drew inspiration from both Fascist Italy and the Third Reich while diplomatically maintaining Greece's 'British connection'. His 'Third Hellenic Civilization' rested upon the state bureaucracy and an elaborate police and surveillance apparatus: an authentic 'police state', it has been suggested. Although the regime described itself as 'totalitarian', developed a fascist-style youth movement, the Neolaia, adopted a corporativist approach to economy and society, and erected a personality cult around Metaxas as (among other things) Greece's 'first peasant', it largely shunned fascism's stress upon the 'new' and, more surprisingly in view of Greece's humiliation in 1922, any renewed pursuit of the 'Great Idea'. Nevertheless, Metaxas's was a more developed authoritarian regime than any other in interwar southeastern Europe. In many respects, indeed, and as Metaxas himself appreciated, it had less in common with other Balkan regimes than with the Iberian dictatorships of Primo de Rivera, Franco and, especially perhaps, Salazar [138].

WAR, COLLABORATION AND THE 'NEW EUROPEAN ORDER', 1939–1945

The outbreak of the Second World War in Europe, and the establishment during 1940–41 of Nazi Germany's military and territorial dominance across most of the continent, transformed not only the international relations and domestic politics of all the countries involved, but also the ways in which, in the future, 'fascism' would be conceived and discussed. Although, as we have clearly seen, fascism between 1919 and 1939 was a Europe-wide phenomenon, albeit one that differed from country to country in strength and significance, Nazi Germany's 'success' down to 1942, its retreat and apocalyptic collapse thereafter, and of course the sheer ghastliness of its most distinctive 'achievement', the Holocaust, have inevitably influenced, and some would say distorted, our understanding of fascism as a whole. Perhaps, however, it is *not* a case of distortion: for if we conclude that in the triumphs, nemesis, bestiality and shame of the Third Reich we are actually observing the direct – which is not to say inevitable – outcome of important elements within *fascism*, our understanding could scarcely be more brutally enhanced.

Between the 1938 Austrian Anschluss and Germany's occupation of Yugoslavia and Greece during early 1941, Hitler's sequence of diplomatic and military successes was effectively uninterrupted and came to seem irreversible. For European fascists, national socialists, and right-wing authoritarians, this meant confronting a tangle of temptations, opportunities, challenges and sometimes unwelcome realities. In one sense, Nazism's triumph seemed to represent the ultimate victory of important fascist ideals: not only anti-liberalism and anti-Marxism, but also ultra-nationalism, national-racial revival, social-Darwinian struggle, and the distinctively fascist worship of power, ruthlessness, virility and violence. In so far as most convinced fascists and national socialists, whatever their nationality, nursed at least some of these ideals, they had scant right to complain if one country's fascism realized them more successfully than the rest. They nevertheless needed to come to terms with the fact and to decide how to respond in the face of German conquest and occupation of, or at the very least suzerainty over, their own nation. For the generally more numerous, and certainly more powerful, authoritarians of the 'establishment' right, who before the war had shared most of fascism's hostility to liberalism and socialism while rejecting its radicalism and aggressiveness, the issue was essentially a practical one. In many countries of interwar Europe, after all, it was they, rather than the out-and-out fascists, who had been the chief agents and beneficiaries of democracy's troubles, and accordingly it was they who now had to treat with Hitler.

Charles Maurras, the intellectual leader of Action Française, described the collapse of French democracy in the wake of its military defeat by

Germany as a 'divine surprise'. Many on the European right, and not only self-confessed fascists and national socialists, reacted similarly to the rapid establishment of a German hegemony in Europe. As the German armies advanced westwards and northwards during 1940, they extinguished the last vestiges of the liberalism so ubiquitous in 1919; in all but completing the destruction of European democracy, they also crushed the 'bolshevist' socialism that democracy had tolerated; and when in 1941 they eventually moved decisively eastwards into Russia, 'bolshevism' too seemed on the point of being obliterated. The means may not have been what non-German fascists and authoritarians would have chosen, but the ends were no less welcome for that.

For fascists and nazis throughout continental Europe, attempting to harmonize their own national and/or racial ambitions with the territorial appetites of the Third Reich necessitated some decidedly intricate ideological footwork. In the circumstances, however, most were willing to give it a try in the hope of thereby achieving power within their own countries and contributing to whatever new Europe Hitler might have in mind [*Doc. 13b*]. As for their less radical 'establishment' rivals, many of them too showed every willingness to adjust to, and take advantage of, the new situation. Neither German dominance nor a seemingly inevitable nazi/fascist future may have been wholly congenial to patriotic, conservative generals, bureaucrats and members of socio-economic elites, but the retention or acquisition of power in an apparently irresistible new order certainly was [161 *pp. 107–43*].

That right-wing super-patriots of various kinds should behave thus was anything but surprising. Before the winter of 1941–42, which saw the German advance into Russia slowed and the United States enter what was now a *world* war, German defeat appeared to most continental Europeans a possibility so remote as to be discountable. Not until late 1942 did possibility become probability. Until then, especially with German propaganda making much of a postwar 'New European Order', German-dominated of course but apparently conceding selected nations some measure of independence, rightists of all kinds embraced the new reality and prepared to work within it. From the summer of 1941 an added inducement to collaborate, for establishment rightists and fascists alike, was Hitler's attack on 'atheistic' Soviet Russia. Inspired by this Nazi 'crusade', several wartime regimes committed substantial forces to the eastern front, and thousands of individual prewar right-wing militants, like the Belgian Rexist leader Léon Degrelle, freely enlisted in the Waffen SS [*Doc. 13a*].

What chiefly determined a defeated, occupied or dependent country's immediate future was, of course, the attitude of Germany itself, which proved to be highly variable and often quite pragmatic. To the east of Germany – former Poland and, with the occupation of Soviet territory from mid-1941, Estonia, Latvia, Lithuania, Belorus and Ukraine – German plans for territorial annexation and 'resettlement', together with Hitler's personal preference for direct rule (and in the case of the Baltic states, complete absorption into Germany), left few openings for political collaboration, much less political advancement. This was as true of prewar rightists, fascists and nazis in Poland and the Baltic states as it was of the anti-Soviet, would-be collaborators who surfaced behind the German lines in Ukraine. (Many nevertheless became committed lower-level collaborators, participating enthusiastically in antisemitic actions and playing their part in the unfolding of the Holocaust.) Elsewhere, however, a variety of arrangements came into being: from actual occupation and more or less direct German rule, to indirect rule through native collaborators, to the exertion of ever-tightening influence over nominally sovereign but actually satellite states.

It quickly became evident that Germany – for which read Hitler, whose views were decisive – had no wish automatically to advance the political careers of the most raucous prewar fascists and nazis. Vidkun Quisling in Norway, Anton Mussert in the Netherlands, Léon Degrelle in Belgium, Frits Claesen in Denmark, and all the would-be leaders of French fascism were at first cold-shouldered in favour of safer alternatives. These mostly involved either direct German rule exercised through the existing bureaucracy and at least accepted by the indigenous conservative establishment, or a semi-autonomous authoritarian regime of essentially traditionalist character. The former option was applied, with local variations, in Norway, Denmark, Belgium and the Netherlands. Examples of the latter were France under the Vichy regime of Marshal Philippe Pétain; Slovakia, where – to the annoyance of local nazis – the right-wing Catholic priest Father Joséf Tiso headed probably the most clerical (or 'clerico-fascist') regime in twentieth-century Europe [140]; and the Serbian part of a now dismembered Yugoslavia, where a 'Vichy-style' regime was installed under General Milan Nedić. Neighbouring Croatia, however, was something of an exception to this pattern, largely because early in the war the Italian Fascist regime was allowed by Germany to act as patron, and did so by more actively sponsoring a fascist regime than Hitler was disposed to do. The Ustaša regime of Ante Pavelić, which later did become a German rather than an Italian satellite, earned its place in history chiefly as one of wartime Europe's bloodiest, waging deadly campaigns not only against Jews but also Serbs. This was a record many Serb survivors were to prove slow to forget [67 *pp. 131–2, 140–2*].

In the rather different cases of Hungary and Romania, which during 1940–41 avoided occupation but settled for what amounted to satellite status, Hitler likewise preferred to deal with the conservative dictators Admiral Horthy and Marshal 'the Conducator' Antonescu, each of whom possessed solid establishment support, rather than the Hungarian Arrow Cross under Szálasi or the resurrected Romanian Legion (Iron Guard) of

Codreanu's mediocre successor Horia Sima. These were, as we have seen, among Europe's most powerful fascist movements, too significant to ignore, too unpredictable to trust with power unless there was no alternative, but useful as a blackmail weapon in dealing with their countries' incumbent leaders. Hitler nevertheless stood by while Antonescu, after briefly sharing power in 1940–41 with the Iron Guard in a short-lived, so-called 'Legionary state', crushed the Guardists when they became over-assertive [147]. Antonescu's regime, like Horthy's and Tiso's, may not have been strictly nazi or fascist in character, but all three were more than happy to assist in Hitler's attack on the Soviet Union, sending large detachments of troops to fight in what they regarded as a crusade against bolshevism.

As the war progressed, as German advances ceased and the tide began to turn, and eventually as conservative collaborators like Antonescu and Horthy began to look uneasily towards a post-Hitlerian future that a short time before had been unimaginable, Hitler sometimes found it expedient to concede indigenous fascists more power, or at least the shadow of power. Quisling in Norway [137] and Mussert in the Netherlands [160] were permitted in 1942 to posture as 'leaders' of their respective countries, while in Hungary in 1944 Szálasi was installed as head of state in place of Horthy, deposed and arrested for showing signs of wanting to pull out of Hitler's war [132 *pp.131–74*]. With German troops now directly occupying Hungary, Szálasi's 'rule' was as brief as it was illusory; within a few months it was not the German but the Soviet army that was in occupation of Hungary, and Szálasi, like his Romanian opposite-number Horia Sima, was in exile in Germany. Szálasi's regime was noteworthy for only one feature: a zeal in the pursuit of antisemitic policies, and the persecution of Hungary's large Jewish population, that equalled anything German Nazism itself could produce [123].

Of all the pseudo-independent, explicitly fascist regimes established under German patronage, unquestionably the most ironical example was the so-called Italian Social Republic. This bizarre regime, often referred to as the 'Salò Republic' after its capital on the shores of Lake Garda, was imposed by the Germans upon occupied northern Italy in the summer of 1943, following Mussolini's deposition and imprisonment in July and his rescue by German paratroopers six weeks later. The Duce, ailing and ineffectual, was now installed as head of a fantasy state behind which the Germans wielded effective power. It was manned by a motley rump of Fascist diehards: old-guardists devoted to the 'Fascism of the First Hour', extremists with nowhere else to go, visionaries and downright crackpots who still believed in Hitler's 'New Europe'. The Salò Republic purported to be inspired by, and to be returning to, the 'pure' Fascist principles – republicanism, anticlericalism, syndicalism, etc. – enunciated in 1919 but then sacrificed through repeated compromises with conservatism. But behind its glossy, radical façade festered a shabby and rotten reality: of deference to the Germans and Nazism, vengefulness against those fascist 'traitors' who had helped overturn Mussolini in 1943, and the ruthless pursuit of resisters and Jews. When in 1945, with the German forces' abandonment of Italy, the Allies' arrival in the north, and Mussolini's assassination by the Italian Resistance, the Salò Republic disappeared, it left nothing solid behind it [131].

This bitter aftertaste of the Italian Fascist regime is nevertheless of interest to students of fascism, for at least four reasons. First, it demonstrates the *subjective* difference, for the Fascist zealots who supported it, between their creed and those of their conservative former allies, and the importance of that difference; second, its critique of the Fascist regime of 1922–43 provides 'internal' support for the view that that regime had been less fully 'Fascist' in practice than it was in theory and superficial appearance; third, it provides further evidence of 'pure' fascism's dependence on powerful allies, in this case not domestic conservatives but foreign Nazis; and fourth, it has provided Italian *neo*-fascists since 1945 with an 'alternative' vision of Fascism that transcends mere nostalgia for the 1922–43 regime's real or supposed achievements.

The Italian Social Republic, notwithstanding its lack of real substance, is therefore one of the very few *regimes* established during the Second World War consideration of which adds something to our understanding of fascism and the right as a whole. Without question, though for rather different reasons, another is the État Français established in the spa-town of Vichy in summer 1940 to replace the defeated French Third Republic [149]. Its head of state, Marshal Pétain, was a elderly, devout, deeply conservative soldier whose collaboration with Germany was pragmatic rather than enthusiastic [*Doc. 13c*], but who was eager to seize the opportunity presented by France's defeat and the discrediting of French democracy in order to introduce a state that would be authoritarian, corporativist, Catholic and socio-culturally traditionalist. His prime ministers Pierre Laval (1940 and 1942–44) and Admiral Darlan (1941–42) lacked his ideological traditionalism but also stopped well short of genuine fascist or nazi enthusiasm; they, too, collaborated pragmatically with Germany, claiming at least to be softening the effects of German dominance and exactions upon France. Whether or not the Vichy regime did succeed in shielding France from the fate meted out to Poland, and whether even if it did the moral price was worth paying, are issues about which historians of France, and indeed the French themselves, continue to debate. What is true is that the Vichy regime, Catholic, authoritarian and traditionalist in its original character, was the most *developed* of the regimes erected autonomously of Germany during the Second World War. By 1943–44, interestingly, it was showing clear signs of a *totalitarian* approach that was moving it in what might be regarded as a more 'fascist' direction [120]. At the same time it was viewed by convinced French fascists such as Jacques Doriot and Marcel Déat as insufficiently radical in domestic terms and insufficiently committed to Hitler's 'New European Order' [134]. Here again, only as the life of the Vichy regime approached its end and it no longer truly mattered were the French fascists admitted to Hitler's political fold.

In reality, all of these cases represented a new and perverted version of the kind of compromise which, ever since 1922, had always been necessary in order for fascism to grasp power; here, however, it was not the local conservative establishment with whom the compromise was being reached – indeed, it was sometimes at that establishment's expense – but a foreign power with little or no intention of allowing native fascists genuine freedom of action or manoeuvre. Either way, it simply confirmed what had been true for much of the interwar period: that in most of Europe authentic fascism could win access to power only with the acquiescence of forces more powerful than itself. And although during the later part of the Second World War fascist and nazi collaborators chose to believe that by clutching to Hitler they were participating in a revolutionary recreation of Europe, this was neither what most of them had dreamed of before 1940 nor, worse still, what was actually happening. By the time these desperate and ulti- mately pathetic men were allowed on board Hitler's ship, it was already holed and sinking fast.

CHAPTER SIX

THEORIES AND INTERPRETATIONS

Fascism's lack of a fundamental, unifying body of theory, its many national and local variants, the ideas/movements/regimes question, and the uniqueness of Nazism and the Third Reich have helped generate a range of interpretations of fascism, on the subject of which, in turn, whole books have been written. This section looks at some of the most important interpretative issues.

MARXISTS, FASCISM, AND CAPITALISM IN CRISIS

Not surprisingly, it was the European left, and more particularly European Marxists, who during the 1920s and 1930s took the lead in attempting to understand fascism and to provide a theoretical framework within which it might be understood and combated [38]. As we have already seen, fascism and the wider rightist advance in interwar Europe represented in part responses to the shock-waves of the Russian Revolution, the challenge of the organized left, and what many Europeans saw as the inability of democracy to contain that challenge. Most fascist movements – and increasingly so – not only assumed an explicitly anti-leftist posture but also based much of whatever appeal they possessed and whatever success they achieved on their anti-Marxism and their promise to suppress the entire organized left if and when they won power. In the few cases where power, or a share of it, did come fascism's way, this was of course the outcome. But much the same also occurred in many of the far more numerous instances where democracy was replaced by a rightist authoritarian regime whose relationship with 'fascism' was less straightforward: to cite some examples, Horthy's Hungary, the Austria of Dollfuss and Schuschnigg, King Carol II's Romania, Metaxas's Greece, Primo de Rivera's and Franco's dictatorships in Spain, Salazar's Portugal, and Vichy France.

But there was more to the left's need to understand 'fascism' than its own prospects and possible fate. In Europe and the wider world of the 1920s and 1930s, the Marxist left especially saw capitalism battered by a series of crises, culminating in the early 1930s in a depression so deep as to raise (briefly as it turned out) the prospect of final collapse. The appeal of fascism and other right-wing movements to many of the human casualties of capitalism's vicissitudes, and the seemingly continent-wide crumbling of 'bourgeois democracy' in the face of varieties of right-wing, pro-capitalist dictatorship, persuaded theorists and propagandists of the European left that 'fascism' and capitalism were inseparably related.

What might be termed the 'official', Soviet- and Comintern-authorized view was promulgated in December 1933, less than a year after Hitler's assumption of power; fascism was 'the open terrorist dictatorship of the most reactionary, most chauvinistic, and most imperialist elements of finance capital' [166]. This definition, which remained current within the Soviet bloc until its collapse, took Nazi Germany as its model, but in practice made little distinction between different forms of right-wing dictatorship; fascism was a *form of state* deliberately created by a doomed bourgeoisie during the final stages of capitalism's collapse; fascist movements were intrinsically uninteresting, artificial creations, with little or no truly autonomous support and no ideas worth speaking about.

The limitations of this approach are obvious, and were so to many independent-minded European Marxists even at the time. From the 1920s onward, many on the European left acknowledged that fascism was something more complex than a mere 'agent' of a monopoly capitalism whose crisis, while undeniably acute, might not actually be terminal. Stalin's most inveterate enemy, Trotsky, viewed fascism as a kind of bourgeois counter-assault following a proletarian failure to seize a genuine revolutionary opportunity [193; *Doc. 15c*]. Numerous interwar and post-1945 Marxists proffered one or other variant of a 'Bonapartism' theory; while naturally embracing fascism's role as defender of capitalism, these Marxists – among them the German August Thalheimer [167], the 'Austro-Marxist' Otto Bauer [165], and (in the 1960s) the Hungarian Mihaly Vajda [191] – recognized the autonomy and significance of fascist *movements*, the importance of a combination of 'class equilibrium' and political paralysis for allowing fascism access to power, and the autonomy (in greater or lesser degree) of the fascist state from the socio-economic forces that had surrendered to it their political freedom in return for its protection against the left.

From a turn-of-the-century perspective it is clear that the cruder Marxist analyses of the interwar years, more or less equating fascism with capitalism or at least regarding fascism as capitalism's tool, were always unsound. They either ignored or failed to explain the fact that explicitly fascist movements possessed other sources and preoccupations besides anti-leftism and pro-capitalism; that the social bases of some fascist movements were highly complex; and that financial, manufacturing and landowning elites almost always preferred more conservative outcomes to the assumption of power by the revolutionary right. Nor, even though they were far more interested in 'fascist' regimes than in fascist ideas or movements, did they recognize in the regimes of Mussolini and Hitler those areas of potential or actual convergence with *left*-wing dictatorship that others were to seize upon after 1945.

Nevertheless, while Marxist and other left-wing analyses and definitions of fascism may nowadays be unfashionable and even in some eyes discredited, we must beware of throwing out the baby with the bathwater. Even the most crass Comintern commentators, while wrong to embrace the simple idea of 'agency' and unwise to enquire little further into the nature of fascism's ideas, support and system of rule, were right to recognize that important relationships *did* exist between European capitalism in a period of successive crises and the emergence of fascist movements and (more particularly) regimes. It remains entirely reasonable to conclude that without the complaisance of established elites neither Italian Fascism nor German Nazism would have won power. In helping us to understand why fascist movements 'took off' in some situations and not in others, and why some achieved power while most did not, the stress of Thalheimer, the 'Austro-Marxists' and others on 'class equilibrium' and political paralysis remains helpful. Moreover many leftists, both before and after 1945, while differing over details, were correct to insist that whatever the differences distinguishing Nazi Germany (certainly) and Fascist Italy (probably) from other right-wing dictatorships, all arose within capitalist economies, presented capitalism with no fundamental threat, allowed capitalism to recover and prosper, and accordingly belong to the same, however extended, family. We would be unwise, therefore, to jettison Marxist analyses of fascism, even if there is much about fascism they cannot tell us.

FASCISM AND MODERNIZATION

Marxist analyses of fascism recognized the importance of profound changes within European society that were driven – in their eyes – by the development, problems and inevitable collapse of capitalism. Many 'liberal' attempts to analyse fascism have also sought explanations in a more complex set of transformations characteristic of twentieth-century Europe and together categorized as 'modernization'. These included urbanization, secularization, industrialization, agricultural commercialization, a revolution in communications, and a 'massification' of culture and politics. Against this background, fascism was seen as embodying some form of response to modernization, although little agreement was apparent among commentators as to whether it was best regarded as a protest against modernity, an embracing of it, or something more complex and subtle than either.

General 'modernization theory' has now lost the voguishness it possessed between the 1950s and the 1970s. Moreover in a supposedly 'post-modern' age, the word 'modernization' no longer carries the overwhelmingly positive associations that it once did. Nevertheless it would be absurd to deny that during the first half of the twentieth century in Europe, and allowing for local variations, most of the ingredients of modernization listed above were at work. Given the pace and profundity of the changes affecting much of Europe, it is obvious that the appearance and, where it occurred, the growth of fascism must have been related to them. The questions remain: how, and how consistently?

Most early commentators on the fascism/modernization relationship regarded fascism as fundamentally anti-modern in theory, composition and practice. For the American political scientist Seymour Martin Lipset, writing in the 1950s, fascism (a term he used very loosely) represented a 'radicalism of the center', that is, of a middle class squeezed between big capital and organized labour, desperate to recover lost status and restore past certainties [176]. The German intellectual historian Ernst Nolte, in the early 1960s, saw it as 'resistance to transcendence', an obscure formulation loosely interpretable as 'resistance to modernization, progress and personal liberation' [182]. Other historians and social scientists, however, have taken a very different position, namely, that Italian Fascism especially, but also other fascist movements and even, in some respects at least, Nazism, have been both 'objectively' and 'subjectively' modernizing; the outstanding example is probably to be found in the work of the American political scientist A.J. Gregor, most notably in his *Italian Fascism and Developmental Dictatorship*, a title that more or less speaks for itself [135].

Fascism's relationship with modernization is another of those aspects of fascism which look different according to whether one is considering the realm of ideas, the support given to fascist movements, or the conduct of fascist regimes (though within each of these categories further variations are evident). In one form or another most sets of fascist theories were critical of selected aspects of 'modernity', for example cultural pluralism and political democracy, and often erected myths around supposed past glories and their future recovery. At the same time, however, they rejected a mere return to traditional values and social relationships in favour of something *new*. Within Italian Fascism particularly, but also among French fascists like Marcel Déat and Jacques Doriot, as well as in Mosley's BUF, there existed a positive celebration of modern technology [190]. Mosley was not alone, even if he was unusually explicit, in his conviction that fascism was a 'modern' movement aimed at controlling and directing change towards a future very different both from the feudal/aristocratic and bourgeois/liberal pasts *and* from the future as viewed by liberal-democrats and socialists [181]. Even Nazism, for all its mythification of the Germanic past, the ruralism and neo-paganism of some of its leaders, etc., looked forward to a futuristic, highly industrialized Germany fed and provided for by agrarian satellites (a vision paralleled, after the Second World War, by Stalin's view of the Soviet Union and *its* satellites) [189]. Allowing for all variations, therefore, it would probably be wiser to regard fascist ideas as representing proposed ways of *dealing with* change rather than of reversing it, part of which involved using versions of the past as a 'mobilizing myth'.

Early proponents of the fascism/modernization approach, notably Lipset and Nolte, tended to regard as 'anti-modern' not only fascist ideas but also fascist mass support. Fascist movements were depicted as overwhelmingly middle-class in composition, with the middle class – and especially the lower middle class – viewed as the chief casualty of modernization. In this, at least, the fascism/modernization theorists largely agreed with many Marxists. Increasingly, however, empirical research into the social base of fascist movements (which was only just beginning when modernization theory was in its heyday) has demonstrated the multi-class character of the larger fascist movements and the attraction of fascism for upwardly mobile, upwardly striving *accepters* of modernity. Ambitious if frustrated members of a 'new' middle class, non-Marxist members of the working class (broadly defined), for example, it is argued were every bit as important to fascism as déclassé petit-bourgeois casualties of 'modernization' [180]. We might therefore conclude, perhaps, that rather than fascism's appealing exclusively to either the casualties or the potential beneficiaries of 'modernization', it attracted a complex (and very varied) range of groups *affected* by those processes and inadequately represented by other political forces.

And what of the relationship of fascist *regimes* with 'modernization'? Two things are obvious: first, that the number of fascist regimes, strictly defined, was (mercifully) small; secondly, that most of the processes habitually lumped together as 'modernization' were, in broad terms, historically irreversible for any European regime. Accordingly, while important aspects of the Fascist, Nazi and early Franco regimes – notably anti-feminism, demographic policy, and ruralization – were explicitly anti-modern in character, these were unsuccessful in the face of historical change. At the same time, other policies tended, admittedly in an idiosyncratic fashion, to advance and even accelerate modernization – in, for example, breaking down traditional social relationships, improving communications, and encouraging industrial development and concentration.

FASCISM, MORAL CRISIS, AND PSYCHOSIS

Ever since fascism first made its appearance, commentators from a variety of disciplines and ideological standpoints have attempted to link it with moral or psychological disorder. Such approaches differ from those of 'totalitarian theorists' (see below) and of many Marxists in their preoccupation with the susceptibility of *individuals* to fascist ideas and values, and the vulnerability of societies, cultures and polities to fascist propaganda, recruitment and, ultimately, takeover. The majority of these analyses were conducted during the heyday of fascism or shortly afterwards, and relied more upon assertion than empirical evidence.

It is not surprising that in the wake of the First World War many observers should have seen European society and culture as having reached the trough of a cultural and moral decline which they mostly dated back to the later nineteenth century. In this situation, they concluded, and amid a climate of socio-economic conflict, political uncertainty, and cultural chaos, new ideas and movements like fascism were able to appear as if from nowhere and to prosper. An outstanding exponent of this outlook was the great Italian historian and philosopher Benedetto Croce [164], who, like the historian Friedrich Meinecke in Germany, saw his country's experience as exemplifying a particular strand within this broader crisis. In retrospect it is possible to see that such approaches were suffused with an understandable nostalgia for a more stable prewar world; that supposed cause (moral crisis) and effect (fascism) were less directly linked than they seemed to suggest; and that there was much about fascism and its appeal that they failed to address and comprehend. Ironically, of course, most fascist theorists shared this notion of 'moral crisis', while differing radically in their interpretation of fascism's relationship with it; for them, fascism was a positive response to, and cure for, the moral ills of their world.

If Croce, Meinecke and others were concerned chiefly with *moral* disorder, many others viewed fascism – its ideas, its appeal and its conduct – as in some way exemplifying collective and/or individual *psychological or sociopsychological* disorder. The notion of the 'revolt of the masses', involving the explosive arrival on the European (and North American) scene of mass culture, mass society and mass politics, was formulated in 1930 by the Spanish philosopher José Ortega y Gasset [184]. After 1945 it was widely used, mainly by American social scientists such as Talcott Parsons, to explain fascism's alleged appeal to 'uprooted' elements within rapidly transformed urban-industrial societies [185]. (The relationship of such views with the 'modernization' issue is clear.) Others looked to supposedly more deep-rooted psychological explanations. Freudians such as Wilhelm Reich [188] and Erich Fromm [170] argued that the fascist personality was attributable to, respectively, sexual repression or the collapse of authoritarian family structures. The so-called 'Frankfurt School', whose most representative figure was Theodor Adorno, also stressed the importance of authoritarian German and central European cultures in producing a supposedly 'authoritarian personality' capable of expressing itself either via the exercise of, or subjection to, authoritarianism [162]. All of these analyses (except perhaps Reich's) helped, and still help, towards our understanding of fascism, while suffering from lack of empirical weight and insufficient recognition of the sheer variety within European society and culture. More recent attempts to unravel the psyche of fascist leaders, notably of course Hitler [192] and Himmler [178], or groups of fascist activists [177] have been suggestive, but their contribution to the wider understanding of fascism's appeal and support has been strictly limited; apart from anything else, the more successful a fascist movement in attracting support, the more difficult its numbers make any attempt at retrospective, collective psychological analysis.

FASCISM AND TOTALITARIANISM

In the wake of the Second World War, and more particularly with the advent of the 'first' cold war from the late 1940s to the 1960s, Western commentators attempting to analyse fascism chose to do so mainly in terms of its 'totalitarianism'. The architects and practitioners of the 'totalitarian school' were chiefly political scientists; at this stage, with archives closed and 'fascism' a no-go area, historians had yet to get in on the act. Like the interwar Marxists (with whom they otherwise had absolutely nothing in common), the exponents of 'totalitarianism' theory were concerned with systems of power, that is with regimes rather than with ideas, movements or the context out of which twentieth-century regimes emerged. Focusing upon such features as the role of a charismatic leader, the single party, the official monopoly of repressive power and the media, and the directed economy, these writers insisted upon the common 'totalitarianism' not only of Fascist Italy and Nazi Germany but also of Soviet Russia, the Soviet bloc in eastern Europe and, after 1949, Communist China. In doing so they were in effect suggesting that the most important ideological and political division in the twentieth century was not so much that between left and right as that between Western pluralism and *all* kinds of totalitarianism; thus the cold war against Communist totalitarianism was in a sense a continuation of the hot war fought between 1939 and 1945 against Fascist and Nazi totalitarianism.

The fortunes of the 'totalitarian theory', identified particularly with such writers as Hannah Arendt [163], Carl Friedrich and Zbigniew Brzezinski [169] and Dante Germino [172], have fluctuated wildly over the years. During the 1960s and 1970s, with the easing of cold war tensions, the explosion of empirical research by historians into interwar fascism, the collapse of right-wing dictatorships in Spain, Portugal and Greece in the mid-1970s, and the (temporary) seizure of the intellectual high ground by the American and European left, it fell utterly out of favour, only to recover with the arrival of the 'second cold war' in the 1980s and the 'collapse of communism' between 1989 and 1992. The implosion of Communist regimes under the pressures of crippling defence budgets, internal conflicts and corruption, and the corrosive success of Western consumerism, undermined their appearance of differentiation from dictatorships of the right. Soon thereafter, the newly available holdings of Soviet and satellite archives revealed realities of government and everyday experience that had little to do with Marxism and everything to do with dictatorship. As devotees of the totalitarian theory had always suggested, for most of the population, life under one form of would-be totalitarian regime tends to be much like life under another, defined less by a particular ideology than by the absence of liberal freedoms and a monopoly of power and economic privilege in the hands of self-perpetuating minorities. Symptomatic of what amounted to a 'new look' at totalitarianism was a major, controversial work by the doyen of 'fascist studies', Ernst Nolte, which, in apparently seeking to 'relativize' the Holocaust, lumped Hitler's Germany and Stalin's Soviet Union together as mutually stimulating perpetrators of mass murder [183].

Looking back from the end of the twentieth century, when few illusions can survive concerning the nature of any dictatorship, it would be ungenerous not to concede that the 'totalitarianism' theory, for all its questionable origins and often superficial analysis, did after all have a point. Yet even if it tells us something about the 'converging' tendencies of would-be totalitarian dictatorships, regardless of their origins, this is not, or should not be, enough to satisfy historians seeking to understand *fascism*. 'Totalitarianism' never sought to explain fully the origins and complexities of fascism and the rest of the political extreme right, and certainly does not do so. It has little to say about fascist ideas, fascism's social base, its road to power, or the great majority of fascist movements that enjoyed no success. Its devotees largely fail to explore – or admit – the distinction between 'fascist' expansionism and the (I would argue) very different foreign policies pursued by the Soviet and other communist regimes. In any case, and as we have clearly seen, in Fascist Italy especially, totalitarianism was a dream so far from fulfilment as to undermine the entire approach. Even in the German case, leading scholars have increasingly tended to see the Third Reich not as a fully realized totalitarian regime but as a 'polyocracy' in which power was actually dispersed among contending interests and blocs, with Hitler an 'inefficient' dictator and far more extensive areas of individual and collective autonomy than would once have been believed [175].

A REVOLUTION OF THE RIGHT?

The decline and collapse of communism since the late 1980s has undoubtedly assisted the emergence of what one of its exponents has recently termed a 'new consensus' on fascism, which treats its ideology seriously and regards it as a revolutionary force in its own right, every bit as worthy of serious consideration as liberalism, conservatism or Marxism. In a specifically Italian context, the colossus among Italian historians of Fascism, Renzo De Felice, and younger followers such as Emilio Gentile, have taken Fascism's revolutionary aims and achievements more seriously than many others would wish to do [126; 171]. Early advocates of applying such a view to fascism more widely were the Israeli scholar Zeev Sternhell, and the Americans A.J. Gregor and George Mosse. Sternhell, publishing chiefly in France, concentrated on French and later Italian fascism to argue that fascism represented an authentically revolutionary fusion of deviant Marxism and radical nationalism [32; 110]. A broadly similar position was taken, and then taken much further, by Gregor, who, in a series of works treated with suspicion by many fellow academics, suggested not only that Fascist Italy had been a genuinely 'developmental dictatorship' but that in this it belonged within a much wider category of twentieth-century dictatorships that included, among others, the Soviet Union, Mao's China and Castro's Cuba [173].

Sternhell and Gregor found it difficult to fit Nazism and the Third Reich into their typologies, but others have been more willing to make the attempt. George Mosse, for example, wrote of fascism, and in particular nazism, as embodying above all a *cultural* revolution, seeking to mobilize the masses behind a programme of national, racial and spiritual renewal, and to replace liberal materialism with a new value system and a 'new man'. Fascism was thus not conservative nor wholly reactionary, but – in its own way – revolutionary [179].

The tendency, which all these examples illustrate, to view fascism in its own terms, as defined by its ideology, and as revolutionary in character, has if anything gathered momentum during the 1990s, as communist dictatorships have become a matter of history, less obviously 'different' from, or more successful than, other forms of supposedly revolutionary regime. Among its leading exponents have been two British scholars, Roger Eatwell and Roger Griffin. The latter in particular, with his 'ideal type' definition of fascism as 'a genus of political ideology whose mythic core in its various permutations is a palingenetic form of populist ultra-nationalism' [174], has unquestionably given a major new twist to our view and understanding of fascism, and forced all students of fascism to take more seriously ideas and ideological packages that previously had been too casually dismissed. Griffin's definition greatly assists the essential task of distinguishing fascism, on the ideological level, from other elements of the right. Eatwell's approach is broadly compatible with Griffin's, both in its stress upon fascist *ideology* and in the manner in which that ideology is viewed; fascism, he writes, is 'a form of thought which preaches the need for social rebirth in order to forge a *holistic-national-radical Third Way'* [168]. Eatwell provides us with a timely reminder as to the historical pedigree of the term 'third way', nowadays used very differently by politicians and, indeed, by social scientists.

'Fascism' has always been far more than merely a set of ideas, however, and it is difficult not to conclude that undue stress upon its ideological and noisily 'revolutionary' aspects devalues the importance of issues just as crucial to our understanding of fascism *in all its aspects and (where appropriate) stages.* These include the sociology of fascist (and other right-wing) movements, the pursuit and acquisition of power, relationships between fascism 'proper' and the rest of the right, and the structure and character of fascist (and, again, other right-wing) regimes. To insist that fascism deserves to take its place as a twentieth-century revolutionary set of ideas raises as many questions as it answers concerning the applicability of those ideas and their centrality to the fascist experience as a whole.

Two American historians, Stanley Payne and Robert Paxton, have within the last few years adopted a more pragmatic approach to these issues. In his monumental *A History of Fascism, 1914–1945,* Payne covers in detail all aspects of fascism, not only in Europe but also in other parts of the world such as Latin America, before concluding with what he terms a 'retrodictive theory of fascism' embracing cultural, political, social, economic and international factors. Readers of this book anxious for more detail will find Payne's impressive study useful [187]. They will also benefit from reading Robert Paxton's (much briefer) attempt, broadly consistent with that mounted here, to cope with fascism's dynamic and shifting character as it moves along the ideas/movement/regime route. Paxton proposes 'five stages of fascism'. These are '(1) the initial creation of fascist movements; (2) their rooting as parties in a political system; (3) the acquisition of power; (4) the exercise of power; and ... (5) radicalization or entropy'. Each stage, Paxton suggests, involves a distinct historical process, and its analysis accordingly requires the deployment of 'different scholarly strategies' [186]. By taking fascist ideology seriously while keeping it firmly in its place, Paxton provides historians with a framework within which fascism, and its relationship with other elements of the right, may be understood in all their shifting and untidy reality. Another attempt at achieving this is made in the next section of this book.

PART THREE   CONCLUSIONS

CHAPTER SEVEN

UNDERSTANDING FASCISM

A HISTORIAN'S VIEW

Between the two world wars, there emerged in most European countries political movements embracing a distinctive combination of ideas, myths and goals to which we may conveniently apply the label 'fascist': a term invented in Italy and widely adopted over the years that followed. Those ideas were self-consciously 'revolutionary' in a sense very different from that understood by the revolutionary left, involving variable combinations of ultra-nationalism, authoritarianism or even totalitarianism, corporativism, belief in a new, 'purified' political and cultural order, and acceptance of a 'leadership principle'. In a few countries – Italy, Germany, Austria, Hungary, Romania – such movements achieved genuine mass support and political potency, yet only in the first two did they actually win political power in what might be termed 'normal', that is to say peacetime, conditions. Even in these cases they did so with the collusion of conservative elites at a time when their success was anything but inevitable. Elsewhere, the Austro-Nazis achieved what little power they were permitted only in the wake of what amounted to German annexation; the Hungarian national-socialist Arrow Cross and the Romanian Iron Guard grasped power only in wartime conditions, as did the much weaker Croatian Ustaša and the assorted fascists and nazis of France, Belgium, the Netherlands and Norway. Even the Spanish Falange, which in some senses might be considered the third most successful European fascist movement, blossomed only amid the peculiar conditions of civil war, won a share of power only as the lackey of Franco's military-conservative dictatorship, and never in the course of thirty-eight years came close to exercising that power independently.

In most of northwestern Europe (Britain, Ireland, the Nordic countries, the Benelux countries, Switzerland and, on balance, France) and in pre-Munich Czechoslovakia, true fascism was essentially a weak, largely imitative, and essentially *artificial* phenomenon, incapable of effectively challenging an entrenched and resilient liberal-democratic system and ulti-mately dependent on German invasion and occupation for a largely illusory and in every case shabby experience of power. Further east and further south (in Poland, the Baltic states, most of the Balkans, Portugal, and even pre-Civil War Spain) authentic fascism was overshadowed by varieties of establishment authoritarianism – royalist, military, religious, bureaucratic – which either suppressed it or domesticated it for their own, essentially conservative, purposes. In several of these cases, nevertheless, the adoption of 'fascism from above' created a situation different in degree rather than in kind from that achieved when fascism proper won and exercised power by compromise. Although it is undeniable that Mussolini's regime retained at least something of the revolutionary quality of the Italian Fascist movement in opposition, in reality it was only in Germany that fascism, or to be precise Nazism, *convincingly* continued its revolution once in power.

When fascism is defined, as at the outset it must be, with some degree of precision, it is accordingly revealed to have been throughout most of Europe a dismal failure. Without placing too much reliance on an ultimately futile counterfactualism, one might suggest that had a few establishment figures behaved differently in the Italy of October 1922 and the Germany of January 1933, not only would the history of the twentieth century have taken a very different course, but 'fascism' might have been a mere historical footnote instead of the basis, as it is, of the academic industry referred to earlier – and of which this book forms a modest part. Counterfactual musings aside, one might reasonably ask whether the actual record of 'generic fascism', as distinct from its unquestionable power of morbid fascination, has really been sufficient to justify such an industry; and whether, perhaps, we should not be concerning ourselves less with the history of 'fascism' and more with that of the 'anti-democratic right' of which it formed merely a part – and, taking pre-1940 Europe as a whole, by no means the most successful part.

Yet while a due sense of proportion concerning fascism's historical importance needs to be maintained, this still does not mean that we can afford to deny or neglect fascist 'distinctiveness'. For one thing, obviously, fascism *did* achieve power, whether avoidably or not, in two of Europe's major countries, Italy and Germany, with cataclysmic consequences for the fate of Europe as a whole. Even if it had never so much as surfaced anywhere else, we would therefore still be forced to recognize its importance to the history of the twentieth century, and to try to understand what it represented.

Secondly, and more subtly, we need to recognize the encouragement that Fascist and Nazi 'successes' gave to authoritarians elsewhere in interwar Europe who, in the strict 'ideological' sense of the term, were not fascists themselves. Before 1940 – and indeed for some time beyond – this had far more significance for most of Europe than the pathetic rantings and struttings of mimetic homegrown fascists. Quite possibly, the anti-democratic, authoritarian soldiers, politicians, bureaucrats, clerics and monarchs who subverted or overthrew liberal democracy throughout much of central, southern and eastern Europe during the course of the 1920s and 1930s would have behaved in much the same way even had Mussolini not got there first or had Hitler not followed him on to the world stage a decade later. We certainly cannot be *sure* of this, however, since the inspirational example of Italian Fascism and then of German Nazism for European rightists of *all* kinds is hard to deny. This is particularly true of the 1930s, when against the backdrop of the depression many Europeans convinced themselves that democracy was finished, and that the future lay with 'fascism', however loosely they may have understood or used the term.

Not only did this growing, Italian- and German-induced sense that Europe's future was 'fascist' assist the overthrow of many interwar European democracies, but the character and conduct of many of the authoritarian regimes then established was strongly if selectively influenced by their leaders' and architects' interpretation of the Italian and/or German reality. Thus the Primo de Rivera regime more closely and deliberately mimicked Fascist Italy the longer it survived, while little over a decade later the Franco regime of the early 1940s began its life with an openly fascist appearance that its leader was soon to find inappropriate and seek to shed. From Greece's dictator Metaxas with his 'Third Hellenic Civilization', to the uniformed youth movements of Carol II's Romania and Stojodinović's Yugoslavia, by the mid or late 1930s much of southern, central and eastern Europe – even for a few years the Portugal of the ultra-conservative Salazar – *looked*, and doubtless to many of its peoples *felt*, fascist, even if, when subjected to the subsequent scrutiny of historians and political scientists, it strictly was not.

Knowing as we now do how insubstantial was much of Fascist Italy's veneer, we need to be particularly careful not to overstate the gulf between Fascist Italy and at least some of the fascist-influenced dictatorships just referred to. As we have seen, the compromise with conservative forces that had permitted Fascism to take power in 1922 and retain it two years later represented an arrangement from which the regime was never able to break free and which in 1943 was crucial to its overthrow. Had this not been so, Fascist restlessness during the 1930s would not have been so evident, nor the Salò Republic of 1943–45, for all its hollowness, so ostentatious in its 'revolutionary' self-presentation. Behind the radical façade of Fascist Italy lurked a conservative reality [100]. Yet this apparent contradiction, it might be argued, was actually not a contradiction at all, since at the time it is doubtful whether any other kind of 'Fascist' regime could have existed. As a supposedly revolutionary movement, Italian Fascism was deficient in at least two vital respects. First, while its mass appeal certainly was considerable, its base remained a long way short of being broad enough to drive it to power unaided. Secondly, once having won power by the only means available to it, namely an alliance with the establishment, it lacked a powerful enough ideological thrust to sweep, or even elbow, that establishment completely aside. As a result, the underlying reality of Fascist Italy may have been less different from that of its many, sometimes selective, imitators than might be expected to have been the case.

Perhaps, therefore, the *fascisant* imitators – Franco, Metaxas, King Carol, Smetona, even Salazar and Pétain, and the rest – intuitively grasped an underlying truth that analyses based on fascist theory and elite culture have tended to avoid. This was that more often than not 'fascism', as ideology and stylistic veneer or as political movement, was something the conservative-authoritarian right could use, and when appropriate discard, but which they had serious reason to fear in only rare instances and exceptional circumstances. To take another perspective, those interwar liberals and left-wingers who categorized all contemporary right-wing dictatorships as 'fascist' may have had a point. That is, that irrespective of the *origins* of such dictatorships, and in particular of whether they represented (as most did not) the fruit of a powerful fascist *movement* based on recognisably fascist *ideas*, the outcome for the person in the street, on the farm, or in political detention was much the same. A 'fascist' *regime*, it might in other words be tentatively suggested, can be established in a variety of ways, of which impulsion from a powerful fascist *movement* is only one. Fascist features grafted on to a conservative-authoritarian body may produce a result little or no less authentically 'fascist' than a fascist movement that sells out to established interests.

This argument will probably not convince devoted pursuers of 'generic fascism', and it must be admitted that it does have to contend with a number of important challenges. First, at one analytical extreme it must cope with the fact that some of the dictatorships mentioned in this book – the presidential 'authoritarian democracies' of Estonia and Latvia, for example, or the royal dictatorship of Bulgaria's Boris III – were not fascist *by any reasonable criteria*; second, it perhaps takes insufficiently seriously the centrality and possible distinctiveness of aggressive, militaristic expansionism within Italian Fascism, something that few other interwar dictatorships displayed; third, and still more problematically, it evades the 'Third Reich question': the fact that the Third Reich simply refuses to conform to the fascism/establishment 'compromise' model that, *mutatis mutandis*, largely applies in all other cases, whether of 'fascism from below' or 'fascism from above'.

The first of these qualifications is easily enough dealt with, essentially by conceding the point: namely, that interwar or wartime European dictatorships which neither (i) drew upon a prior fascist or nazi mass movement, nor (ii) used the Italian and/or German models to develop 'fascism from above', nor (iii) took advantage of wartime circumstances to pursue fascist or nazi goals, cannot be regarded as fascist even in the 'objective' sense.

The second qualification may at first sight appear more awkward but in fact is also not too difficult to deal with. The importance of militarism, international aggressiveness, territorial expansionism, and even imperialism to Italian Fascism and Nazism is inescapable, while similar tendencies can easily be observed in (for example) Spanish Falangism and Hungarian national socialism. There nevertheless remain numerous fascist movements – the BUF, most of the French examples, those in the Netherlands and Scandinavia, even the Romanian Legion – which, while some may have wished to hold on to and exploit empires or territories already possessed, cannot be said to have nursed aggressive ambitions towards neighbours or the alien world at large. International aggressiveness is better regarded, therefore, as a central feature of (significantly enough, to be sure) the Italian, German and *some* other variants of fascism, related to the historical development and geopolitical positions of the countries concerned, rather than as an integral feature of fascism itself. Antagonism and frequently violence towards *internal* minorities, enemies and dissidents, however, were characteristic of all fascist movements and regimes – though obviously not exclusive to them.

The 'Third Reich question', however, it must be conceded, remains an intractable one. Clearly it would be absurd to suggest (though some have tried) that Nazism and Italian Fascism were generically unrelated, that they were not members of the same family; nevertheless it equally cannot be denied that like siblings sharing genetic material they also exhibited major behavioural differences. If, as Geoff Eley has usefully and trenchantly written, fascism compared with the rest of the right was simply 'more extreme in every way' [194], then Nazism, as movement but even more as regime, was more extreme still. Unlike Italian Fascism, which after all enjoyed power much longer, Nazism (i) refused to live with the compromise which brought it to power and (ii) demonstrated that it did not have to. Papen was wrong: Hitler was not after all for hire, while Nazism proved to contain enough revolutionary material to proceed with the removal and replacement of old elites whose Italian counterparts survived Fascism pretty much unscathed.

Does, then, the history of Nazism and the Third Reich invalidate the 'compromise' argument that has run like a thread through this book: that is, that European fascist ideas and movements, for all their dramatic effect and revolutionary rhetoric, were generally too intellectually weak and contradictory, and the support they attracted too limited, to produce true revolutions, so that their devotees were forced to settle for something less: either power-sharing with established elites, influencing those elites from outside, or grovelling for power in the wake of Hitler's advances? In general terms it does not, since Nazism and the Hitler regime clearly represented an extreme exception to a rule they thereby help to prove. Nazism offers us, just the same, a graphic and appalling illustration of what, in an exceptional form, fascism *can* be and *can* do – something of which we need to be fully aware when reflecting upon present-day fascist activity and the possible emergence of serious, though no doubt very different, forms of fascism in the future.

'NEO-FASCISM' AND 'POST-FASCISM': SOME TURN-OF-THE-CENTURY REFLECTIONS

The main purpose of this book has been to consider fascism in its heyday: the interwar period and the years of the Second World War. It is a work of history, not of contemporary politics or prophesy. Nevertheless, just as it was necessary, in order to understand fascism, to go back to the years before it actually existed, so it is at least desirable to reflect briefly on the phenomenon of neo-fascism in the Europe of the last half-century [195].

It would have been surprising, in the pluralist politics of non-communist Europe after 1945, and indeed of post-communist eastern Europe since 1989, if political minorities had not seized upon the former ideals, myths and 'achievements' of fascism and nazism and embraced them for their own purposes. And indeed, most European countries have produced examples of such organizations, ranging in size from the significant to the barely visible, and in character from the highly 'political' to the psychotically violent. At the more 'political' end of the spectrum have stood parties such as the Italian Social Movement; the German National Democrats, Republikaner and German People's Union; in Britain the Union Movement, the National Front and the British National Party; in Belgium the Vlaamse Blok; and so on. At the more unabashedly violent end (though most of the aforementioned parties have housed a thuggish element) have seethed a profusion of *groupuscules* far too numerous to mention – and mostly too tiny to be worth mentioning.

It would be wrong to seek to play down the significance or repulsiveness of explicitly neo-fascist ideas and activity, their denial or at best attempted relativization of the Holocaust, their scapegoating of and violence against ethnic minorities, etc. Nevertheless what should reassure antifascists is that despite periodic alarms over the rise or revival of fascism in one or more European countries, open neo-fascism and neo-nazism *have* mostly remained fringe affairs, fed above all by ethnic prejudice – against north African immigrants in France, Asian and West Indian immigrants in Britain, Turkish and east European workers in Germany and Austria, Moroccans in Spain, gypsies in parts of eastern Europe, and of course Jews everywhere. Prejudice against immigrants, suspicion of Europeanization

and 'globalization', and genuine if misdirected economic and social griev-
ances, have for some marginalized elements become caught up with a sad
and highly selective nostalgia for the supposed certainties and glories of a
fascist or nazi past. This combination has helped nourish the far-right fringes
in Germany, where explicit neo-nazism has none the less been constrained by
the law; in Italy, where by and large neo-fascism has operated legally and
achieved some electoral success; in Austria; in post-communist Hungary and
Romania, where the spirits of Szálasi and Codreanu have once again been
invoked by mainly youthful nationalists. The emergence on a potentially
larger scale, during the 1990s, of a populistic and antisemitic ultra-
nationalism in Russia, Poland, and other countries of eastern Europe, however, probably reflects not so much nostalgia for a fascist past as ignorance
of what fascism – as distinct from the recently experienced excesses of
Soviet-style communism – can mean. And recent experience certainly counts:
nothing could be more telling than the utter marginality of neo-fascism in
precisely those European countries – Spain, Portugal and Greece – which
have had the most recent experience of right-wing dictatorship.

There is, however, another aspect to this picture, and one which particularly merits attention in a book that has stressed the protean quality of
fascism and its 'presence' within movements that may not themselves wear,
or quite deserve, the fascist label. Nostalgia for selected aspects of a fascist
past, together with some of the characteristic impulses of fascism, can and
do express themselves in forms less obvious and, it might be argued, less
dated than a neo-fascism of swastikas, salutes and coloured shirts. During
the 1980s and 1990s, Europe has witnessed the emergence of significant
organizations of what might best be termed 'post-fascist' character: for
example, the French Front National of Jean-Marie Le Pen; Alleanza
Nazionale, the reconstructed Italian far right of the mid and late 1990s; and
Jörg Haider's Freedom Party in Austria. For reasons of political acceptability these parties have sought to distance themselves from outright
fascism or neo-fascism, while displaying clear signs of not having turned
their backs completely on the past. Former neo-fascists have already
participated (though not for long) in an Italian coalition government; the
Front National (though now split into two) continues to play an important
part in French political life, especially at regional level; and of course in
Austria the Freedom Party, to the horror of European liberal opinion, in
early 2000 translated its growing support and influence into a major share
of power at national level. As yet it remains uncertain whether this new,
'post-fascist' form of compromise, whereby the 'respectable' far right (as
distinct from the violent fringe) appears to embrace the machinery and
values of democracy, truly represents fascism's final, reluctant capitulation
to liberalism, or merely a potential *subversion* of democracy by forces
whose conversion is purely tactical and ultimately cynical. Time will tell.

All in all, it seems reasonable to conclude that, as we look back upon what Mussolini predicted would be 'the Fascist century' and forward to its successor, outright neo-fascism and neo-nazism as they are currently understood, while a pernicious nuisance and for some minorities a life-ruining and sometimes life-threatening evil, hardly offer a major threat to democracy itself. However, the role of the 'parliamentary', post-fascist extreme right, the authenticity of whose democratic credentials is to say the least debatable and whose future evolution is difficult to predict, does raise serious questions for European democracies and their supporters. The possibility cannot be entirely ruled out, even if the prospect may not be an immediate one, that European democracy in the early twenty-first century may begin to find itself being challenged or undermined by an extreme right infected by at least some elements of post-fascist nostalgia or fascist-style ethno-racial prejudice. The dramatic accession to power of the Austrian Freedom Party ought to be sufficient to counsel us against complacency. As a new century and a new millennium dawn, and as the times and memories of fascism's heyday recede, it would be dangerous to conclude that new versions of this menace will never reappear to threaten the safety and the lives of minorities, the security of democracy, and even international peace. Remembering and understanding the past is one way of preparing ourselves.

CHAPTER EIGHT

APPENDIX: FASCISM, A TEMPLATE

It was not the intention, in writing this short book, to offer yet another *definition* of fascism. As must have become obvious, fascism continues to elude satisfactory precise – and especially concise – definition owing to its intrinsic fluidity and the metamorphoses through which it must go on the journey from ideas, through movement, to regime. It is as if one were to attempt a single definition or description embracing larva, pupa and insect; even if scientifically possible, it would be unlikely to bear much resemblance to visible reality.

Nevertheless to opt out of the definition game entirely would be an act of authorial cowardice and unhelpful to the reader. What this brief appendix offers, therefore, is not so much a *definition* as a kind of three-part *template* which attempts to embrace that process of metamorphosis which historians ought surely to consider crucial to the understanding of fascism, but which too many static definitions fail squarely to confront.

Fascism, therefore, may be said to be:

1. *A body of ideas and 'myths'*, generally arising within a particular national or ethnic context and accordingly subject to considerable local variations. Its core may nevertheless be said to consist of:
   (i)   extreme nationalism and sometimes racism, these involving →
   (ii) belief in national and/or racial revolution embodying rebirth from an existing condition of subjection, decadence or 'degeneracy'; this in turn requires →
   (iii) rejection of (a) pluralist liberalism and democracy; (b) uncontrolled capitalism; (c) 'materialistic' socialism; (d) notions of class conflict, all in favour of →
   (iv) authoritarian or more probably 'totalitarian' rule involving (a) a single party; (b) the 'leadership principle', and (c) an 'integrative' or 'corporate' state. This will be accompanied by →

(v) the creation and (given time) constant *re*-creation of new ruling elites made up of examples of a 'new fascist man'.

2. *A type of political movement* (party, society, etc.) whose leaders, intellectuals and to some degree militants embrace, and seek to implement, all or most of the above ideas. It should be noted, however:
   (i)   that the depth, clarity and consistency with which such ideas are held, even at a movement's higher levels and especially at rank-and-file level, may vary wildly;
   (ii) that appeal, recruitment and accordingly mass potency may depend less upon successfully transmitting the stated ideas than upon more pragmatically adopted policies and propaganda; and
   (iii) that *invariably*, in order to win even a share of power, fascist movements must compromise with established elites and interests.

3. *A type of political regime* within which a fascist movement or party plays a monopolistic, dominant or strongly influential role. Here it should be noted:
   (i)   that while the definition just offered may appear self-evident, the inevitable compromise noted in part 2 (iii) may mean that the fascist ideas listed in part 1 remain matters of rhetoric, propaganda and long-term mission, rather than genuinely driving the regime's affairs, the underlying reality being a more conservative one;
   (ii) that because of the limitations of 'fascistization' and consequent underlying conservatism of fascist regimes as defined above, other (far more numerous) regimes with 'authoritarian conservative' origins but deliberately adopting 'fascist' characteristics may in reality be less distant from supposedly 'authentic' fascism than is sometimes suggested;
   (iii) that history does not stand still, or the central characteristics of a regime necessarily remain unchanging; regimes can evolve and alter their core character; thus the Franco regime became less 'fascist' over time, while the Smetona and Vichy regimes became more so; and, finally,
   (iv) that while Nazism clearly conforms to the whole of parts 1 and 2 of this template, it is the *only* regime to which the word 'monopolistic' in part 3 can truly be said to apply, and the only one in which the 'fascist' ideas and movement transcended the compromise from which others never escaped.

PART FOUR   DOCUMENTS

The intellectual, cultural and ideological world of Europe, roughly from 1880 to 1914, was extraordinarily fertile and varied, and the fascism of the next generation drew upon numerous prewar sources. The examples here (countless others could be offered) are: (a) the German Julius Langbehn's voicing of a fin de siècle 'cultural despair'; (b) Georges Sorel's invocation of 'myth' as a means of mobilizing masses and achieving revolution – a message directed at the left but seized upon by the right; (c) the Italian Nationalist Enrico Corradini's reflections on war and his conception of 'national socialism'; and (d) the Frenchman Edouard Drumont's depiction of an international Jewish conspiracy subverting Western, Christian civilization and his advocacy of an organized, cross-class response.

[a]

It has gradually become an open secret that the contemporary spiritual life of the German people is in a state of slow decay: according to some, even of rapid decay. Science everywhere is dissipated into specialization; in the field of thought and literature, the epoch-making individuals are missing. The visual arts, though represented by significant masters, lack monumentality; ... musicians are rare, performers abound. Without question the democratizing levelling atomistic tendency of this country expresses itself in all this. Moreover, the entire culture of the present is ... turned backward; it is less concerned with the creation of new values than with the cataloguing of old ones.... The more scientific [culture] becomes, the less creative it will be.

Julius Langbehn, *Rembrandt als Erzieher. Von einem Deutschen*, 1891, p. 1, quoted in Fritz Stern, *The Politics of Cultural Despair. A Study in the Rise of the Germanic Ideology*, Anchor Books, London, 1965, pp. 159–60.

[b]

A knowledge of what the myths contain in the way of details which will actually form part of the history of the future is then of small importance; they are not astrological almanacs; it is even possible that nothing which they contain will ever come to pass, – as was the case with the catastrophe expected by the first Christians. In our own daily life, are we not familiar with the fact that what actually happens is very different from our preconceived notion of it? And that does not prevent us from continuing to make resolutions. Psychologists say that there is heterogeneity between the ends in view and the ends actually realized: the slightest experience of life reveals this law to us....

The myth must be judged as a means of acting on the present; any attempt to discuss how far it can be taken literally as future history is devoid of sense. *It is the myth in its entirety which is alone important*: its parts are only of interest in so far as they bring out the main idea. No useful purpose is served, therefore, in arguing about the incident which may occur in a social war, and about the decisive conflicts which may give victory to the proletariat; even supposing the real revolutionaries to have been wholly and entirely deluded in setting up this imaginary picture of the general strike, this picture may yet have been, in the course of the preparation for the Revolution, a great element of strength, if it has embraced all the aspirations of Socialism, and if it has given to the whole body of Revolutionary thought a precision and a rigidity which no other method of thought could have given.

Georges Sorel, *Reflections on Violence* (trans. T.E. Hulme, introduced by E.A. Shils), Collier-Macmillan, London, 1970 edn, pp. 126–7.

[c]

[Socialism] urged [the working class] to fight and, through that fight, forged their unity, their awareness, their strength, their very weapons, their new rights, their will to win, their pride in abusing their victory; it freed them and enabled them to dictate their class law to the other classes, to the nation and to other nations.

Well, my friends, nationalism must do something similar for the Italian nation. It must become, to use a rather strained comparison, our national socialism. This is to say that just as socialism taught the proletariat the value of the class struggle, we must teach Italy the value of the international struggle.

But international struggle means war.

Well, let it be war! And let nationalism arouse in Italy the will to win a war.... In a word, we propose a 'means of national redemption' which we sum up ... in the expression 'the need for war'. War is the last act, but asserting the necessity of war means acknowledging the need to make ready for war and to prepare ourselves for war, that is to say, it involves both technical and moral methods. It is a means of national discipline. A means of creating an overwhelming and inevitable reason for the need for national discipline. A means of creating an irresistible need to return to a sense of duty ... And a means, finally, of reviving a pact of family solidarity between all classes of the Italian nation....

There is a need for a change of system in order to find a better one, both human and material. Nationalism wants to find such a system. Herein lies its justification.

Enrico Corradini, Report to the First Nationalist Congress, Florence, 3 December 1910, quoted in Adrian Lyttelton (ed.), *Italian Fascisms from Pareto to Gentile*, Jonathan Cape, London, 1973, pp. 146–8.

[d]

The Semites, those restless people, were happy to destroy the foundations of the old society, and to use the money they extorted from it to found a new one. They have created a social problem, and it will be solved at their expense. The property which they have wrongfully acquired will be distributed to all those who take part in the great struggle which is getting under way, just as, in days gone by, land and fiefs were distributed to the most valiant.

In Germany, in Russia, in Austria-Hungary, in Rumania, and in France itself where the movement is still dormant, the nobility, the middle classes, and intelligent workers, in a word everyone with a Christian background – often without being practising Christians – are in agreement on this point: the Universal Anti-Semitic Alliance has been created, and the Universal Israelite Alliance will not prevail against it.

Edouard Drumont, *La France juive* (1886), quoted in J.S. McClelland (ed.), *The French Right from de Maistre to Maurras*, Jonathan Cape, London, 1970, pp. 115–16.

DOCUMENT 2   THE FOUNDATION OF ITALIAN FASCISM AND GERMAN NATIONAL SOCIALISM

At their foundation in 1919 the Italian Fasci di Combattimento issued a series of demands ('We insist upon ...') that then, briefly, became the movement's programme. Mussolini's speech (a) to the founding meeting of the Fasci encapsulates Fascism's initial posture as an alternative to socialism, radical on such matters as monarchy v. republic, worker–employer relations, etc. This was soon to change (see pp. 32–4, 129). The Twenty-Five Points (b) of the German Workers' Party, later the NSDAP, drafted by Hitler and Anton Drexler, likewise contain socially radical elements that were largely discarded as time passed, but are also striking for their stress upon 'German-ness', racial policy, etc., which remained hallmarks of Nazism. In general these passages illustrate the greater ideological drive and consistency characteristic of Nazism compared with Italian Fascism.

[a]

We declare war against socialism, not because it is socialism but because it has opposed nationalism ... It is plain that the Socialist party will be unable to lead a programme of renewal and reconstruction.... We intend to be an active minority, to attract the proletariat away from the official Socialist party. But if the middle class believes that we shall be their lightning conductors, they are wrong. We must meet the workers half-way. At the time of the Armistice I wrote that we must approach the workers who were returning from the trenches, since it would be odious and Bolshevik not to recognize the rights of those who had fought in the war. We must therefore accept the working classes' demands. Do they want an eight-hour day?... Sickness and old-age insurance? Workers' control over industry? We shall support these demands....

I have the impression that the present regime in Italy has failed.... We must not be fainthearted, at a moment when the future nature of the political system is to be decided. We must act quickly. If the existing regime is going to be superseded, we must be ready to take its place. We are accordingly setting up the Fasci as organs of creativity and agitation which will be ready to rush into the piazzas and cry: 'The right to the political succession is ours, for it was we who pushed the country into the war and led it to victory!'

Our programme includes political reforms. The Senate must be abolished.... We demand universal suffrage for both men and women; a system of voting by list on a regional basis; and proportional representation. New elections will produce a national assembly, which we insist must decide the question of what form of government the Italian state is to possess. It will choose between a republic and a monarchy, and we who have always been inclined towards republicanism declare here and now that we favour a republic.

Mussolini, speech to founding meeting of the Fasci di Combattimento, Milan,
23 March 1919, reported in *Il Popolo d'Italia*, 24 March 1919.

[b]

We demand the union of all Germans in a Greater Germany on the basis of the right of national self-determination.

We demand equality of rights for the German people in its dealings with other nations, and the revocation of the peace treaties of Versailles and Saint-Germain.

We demand land and territory (colonies) to feed our people and to settle our surplus population.

Only members of the nation may be citizens of the State. Only those of German blood, whatever their creed, may be members of the nation. Accordingly, no Jew may be a member of the nation.

Non-citizens may live in Germany only as guests and must be subject to laws for aliens.

The right to vote on the State's government and legislation shall be enjoyed by the citizens of the state alone. We demand therefore that all offcial appointments ... shall be held by none but citizens....

We demand that the State shall make it its primary duty to provide a livelihood for its citizens. If it should prove impossible to feed the entire population, foreign nationals ... must be deported from the Reich.

All non-German immigration must be prevented. We demand that all non-Germans who entered Germany after 2 August 1914 be required to leave the Reich forthwith.

All citizens shall have equal right and duties.

It must be the first duty of every citizen to perform physical or mental work. The activities of the individual must not clash with the general interest ... *We demand therefore*:

The abolition of incomes unearned by work....

... We demand the ruthless confiscation of all war profits.

We demand the nationalisation of all businesses which have been formed into [trusts].

We demand profit-sharing in large industrial enterprises.

We demand the extensive development of insurance for old age.

We demand the creation and maintenance of a healthy middle class, the immediate communalising of big department stores, and their lease at a cheap rate to small traders ...

We demand a land reform suitable to our national requirements, the passing of a law for the expropriation of land for communal purposes without compensation, ... the prohibition of all speculation in land.

We demand the ruthless prosecution of those whose activities are injurious to the common interest. Common criminals, usurers, profiteers, etc., must be punished with death, whatever their creed or race.

We demand that Roman Law ... be replaced by a German common law.

The State must consider a thorough reconstruction of our national system of education ...

The State must ensure that the nation's health standards are raised ...

We demand the abolition of the mercenary army and the formation of a people's army.

[Close scrutiny of, and where appropriate censorship of, press and publication.]

We demand freedom for all religious denominations ..., provided they do not threaten its existence or offend the moral feelings of the German race....

To put the whole of this programme into effect, we demand the creation of a strong central state power for the Reich; the unconditional authority of the political central Parliament over the entire Reich and its organisations; and the formation of Corporations based on estate or occupation for the purpose of carrying out the general legislation passed by the Reich in the various German states.

The leaders of the Party promise to work ruthlessly – if need be to sacrifice their very lives – to translate this programme into action.

Twenty-Five Point Programe of the DAP (later NSDAP), 24 February 1920, quoted in J. Noakes and G. Pridham (eds), *Nazism 1919–1945. 1: The Rise to Power 1919–1934*, Exeter University Press, Exeter, 1983, pp. 14–16.

DOCUMENT 3   THE FASCIST INFLUENCE

Many parties and movements of the extreme right founded during the 1920s and 1930s lacked something of 'true' fascism's radicalism but were nevertheless strongly influenced by aspects of Italian Fascism and/or German National Socialism. Examples abound; here are two pronouncements by organizations many would deny were fully fascist, but few could dispute were firmly in the fascist-influenced camp: the Austrian Heimwehr and the Bloque Nacional, an alliance of extreme right-wing forces in the Spain of 1934–36, from which the indisputably fascist Falange nevertheless remained aloof.

[a]
We want to renew Austria from the ground up!

We want the people's state [*Volksstaat*] of the Heimatschutz.

We demand of each comrade: indomitable faith in the fatherland, indefatigable zeal in serving, and passionate love of homeland.

We want to reach for the power in the state and to remould the state and economy for the benefit of the whole people.

We must [completely] forget individual advantage, must unconditionally subordinate connection with, and demands of, the parties to the objective of our struggle, for we want to serve the community of the German people!

We reject western democratic parliamentarism and the party state.

We want to put in its place the self-administration of the corporations [*Stände*] and a strong state leadership, which will be formed, not by party representatives, but by the leading persons of the large corporations and by the most capable and proven men of our popular movement.

We fight against the disintegration of our people by the Marxist class struggle and the liberal capitalistic economic order.

We want to realize the self-administration of the economy on an occupational-corporative basis. We will overcome the class struggle and establish social dignity and justice.

We want to improve the welfare of our people by a fundamentally sound and commonly shared economy.

The state is the embodiment of the whole people; its power and leadership see to it that the corporations remain subservient to the needs of the whole people.

Every comrade should feel and confess himself to be a bearer of the new German conception of the state; he should be prepared to risk possessions and life; he should recognize three powers: faith in God, his own hard will, and the command of his leaders.

The Austrian Heimwehr's Korneuberg Oath, *Wiener Zeitung*, 20 May 1930, quoted in C.E. Edmondson, *The Heimwehr and Austrian Politics 1918–1936*, Georgia University Press, Athens, 1978, pp. 98–9.

[b]

We want an INTEGRATIVE State that, by contrast with the present anarchic State, imposes its special authority upon all classes, be they social or economic. The ruinous era of the class struggle is playing itself out. The State, arbiter in every dispute – be it civil, administrative or criminal – must also be arbiter in those of a social nature. No more strikes, no more lock-outs as instruments of economic strife, and still less of political strife. The State must determine the life of labour, by imposing a distributive social justice, granting, what is more, to the weak a just recompense, and stimulating, where this falls short, Christian charity. Faced with an inhibited State, with folded arms, the combative trade-unionist phenomenon has reason for existence. Faced with a State ready to realize social justice by force, the trade-unionist anti-State is a crime. Economic life must be fitted into the framework of professional corporations; the accession of the proletariat to property must be made easy; the consciousness that they are serving a supreme national interest which integrates one-sided class interests must be infused into employers, workers and experts. This will be achieved when the life of labour is regulated by a State with MORAL UNITY, POLITICAL UNITY AND ECONOMIC UNITY....

We therefore propose to you, Spaniards, the constitution of a BLOQUE NACIONAL which has: for OBJECTIVE, THE CONQUEST OF THE STATE, complete conquest, with no conditions, no silent partnerships; for PURPOSE, the formation of a new State, with the characteristics already described, plus the two essentials of UNITY OF COMMAND AND TRADITIONAL HISTORICAL CONTINUITY: for MEANS, the coming together of all citizens who share our ideas, whatever may be their present party affiliations, respected and compatible, and of those associations economic and social in character which want to co-operate in this great undertaking: and as FIELD OF ACTION, platform, press and street, that is to say, extraparliamentary political activity.... If, sheltered by Divine protection and at the entreaty of the national will, we attain the desired goal, we shall be ready – may Spain know it well – to install in the head and in the heart of the Spanish State the principles of UNITY, CONTINUITY, HIERARCHY, COMPETENCE, CORPORATION AND SPIRITUALITY ...

Manifesto of the Bloque Nacional, December 1934, in Richard A.H. Robinson, 'Calvo Sotelo's *Bloque Nacional* and its manifesto', *University of Birmingham Historical Journal*, 10, 1966, pp. 160–84.

DOCUMENT 4   VARIETIES OF FASCISM: (i) ROMANIA – CODREANU AND 'SPIRITUAL' FASCISM

The Legion of the Archangel Michael, more generally known as the Romanian Legion or the Iron Guard, was one of the most successful of Europe's fascist movements between 1919 and 1945. Its impact upon Romanian life and politics was massive, and briefly, in 1940–41, it became one of the few fascist movements truly to exercise power. By then its charismatic founder and 'Captain', Corneliu Codreanu, was dead, assassinated by agents of King Carol II's conservative-authoritarian regime. In this passage, Codreanu reveals his movement's contempt for political programmes and stress upon a spiritually reborn, heroic, idealistic 'new man' as the vehicle for Romania's national reawakening.

The 'nest' of young men was the beginning of legionary life, the foundation stone that had to be placed on firm ground.

I therefore did not say: 'Let us go forth and conquer Romania! Go into the villages and cities and cry: "A new political organization has been founded – everyone join it!" '

I did not formulate a new *political programme* alongside the other ten that exist in Romania, all of them perfect in the minds of their authors and adherents, and I did not send the legionaries to throw it around everywhere, calling on men to join together to save the nation. In this respect we are different from all the other political organizations ...They all believe that the country ... is dying for want of good programmes, and accordingly each puts together a perfectly honed programme and then sets out with it to collect men. Thus everyone asks: 'What is your programme?'

The country is dying for want of *men*, not for want of *programmes*. That is our opinion. And that is why it is not programmes that we must create but *men, new men*. Because the men of today, educated by politicos and infected by Jewish influence, would compromise the most splendid programme. This kind of man, who inhabits present-day Romanian politics, I have already met in history; under his leadership nations have perished and States have been destroyed ...

Therefore the keystone for the Legion is not the political programme but *man*; the reform of man, not the reform of political programmes. The Legion of the Archangel Michael, it follows, will be *more of a school and an army than a political party* ...This hero, this legionary of heroism, of labour, of justice, with the power that God has given his soul, will lead our race on the path of glory.

Corneliu Codreanu, *Pentru Legionari* (For the Legionaries), Editura 'Totul pentru Țara',

Bucharest, 1936, pp. 284–6.

DOCUMENT 5   VARIETIES OF FASCISM: (ii) FRANCE – GEORGES VALOIS
AND 'EUROPEAN' FASCISM

Georges Valois had before the Great War been a militant of Action Française, eager to woo working-class support. In the 1920s he founded and led France's first openly fascist party, the Faisceau. Valois's career and outlook as a fascist illustrate fascism's attraction in many countries to patriotic but not necessarily chauvinistic radicals for whom socialism was unacceptably materialistic and internationalist. Valois's idealistic fascism made little headway and he dissolved the Faisceau in 1928. Significantly, the 'Europeanist' Valois spurned the allure of collaboration in 1940, joined the French Resistance, and died in Bergen-Belsen concentration camp.

[Fascism is a] European Historical Necessity. Fascism absorbs and goes beyond liberalism, democracy and Socialism. Just as, whether monarchy or republic, the modern State will be Fascist, that is, non-parliamentary, unitary and syndical .... [As to] whether Fascism is peculiarly Italian: here too, only the results of actions will tell. If Fascism succeeds in Europe, no one will gainsay that it is European. Going by what one can see in every European country, Fascism is the name given to the movement by which modern nations seek to break the framework of old parties, break out of the parliamentary matrix and create the modern State....

[That] fascism has a European (not merely a purely local) character ... is true to such an extent that in all countries and in almost all parties Fascist tendencies show themselves .... And while parliamentary groups continue to oppose each other according to the old party spirit, the anti-parliamentary and syndicalist groups of all parties attempt to get together in order to act together, according to the unitary spirit of the *faisceau*....

Fascism is ... the movement by which Europe will absorb and transcend all democratic and Socialist experiments, and will create the modern State endowed with indispensable economic structures and capable of giving the economic forces of the modern world the national and social discipline which will make them beneficial.

Georges Valois, *Le Nouveau Siècle*, 13 December 1925, quoted in Eugen Weber,
Varieties of Fascism. Doctrines of Revolution in the Twentieth Century, Van Nostrand,
New York, 1964, pp. 183–5.

DOCUMENT 6   VARIETIES OF FASCISM: (iii) BRITAIN –
MOSLEY AND FASCISM AS 'PROGRESS'

Like Valois and many others, Sir Oswald Mosley viewed and represented fascism as a 'modern' movement for dealing with modern economic and social problems. In The Greater Britain, *published in 1932 as his manifesto to the nation, Mosley made clear his admiration for the Italian Fascist regime, and his belief in the necessity of 'order', 'authority' and 'discipline' as the bases of a successful state, economy and society. This outlook exemplifies the tendency of 'second wave' fascists in the 1930s, as well as other right-wing authoritarians, to draw inspiration from the Fascist and Nazi regimes in action, rather than from the original ideas and movements from which they had developed.*

In all countries, Fascism had been led by men who came from the 'Left', and the rank and file has combined the Conservative and patriotic elements of the nation with ex-Socialists, ex-Communists and revolutionaries who have forsaken their various *illusions* of progress for the new orderly *reality* of progress. In our new organization we now combine within our ranks all those elements in this country who have long studied and understood the great constructive mission of Fascism; but we have no place for those who have sought to make Fascism the lackey of reaction, and have thereby misrepresented its policy and dissipated its strength. In fact Fascism is the greatest constructive and revolutionary creed in the world. It seeks to achieve its aim legally and constitutionally, by methods of law and order; *but in objective it is revolutionary or it is nothing.* It challenges the existing order and advances the constructive alternative of the Corporate State. To many of us this creed represents the thing which we have sought throughout our political lives. *It combines the dynamic urge to change and progress, with the authority, the discipline and the order without which nothing great can be achieved.*

The essence of Fascism is the power of adaptation to fresh facts. Above all it is a realist creed.... The steel creed of an iron age, it cuts through the verbiage of illusion to the achievement of a new reality.

Oswald Mosley, The Greater Britain, BUF, London, 1932, pp. 15–16.

DOCUMENT 7   PURSUING POWER BY COMPROMISE

No fascist movement has ever achieved power purely through its own strengths and efforts. In the most important Italian, German and Spanish cases, some kind of compromise with established forces was necessary in order that power could be effectively pursued and won. In (a) the Italian Fascist movement, in becoming a political party, shows clear signs of modifying early radical positions on monarchy, Church, and capital–labour relations; in (b) Hitler (actually with only limited success at the time) attempts to persuade Rühr industrialists that they, and Germany, need Nazism to overcome 'bolshevism' and restore the order required for successful business; and in (c) the Spanish Falange is admitted to a version of power – but entirely on General Franco's terms.

[a]

The National Fascist Party declares that at this moment in history the dominant form of social organization in the world is *national society*; and that the essential law of life in the world is not the consolidation of different societies into one single, immense society called 'Humanity', as internationalist-minded theoreticians believe, but is rather a fruitful and, let us hope, peaceful competition among different national societies....

The state is sovereign. Such Sovereignty cannot and must not be infringed or diminished by the Church, and the latter, for its part, must be guaranteed the broadest freedom in the exercise of its spiritual mission.

With respect to the specific form of political institutions [i.e. monarchy or republic], the National Fascist Party subordinates its own attitude to the moral and material interests of the nation as understood in all aspects of its historic destiny....

Corporations must be promoted for two basic purposes – as the expression of national solidarity, and as the means for increasing production....

The prestige of the Nation-State must be restored ... the State must not watch with indifference the unleashing of arrogant forces that attack and otherwise threaten to weaken the material and spiritual qualities of our national life. Instead, it must act scrupulously as the custodian, defender, and promoter of our national traditions, national feeling, and national will....

Fascism does not believe in the validity of the principles that inspire the so-called League of Nations....

Fascism recognizes the social utility of private property, which involves both a right and a duty.... The National Fascist Party is in favour of a regime that encourages the growth of national wealth by spurring individual initiative and energy ... and it absolutely repudiates the motley, costly, and uneconomic machinery of state control, socialization, and municipalization.

National Fascist Party programme, adopted by Third Congress, Rome, November 1921.

[b]

That [fundamental] solution [to Germany's problems] rests upon the realiz-ation that economic systems in collapse have always as their forerunner the collapse of the State and not vice versa – that there can be no flourishing economic life which has not before it and behind it the flourishing powerful State as its protection ...

I know quite well, gentlemen, that when National Socialists march through the streets, and suddenly a tumult and commotion breaks out in the evening, then the bourgeois draws back the window curtain, looks out, and says: 'Once more my night's rest is disturbed; no more sleep for me.' ... But remember there is sacrifice involved when those many hundred thousands of S.A. and S.S. men of the National Socialist movement every day have to climb into their trucks, protect meetings, stage marches, exert themselves night after night and then come back in the grey dawn either to workshop and factory or as unemployed to take the pittance of the dole.... If the whole German nation today had the same faith in its vocation as these hundred thousands, if the whole nation possessed this idealism, Germany would stand in the eyes of the world otherwise than she stands now! (Loud applause.)

> Hitler, speech to the Industry Club of Düsseldorf, 26 January 1932, quoted in J.C. Fest,
> *Hitler*, Weidenfeld and Nicolson, London, 1974, pp. 458–62.

[c]

Efficient government ... demands regimentation of both the individual and the collective activities of all Spaniards towards a common destiny.

This truth, which the good sense of the Spanish people has grasped so clearly, is incompatible with the conflicts of parties and political organizations.... Now that the war has reached an advanced stage and the hour of victory draws near, it is urgent to undertake the great task of peace and to crystallize in the New State the thought and style of our National Revolution.... The unification that I am demanding ... does not mean a conglomeration of forces, or a mere governmental concentration, or a temporary union.... In Spain, as in other countries with totalitarian regimes, traditional forces are now starting to integrate themselves with new forces. Falange Española has attracted masses of young people through its programme and its new style of propaganda, and has provided a new political and heroic framework for the present and a promise of future Spanish fulfilment. The Requetés [Carlist militia], as well as possessing martial qualities, have served through the centuries as the sacred repository of Spanish tradition and of Catholic spirituality, which have been the principal formative elements in our nationality ...

In view of all the foregoing,

I ORDER THAT

Article 1: Falange Española and the Requetés, along with all their existing services and units, shall be integrated, under my leadership, into a single political entity of national character which hereafter shall bear the name Falange Española Tradicionalista y de las JONS....

Boletín Oficial del Estado, 2 April 1937 (author's translation).

DOCUMENT 8   THE CORPORATE STATE

Although in practice the Third Reich was never strictly corporativist, the great majority of fascist and fascist-influenced movements and regimes between the two world wars subscribed to the principle of corporativism. In (a) the ex-Nationalist Alfredo Rocco, one of the chief architects of the Fascist state, sets out the purpose of the Corporate State in Italy; in (b) the role of corporativism within the Portuguese Estado Novo of Salazar is affirmed. In principle, the second version, inspired by Catholic ideas, places less stress on the corporations' economic role and more on their participatory function; in practice the differences were probably less significant than this suggests.

[a]
The key body in this new Fascist economy is the corporation, in which are all represented the various categories of producers, employers and workers, and which is unquestionably the body best suited to regulate production – not in the interest of any one producer but in order to achieve maximum output, which is in the interests of all the producers but above all in the national interest.... This is why the corporations are state bodies and must remain so. This does not mean that the state takes over production – any more than it means the corporations take it over either. Except in special cases where the state takes over directly for important political reasons ... production remains in private hands. The corporations are merely entrusted with overall control, organization and improvement of production; while state bodies, they are autonomous and are composed of representatives of those groups that themselves are responsible for production .... The Fascist corporation ... regulates production through the producers, not only in their interest but primarily in the interests of all concerned, under the effective guidance of the state.

Alfredo Rocco, on introducing Bill on Corporations to the Italian Chamber of Deputies,
January 1934.

[b]
It is the duty of the State to authorize, unless otherwise provided by law to the contrary, all corporative, collective, intellectual or economic bodies, and to promote and assist their formation.

The principal aims of the corporative bodies ... shall be scientific, literary or artistic, or physical training, relief, alms, or charity; technical improvement or solidarity of interests....

In the corporate organization, all branches of the nation's activities shall be represented through their association in the corporative organizations, and it shall be their duty to participate in the election of town councils and provincial boards and the constitution of the Corporative Chamber....

The State shall promote the formation and development of the national corporative economic system, taking care to prevent any tendency among its constituent bodies to indulge in unrestricted competition with each other, contrary to their own proper aims and those of society, and shall encourage them to collaborate as members of the same community.

Constitution of the Portuguese Republic under the *Estado Novo* (1933), quoted in C. Delzell (ed.), *Mediterranean Fascism 1919–1945*, Macmillan, London, 1970, pp. 338–46.

DOCUMENT 9   THE CULT OF LEADERSHIP

A belief in the virtue of dynamic, charismatic leadership, and the construction of personality cults around individual leaders, were hallmarks of fascist and national socialist movements and, even more, regimes. Extract (a) comes from a letter sent by a rank-and-file Nazi to Hitler in 1936. Typical of countless such messages, it not only demonstrates the power of the 'Hitler myth' that was deliberately constructed around the Führer, but also provides insights into why so many ordinary Germans, and especially war veterans, came to support Nazism. Extract (b) illustrates how Mussolini's (and later of course Hitler's) style of leadership impressed many foreigners, and played its part in spreading the fascist contagion abroad. Here, the incipient leader of British Fascism, Sir Oswald Mosley, treats Daily Mail *readers to an account of his recent meeting with Mussolini, together with his own views on leadership. The military imagery and stress upon masculinity are characteristically fascist in character.*

[a]
My Führer! ... I feel compelled by unceasing love to thank our creator daily for, through his grace, giving us and the entire German people such a wonderful Führer, and in a time ... where our beautiful dear Fatherland was threatened with the most horrible destruction through Jewish bolshevism. It does not bear thinking about what floods of tears, what blood after the scarcely healed wounds of the World War, would have flowed, if you, my beloved Führer, in all your anguish for such a great people had not found the courage, with at that time a small band of seven men, to win through as the saviour of 66 million Germans, in that through your great love of every individual, from the smallest child to the most aged, you captured all, all,

women, men, and the whole of German youth.... It is a pleasure for me, not a compliment, not hypocrisy, to pray for you, my Führer, that the Lord God who has created you as a tool for Germany should keep you healthy, that the love of the people towards you should grow, firm and hard like the many oak trees which have been planted in love and honour to you, my Führer, even in the smallest community in Germany.... A Heil to the Führer for victory with all the former front-line fighters who still remain today devoted to the Führer to death. For Germany must live even if we must die. Your unto death loyally devoted front-line comrade, Adolf Dörn.

Letter from a 'party comrade' to Hitler, 1936, quoted in Ian Kershaw, *The Hitler Myth*,
Oxford University Press, Oxford, 1987, p. 81.

[b]
A visit to Mussolini ... is typical of that new atmosphere. No time is wasted in the polite banalities which have so irked the younger generation in Britain when dealing with our elder statesmen....

Questions on all relevant and practical subjects are fired with the rapidity and precision of bullets from a machine gun; straight, lucid, unaffected exposition follows of his own views on subjects of mutual interest to him and to his visitor. Every moment possible is wrung from time; the mind is hard, concentrated, direct – in a word, 'Modern'.

The great Italian represents the first emergence of the modern man to power; it is an interesting and instructive phenomenon. Englishmen who have long suffered from statesmanship in skirts can pay him no less, and need pay no more, tribute than to say, 'Here at least is a man.'

Sir Oswald Mosley, *Daily Mail*, 1 February 1932, cited in R. Skidelsky, *Oswald Mosley*,
Macmillan, London, 1975, p. 285.

DOCUMENT 10   TENSION AND DISSENT WITHIN FASCISM

The fluid character of many fascist movements and the shifts and compromises necessary to acquire power and adjust to its use inevitably meant that some fascists became disgruntled, disillusioned and even marginalized within the regimes they had helped to create. In particular, and most notably in Fascist Italy and Franco's Spain, selfconsciously radical fascists wondered when the real fascist revolution was actually going to take place. Extract (a) shows how some, in this case young, Spanish Falangists struggled in the years following the Spanish Civil War to shift the Franco regime in a truly, i.e. radically, fascist direction. A different kind of dissent is present in (b), where a former Nazi office-holder, by now in exile, berates Hitler's regime for conducting a 'nihilistic' revolution that, in his view, destroys German traditions rather than building upon them.

[a]

I know that this proposal for a strong vanguard of the young will seem dangerous and out of line to excessively cautious spirits.

The same people who were interested in prolonging our war are today desirous of a hungry, rancorous, downtrodden Spain, for the same reasons multiplied a hundred times. The same people who for centuries have come to us enclosing and conquering, those who were counting coin after coin while we were losing man after man, are now waiting for us to lose our enthusiasm in order to begin spreading their old corrosive negations.

The negative slogans return once more. Not this. Not that.

But once and for all, what do they bring? What does the Spanish reaction represent and pretend today?

Perhaps nothing encourages us so much as the rage of those who oppose us.

We entertain the immense joy of being hated by them!

Let those who so happily join the chorus of murmurers consider the terrible responsibility they share.

There is only one road open: Revolution.

NOW OR NEVER!

Enrique Sotomayor, speech to the Falange of Madrid, November 1939, quoted in Stanley G. Payne, *Falange. A History of Spanish Fascism*, Stanford University Press, Stanford, Calif., 1961, pp. 210–11.

[b]

Never did a Government have a finer chance of serving both the recovery of its own nation and the creation of a common supernational order than the new German Government of January 1933. A powerful Germany, ready to assume leadership in honourable and statesmanly collaboration with the smaller states, instead of dominating them, would have had in its hands the key positions of European advance.... In 1933 it was by no means inevitable that this doctrineless nihilistic revolution should obtain the mastery over the nation and its future. By violent means National Socialism has for the present determined Germany's course both at home and abroad.

Hermann Rauschning, *Germany's Revolution of Destruction*, Heinemann, London, 1938, p. 316.

DOCUMENT 11 TOTALITARIAN DICTATORSHIP

That the Italian Fascist regime and the Third Reich went, or attempted to go, well beyond mere authoritarianism is beyond dispute, even if Fascist totalitarianism was more myth than reality and the Third Reich anything but the monolith it was once believed to be. As (a) illustrates, Italian Fascist totalitarianism was ultimately based upon a view of the state as embodying supreme and eternal values, to the service of which Fascism and even the Duce were subject. In the Third Reich, however, as (b) vividly demonstrates, the state (associated by many Nazis with the old order) was viewed as completely subordinate to the interests and imperatives of Volk and race, and the Führer's will – legitimized not by constitution but by charisma and achievement – as supreme.

[a]

The foundation of Fascism is the conception of the State, its character, its duty, and its aim. Fascism conceives of the State as an absolute, in comparison with which all individuals or groups are relative, only to be conceived of in their relation to the State.... the Fascist State is itself conscious, and has itself a will and a personality – thus it may be called the 'ethic' State.... The State is the guarantor of security both internal and external, but it is also the custodian and transmitter of the spirit of the people, as it has grown up through the centuries in language, in customs, and in faith. And the State is not only a living reality of the present, it is also linked with the past and above all with the future, and thus transcending the brief limits of individual life, it represents the immanent spirit of the nation....

Fascism desires the State to be a strong and organic body, at the same time reposing upon broad and popular support. The Fascist State has drawn into itself even the economic activities of the nation, and, through the corporative social and educational institutions created by it, its influence reaches every aspect of the national life and includes, framed in their respective organizations, all the political, economic and spiritual forces of the nation.... The Fascist State organizes the nation, but leaves a sufficient margin of liberty to the individual; the latter is deprived of all useless and possibly harmful freedom, but retains what is essential; the deciding power in this question cannot be the individual, but the State alone.

Benito Mussolini, *La Dottrina del Fascismo* (1932), quoted in C. Delzell (ed.),
Mediterranean Fascism, Macmillan, London, 1970, pp. 104–6.

[b]

Even if no further decisions or legal formulations were added to the present laws of the Third Reich governing its legal structure, as a result of five years' government by the Führer there can be no juridical doubts about the following absolutely clear principles of the Reich:

1. At the head of the Reich stands the leader of the NSDAP, leader of the German Reich for life.

2. He is, on the strength of his being leader of the NSDAP, leader and Chancellor of the Reich. As such he embodies simultaneously, as Head of State, supreme State power and, as chief of the Government, the central functions of the whole Reich administration. He is Head of State and chief of the Government in one person. He is Commander-in-Chief of all the armed forces of the Reich.

3. The Führer and Reich Chancellor is the constituent delegate of the German people, who without regard for formal pre-conditions decides the outward form of the Reich, its structure and general policy.

4. The Führer is supreme judge of the nation.... There is no position in the area of constitutional law in the Third Reich independent of the elemental will of the Führer.

The real characteristic of constitutional law in the Third Reich is that it does not represent a system of competencies but the relation of the whole German people to a personality who is engaged in shaping history. We are in a juridical period founded on the Führer's name, and shaped by him. The Führer is not backed by constitutional clauses, but by outstanding achievements which are based on the combination of a calling and of his devotion to the people. The Führer does not put into effect a constitution according to legal guidelines laid before him but by historic achievements which serve the future of his people. Through this, German Constitutional Law has produced the highest organic viewpoint which legal history has to offer. Constitutional Law in the Third Reich is the legal formulation of the historic will of the Führer, but the historic will of the Führer is not the fulfilment of legal preconditions for his activity. Whether the Führer governs according to a formal written Constitution is not a legal question of first importance. The legal question is only whether through his activity the Führer guarantees the existence of his people.

Hans Frank, head of the Nazi Lawyers' Association, speech in 1938, quoted in J. Noakes and G. Pridham (eds), *Nazism 1919–1945. 2: State, Economy and Society*, Exeter University Press, Exeter, 1984, pp. 199–200.

DOCUMENT 12   AUTHORITARIAN DICTATORSHIP

Most interwar European dictatorships were neither explicitly fascist nor officially totalitarian. Many, while denying that they were fascist, nevertheless showed signs of fascist influence or adopted fascist trappings – uniforms, salutes, youth movements, leadership cults, etc. Not surprisingly, their liberal and left-wing critics – who were often also their victims – recognized little distinction between such authoritarian dictatorships and outright fascism. In (a), an Austrian socialist labels the Dollfuss–Schuschnigg regime 'Clerico-Fascist' but stresses some of its important differences from outright 'Nazi-Fascism'. In (b), Salazar, dictator of Portugal, insists that his regime is not a totalitarian (or a fascist) one.

[a]
The Clerico-Fascist counter-revolution had not ... fully achieved its aim. It had abolished the democratic Republic and had replaced it by a dictatorship ...; it had restored the privileges of the Catholic Church, the aristocracy and the bureaucracy; it had elevated the status of the possessing classes and reduced the working class to an inferior position. It had put back the clock by a century....

The difference between Clerico-Fascist despotism and Nazi-Fascism was merely one of degree and not of essence.... Dollfuss' idea was to oppose Nazi-Fascism by Clerico-Fascism. But it was very soon revealed that Catholicism had lost its political preponderance among the peasant youth. It was able to permeate them with Fascist doctrines; it was not able to immunise them against Nazi-Fascism; they flocked in masses into the Nazi camp....

The Clerico-Fascist propaganda ... vilified democracy, maligned parliamentarism and inculcated the peasant with nationalism and anti-Semitism. It appealed to men's meaner instincts. But the negative aspects of Fascism – anti-Marxism, anti-Democracy, anti-Humanitarianism, anti-Semitism – were preached also, and more boldly, by the Nazis. Yet Nazism was able to offer also some positive aspects: for instance, national unity and economic prosperity. Clerico-Fascism had only national humiliation to offer, by subjecting Austria to the hegemony of the Italians, whom they despised, and the economic distress under which they groaned. Small wonder that ultimately Nazi-Fascism prevailed over Clerico-Fascism.

Julius Braunthal, *The Tragedy of Austria*, Victor Gollancz, London, 1948, pp. 102–7.

[b]

The State which would subordinate all without exception – its morality, its law, its politics, its economy – to the idea of nation or race as represented by itself would come forward as an omnipotent being, a beginning and end in itself, to which all existences, both individual and collective, must be subjected, and would give rise to a worse form of absolutism than that to which the Liberal regimes succeeded. Such a State would be essentially pagan, of its nature incompatible with the spirit of our Christian civilisation.

The [Portuguese] Constitution ... rejects as irreconcilable with its ends all that proceeds, directly or indirectly, from this totalitarian conception. It begins by establishing the moral law and justice as limits to its own sovereignty; it obliged the State to respect its natural obligations towards the individual, the family, the corporation, and local government; it assures liberty and inviolability of religious beliefs and practices; it acknowledges the right of parents to educate their own children; it guarantees the rights of property, capital, and labour, within the social harmony, it recognises the Church, with the organisations which are proper to her, and leaves her free to carry on her spiritual work.

It will one day be recognised that Portugal is governed by a unique system, which accords with her own historic and geographical situation, quite different from all others; and we wish it to be clearly understood that we have not put aside the errors and wrongs of false Liberalism and false democracy merely in order to adopt others which may yet be worse; but, on the contrary, to reorganise and strengthen the country according to the principles of authority, order, and national tradition, in harmony with those eternal verities which are happily the heritage of humanity, the appanage of Christian civilisation.

> António Oliveira Salazar, speech of 26 May 1934, quoted in Michael Derrick,
> *The Portugal of Salazar*, Paladin Press, London, 1938, pp. 148–9.

DOCUMENT 13   WHY COLLABORATE?

A wide range of motives persuaded Europeans to collaborate with the Nazi conqueror between 1940 and 1945. Fascist zealots, as (a), by a French volunteer on the Russian front, indicates, were often ideologically committed to the cause of Nazism and a New European Order, but as (b), a comment on the French fascist leader Marcel Déat, suggests, frustrated personal ambition and bitter hatred of political foes and rivals may in many cases have been just as important. In (c) a depressed Marshal Pétain expresses the sincere, whether or not misguided, conviction of many col-

laborators that they were serving their country's best (perhaps short-term) interests and protecting their fellow-nationals from 'polonization' (being treated like Poland).

[a]

I dream of the Europe of tomorrow 'Luminous spring dawn, risen, magnificent and serene, from a long and bloody winter!'

Don't you anticipate this dawn, sooner or later?

What matter! Does not our noble sacrifice, freely consented to, have as its stake peace and the regeneration of a triumphant Europe? A long era of happiness will be born from the conflict joined in the East.

A glorious past is at stake. France is taking an active part in annihilating the savage hordes of the base Caucasian. What matter the dangers! We are indifferent to death itelf. 'Conquer or die!' Is that not the true motto of the warrior?

Our glorious conquerors of yesterday, brothers in arms today, tomorrow reconciled forever, have traced for us the road to follow: the protection of our threatened peoples and our ancient civilization. We have deliberately followed them in this most sacred task.

> Member of Légion des Volontaires Français contre le Bolshevisme, 'Rêve du Légionnaire',
> in *Le Combattant Européen*, 15 October 1943, quoted in Bertram M. Gordon
> *Collaborationism in France during the Second World War*, Cornell University Press,
> Ithaca and London, 1980, p. 255.

[b]

I dare not think about [Déat's] faith, his sincerity. Without doubt he has the sincerity of his profession: for twenty years he has aspired to power; he still does. A political man should want to exercise power, he says to justify himself. He wants to be a leader, he will be one in German if he cannot be in French. He will be Führer if this is the language of the new Europe. What do the flock matter to him as long as he is the herdsman? One passion alone inspired him yesterday: hatred of the Vichy government which did not make him a minister.

> Jean Guéhenno, *Journal des années noires (1940–1944)*, Gallimard, Paris, 1947,
> quoted in Bertram M. Gordon, *Collaborationism in France during the Second World War*,
> Cornell University Press, Ithaca and London, 1980, p. 98.

[c]

Frenchmen: When this message reaches you, I will no longer be free. In the extremity to which I am reduced, I have nothing to tell you which is not the simple confirmation of all that has dictated my conduct up till now. For more than four years, determined to stay among you, I have, every day, sought what was most fitted to serve the permanent interests of France. Straightforwardly, and without compromise, I have had only one aim: to protect you from the worst. And everything that has been done by me, everything I have accepted, admitted, put up with, whether willingly or by force, has only been so for your safe-keeping. For if I could no longer be your sword, I wished to remain your shield..... My sole concern is Frenchmen. For you, as for me, there is only one France, that of our ancestors.

Marshal Philippe Pétain's last statement to the French people, quoted in Richard Griffiths, *Marshal Pétain*, Constable, London, 1970, pp. 331–2.

DOCUMENT 14   THE DEATH OF ITALIAN FASCISM AND THE THIRD REICH

With the exceptions of the Franco and Salazar regimes in the Iberian peninsula, all the fascist and authoritarian regimes considered in this book collapsed or were overthrown as military defeat overtook the Axis powers themselves. The respective deaths of the Italian Fascist regime proper (as distinct from the puppet Italian Social Republic of 1943–45) and of the Third Reich point up some of the contrasts between the two regimes: among them the far greater constitutional vulnerability of Mussolini; the more enduring ideological and psychological commitment to the war effort of Nazis compared with Italian Fascists; and the deeper penetration of society by Nazism. In response to (a), the Fascist Grand Council, nominally at least the governing body of the National Fascist Party, voted by a decisive majority to remove Mussolini and in effect surrender power to the king; in (b) we see how only Hitler's death cleared the way for the Third Reich's capitulation and final collapse, and are once more reminded how powerful was his personal spell over his closest followers.

[a]
The Grand Council, meeting at this time of great hazard, turns its thoughts first of all to the heroic warriors of every Service who, shoulder to shoulder with the proud people of Sicily, in whom the unanimous faith of the Italian people shines at its brightest, are renewing the noble traditions of hardy valour and undaunted spirit of self-sacrifice of our glorious Armed Forces.

Having examined the internal and international situation and the political and military conduct of the war:

IT PROCLAIMS the duty of all Italians to defend at all costs the unity, independence, and liberty of the motherland, the fruits of the sacrifice and labour of four generations, from the Risorgimento down to today, and the life and future of the Italian people.

IT AFFIRMS the need for the moral and material unity of all Italians in this grave and decisive hour for the destiny of our country.

IT DECLARES that for this purpose the immediate restoration is necessary of all State functions, allotting to the King, the Grand Council, the Government, Parliament and the Corporations the tasks and responsibilities laid down by our statutory and constitutional laws.

IT INVITES the Head of the Government to request His Majesty the King – towards whom the heart of all the nation turns with faith and confidence – that he may be pleased, for the honour and salvation of the nation, to assume, together with the effective command of the Armed Forces, on land, sea, and in the air, according to Article 5 of the Statute of the Realm, that supreme initiative of decision which our institutions attribute to him and which, in all our national history, has always been the glorious heritage of our august dynasty of Savoy.

GRANDI.

Grandi's resolution to the Fascist Grand Council, 24–25 July 1943, in Benito Mussolini, *Memoirs 1942–1943*, Weidenfeld and Nicolson, London, 1949, pp. 65–6.

[b]

Karl Doenitz, the new Chief of State, was still caught up in the ideas of the National Socialist regime, just as I was, and more than either of us imagined. For twelve years we had served that regime; we thought it would be cheap opportunism now to make a sharp turnabout. But the death of Hitler broke that mental bind which had for so long warped our thinking. For Doenitz this meant that the objectivity of the trained military officer came to the fore. From the moment he took over, Doenitz held that we should end the war as quickly as possible, and that once this task was done, our work was over.... [Field Marshal Ernst] Busch made a great to-do about [Doenitz's] no longer acting in Hitler's spirit. But Doenitz was no longer moved by such exhortations.

Albert Speer, *Inside the Third Reich*, Sphere Books, London, 1971, p. 657.

DOCUMENT 15   MARXISTS AND FASCISM

All contemporary Marxists viewed fascism as closely linked with capital-ism, and in particular with the crisis through which interwar capitalism was passing. The 'official' Soviet and Comintern line on fascism, representing fascism and financial capitalism as all but synonymous, was enunciated at the Thirteenth Plenum of the Comintern's executive committee in 1933. It was quoted and embraced by Dimitrov at the Seventh Comintern Congress in 1935, in a speech which was actually more nuanced than is sometimes suggested. In his address, (a), Dimitrov dismissed the approach of more moderate 'Austro-Marxists' such as Otto Bauer, who, as in (b), saw fascism as an at least partially autonomous force, employed by capitalists to destroy a 'class equilibrium' and overturn gains made by social democrats. For Trotsky (c), fascism's success, notably in Germany and later Spain, was evidence of wasted revolutionary opportunities, with revolution the key to its overthrow.

[a]

Comrades, fascism in power was correctly described by the Thirteenth Plenum of the Executive Committee of the Communist International as the open terrorist dictatorship of the most reactionary, most chauvinistic and most imperialist elements of finance capital ... [Fascism] is not a power standing above class, nor a power of the petty bourgeoisie or the lumpen-proletariat over finance capital. Fascism is the power of finance capital itself. It is the organization of terrorist vengeance against the working class and the revolutionary section of the peasantry and intelligentsia. In foreign policy, fascism is jingoism in its most brutal form, fomenting bestial hatred of other nations.

Georgi Dimitrov, *Report to the 7th Congress Communist International 1935. For the Unity of the Working Class Against Fascism*, Red Star Press, London, 1973, pp. 40–1.

[b]

The fascist dictatorship ... comes into existence as the result of a unique balance of class forces. On one side stands the bourgeoisie, controlling the means of production and circulation, and also state power. But the economic crisis has destroyed its profits, and democratic institutions prevent it from imposing its will on the proletariat to the extent that seems necessary to retrieve its loss. The bourgeoisie is too weak to enforce its will any longer through the use of those cultural and ideological means by which it controls the mass electorate in a bourgeois democracy. Constrained by the democratic legal order, it is too weak to crush the proletariat by legal means, through the use of the legal state apparatus. But it is strong enough to equip a lawless and illegal private army, and to unleash it on the working class.

On the other side stands a working class led by reformist socialism and the trade unions, both of them stronger than the bourgeoisie can tolerate.... The result of this balance of forces ... is the triumph of fascism, which serves the capitalists by crushing the working class, and yet, despite being in their pay, so far outgrows them that they cannot help making it the undisputed master over the whole people, themselves included ...

However the process of stabilization of the fascist dictatorship destroys the balance of class forces from which it originally arose. When the capitalist class surrendered power to fascism, it had to sacrifice to fascism its own governments, parties, institutions, organs, traditions, a whole massive retinue of followers who had given it service and enjoyed its confidence. But once the fascist dictatorship was established, the leading stratum of the bourgeoisie, the big capitalists and landowners, succeeded extremely quickly in transforming even this new system of rule into an instrument of its own class domination, and the new rulers into its servants.

Otto Bauer, *Zwischen zwei Weltkriegen?*, Bratislava, 1936, pp. 126–30, 321–5,

quoted in David Beetham, *Marxists in Face of Fascism*, Manchester University Press,

Manchester, 1983, pp. 296–7.

[c]

Fascism did not at all come 'instead' of socialism. Fascism is the continuation of capitalism, an attempt to perpetuate its existence by means of the most bestial and monstrous measures. Capitalism obtained an opportunity to resort to fascism only because the proletariat did not accomplish the socialist revolution in time. The proletariat was paralysed in the fulfilment of its task by the opportunist parties. The only thing that can be said is that there turned out to be more obstacles, more difficulties, more stages on the road of the revolutionary development of the proletariat than was foreseen by the founders of scientific socialism. Fascism and the series of imperialist wars constitute the terrible school in which the proletariat has to ... prepare for the solving of the task apart from which there is not and cannot be any salvation for the development of mankind.

Leon Trotsky, 'Bonapartism, fascism and war' (20 August 1940), in Leon Trotsky,

The Struggle against Fascism in Germany, Penguin Books, Harmondsworth, 1975,

pp. 459–68.

CHRONOLOGY

1914
General   Outbreak of Great War (First World War).
Italy   Mussolini breaks with Italian Socialist Party.

1915
Italy   Formation of Fasci di Azione Rivoluzionaria; Italian
               intervention in war.

1917
Russia   February and October revolutions.

1918
General   Armistice ends First World War fighting.

1919
General   Peace treaties of Versailles, St Germain, Trianon, etc.
Germany   Foundation of German Workers' Party (DAP);
               Hitler becomes member.
Italy   Foundation of Fasci di Combattimento (Milan) by Mussolini
               and colleagues; D'Annunzio occupies Fiume (until December
               1920).

1920
Germany   DAP renamed National Socialist German Workers' Party
               (NSDAP); Kapp Putsch.

1921
Germany   Hitler becomes leader of NSDAP.
Italy   Foundation of Italian National Fascist Party (PNF).

1922
Italy   March on Rome; Mussolini appointed prime minister of
               coalition government.

1923
Germany   Munich 'Beer-Hall' Putsch.
Italy   Italian Nationalist Association joins National Fascist Party.
Spain   Military coup and start of Primo de Rivera dictatorship.

1924
France   Foundation of Jeunesses Patriotes.
Germany   Hitler in jail, writes *Mein Kampf*.
Italy   Matteotti affair and crisis of Fascist regime.

1925
France   Foundation of Faisceau.
Germany   Refoundation of NSDAP.
Greece   Pangalos dictatorship (to 1926).
Italy   Fascist regime becomes dictatorship.

1926
Lithuania   Smetona authoritarian regime inaugurated.
Poland   Piłsudski coup introduces authoritarian regime.
Portugal   Military coup overthows democratic Republic.

1927
France   Formation of Croix de Feu.
Lithuania   Foundation of Iron Wolf.
Romania   Foundation of Romanian Legion.

1928
Portugal   Salazar appointed finance minister.

1929
General   Wall St Crash and start of depression.
Finland   Foundation of Lapua.
Yugoslavia   Dictatorship introduced by King Alexander.

1930
Austria   *Heimwehren* adopt Korneuberg Oath.
Germany   NSDAP electoral breakthrough; introduction of emergency
                rule.
Spain   Collapse of Primo de Rivera dictatorship.

1931
Britain   Mosley leaves Labour Party and forms New Party.
Spain   Fall of monarchy and birth of Second Republic; foundation of
                JONS.

1932
Britain   Mosley founds British Union of Fascists.
Finland   Lapua defeated in challenge for power.
Germany   NSDAP electoral success (July) and subsequent slight decline
                (November).
Hungary   Gömbös prime minister.
Portugal   Salazar prime minister and inaugurates New State.

1933
Austria   Dollfuss moves to dictatorship.
Finland   Lapua reorganized as IKL.
France   Foundation of Solidarité Française and Francistes.
Germany   Hitler becomes chancellor; Third Reich established;
                Gleichschaltung.

Latvia	Foundation of Thunder Cross.
Spain	Foundation of CEDA, Renovación Española and Falange Española.

1934

Austria	Dollfuss regime crushes left; unsuccessful Nazi putsch: Dollfuss assassinated; Schuschnigg premier.
Britain	BUF Olympia rally.
Bulgaria	Semi-authoritarian regime imposed by King Boris.
Estonia, Latvia	Semi-authoritarian regimes imposed by (respectively) Päts and Ulmanis.
France	Right-wing Parisian riots.
Germany	'Night of the Long Knives'.
Norway	Quisling forms Nasjonal Samling.
Spain	Foundation of Bloque Nacional.

1935

Belgium	Degrelle founds Rex.
Germany	Introduction of Nuremberg Laws against Jews.
Italy	Invasion of Abyssinia.
Poland	Death of Piłsudski; start of pronounced rightward shift in Polish politics.
Portugal	Salazar crushes Preto's National Syndicalists.

1936

Belgium	Election success for Rex
France	Popular Front election victory; foundation of Parti Populaire Français (Doriot) and Parti Social Français (La Rocque).
Germany	Remilitarization of Rhineland.
Greece	Metaxas coup and establishment of '4 August' regime.
Hungary	Death of Gömbös; rising and suppression of Scythe Cross.
Spain	Popular Front election victory; right-wing rising and start of Spanish Civil War; Franco becomes *Caudillo* (Leader) of Nationalist Spain.

1937

Belgium	Electoral reverse for Rex.
Spain	Franco creates Falange Española Tradicionalista y de las JONS (FET).

1938

Austria	Anschluss with Germany: end of Austrian dictatorship.
Czechoslovakia	Sudeten crisis, Munich agreement, German occupation of Sudetenland.
Germany	Kristallnacht anti-Jewish pogrom.
Italy	Introduction of Racial Laws.
Romania	Murder of Codreanu, suppression of Legion, and establishment of Carolist dictatorship.

1939

Albania	Albania occupied by Italy; flight of King Zog.
Baltic states	German–Soviet invasion and destruction of Baltic states' independence.
Czechoslovakia	German occupation of Prague and rest of Czechoslovakia; Slovakia becomes German satellite state.
Hungary	Electoral advance of Szálasi's Arrow Cross.
Poland	German invasion and destruction of Polish independence.
Spain	Franco victory in Spanish Civil War.
Second World War	Start of Second World War in Europe.

1940

Second World War	German occupation of France, Belgium, Netherlands, Luxembourg, Denmark, Norway; Italian invasion of Greece.
Britain	Mosley interned for duration of war.
France	Fall of France and establishment of Vichy regime under Pétain.
Romania	Fall of Carolist dictatorship; Antonescu *Conducator* in 'Legionary' regime.

1941

Second World War	German invasion of Yugoslavia and Greece; German invasion of Soviet Union; USA enters war; start of Holocaust.
Romania	Antonescu crushes Romanian Legion following revolt.
Yugoslavia	Croatia becomes German satellite state under Pavelić. Serbia subjected to 'Vichy-style' Nedić collaborationist regime.

1942

Second World War	Allied invasion of North Africa; German defeat at El Alamein.
Netherlands	Mussert puppet head of government.
Norway	Quisling puppet head of government.

1943

Second World War	German reverse at Stalingrad; Allied invasion of Sicily and southern Italian mainland.
Italy	Overthrow and imprisonment of Mussolini; end of original Fascist regime; Italian surrender to Allies; German rescue of Mussolini and imposition of Italian Social Republic.

1944

Second World War	Allied invasion of France.
France	End of Vichy regime and flight of leading French fascists to Germany.
Germany	Unsuccessful attempt to assassinate Hitler ('Bomb plot').
Hungary	Horthy replaced by Szálasi.

1945

Second World War	Victory of Allies; Russian occupation of much of eastern Europe; collapse of all collaborationist regimes.
Germany	Collapse of Third Reich; suicide of Hitler.
Italy	Collapse of Italian Social Republic; Mussolini killed by Resistance.
Spain/Portugal	Franco and Salazar regimes survive Axis defeat.

GLOSSARY

Academic Karelia Society   Finnish cultural and intellectual society, central to the development of Finnish interwar nationalism.

Action Française   French cultural organization and political movement, founded in late 1890s. Its most prominent figure was Charles Maurras.

Arrow Cross   Hungarian national-socialist organization of later 1930s and 1940s, led by Ferenc Szálasi.

Bloque Nacional   = National Bloc. Spanish alliance of extreme-right organizations and individuals, 1934–36.

Blue Shirts   Irish fascist movement of the 1930s, led by Eoin O'Duffy.

British Fascisti, Fascists   Small British fascist movement of the 1920s, later absorbed by British Union of Fascists.

British Union of Fascists   Most important British fascist movement, founded (in 1932) and led by Sir Oswald Mosley.

Boulangism   French nationalist protest movement of the 1880s, whose figurehead was General Boulanger.

Cagoule, Cagoulards   Clandestine and terroristic French fascist society of the late 1930s ('cagoule' = 'hood').

Camp of Great Poland (OWP)   Polish ultra-nationalist, mainly youth movement of the late 1920s.

Camp of National Unity   Emerging 'single party' of late 1930s Poland.

CEDA (Confederación Española de Derechas Autónomas)   Spanish Catholic right-wing party, 1933–37, led by Gil Robles.

Christian Social Party   Austrian Catholic right-wing party led in 1930s by Dollfuss and then Schuschnigg; dominant element within Fatherland Front (q.v.).

Christus Rex   Right-wing, authoritarian, fascist-style Belgian Catholic movement founded in 1935 by Léon Degrelle. Often known simply as 'Rex'.

corporatism/corporativism   Collection of socio-political theories, originating in late nineteenth century and advocating the state's organization on the basis of professional and functional interests. Embraced by many fascist and right-wing authoritarian regimes, including Italian Fascism.

Croix de Feu   = Fiery Cross. French right-wing political league, founded in 1920s under leadership of Colonel François de la Rocque. In 1936 became Parti Social Français (q.v.).

Dopolavoro   = After Work. Fascist Italy's system of organized leisure and recreation.

Estado Novo = New State. Portuguese authoritarian regime installed after 1932 by Salazar.

Etat Français = French State. French authoritarian regime installed in 1940 under leadership of Pétain.

Falanga = Phalanx. Polish fascist movement of 1930s.

Falange Española = Spanish Phalanx. Spanish fascist movement founded in 1933 by José Antonio Primo de Rivera. See also Falange Española de las JONS.

Falange Española de las JONS Spanish fascist movement created in 1934 by fusion of Falange Española (q.v.) and JONS (q.v.); forcibly merged in 1937 into Falange Española Tradicionalista y de las JONS (q.v.).

Falange Española Tradicionalista y de las JONS Single party of Franco's regime in Spain, formed in 1937 when the Falange Española de las JONS was forcibly merged with organisations of the Catholic and monarchist right.

Fasci de Azione Rivoluzionaria = Revolutionary Action Groups. Squads formed in 1915 to agitate for Italy's intervention in the First World War.

Fasci di Combattimento = Combat Groups. Italian organizations formed in 1919 by Mussolini and collaborators, from which PNF (q.v.) was formed in 1921.

Fatherland Front Authoritarian 'single party' formed in Austria following right-wing takeover in 1933–34.

Flemish National Federation (VNV) Belgian Flemish fascist-style movement of the 1930s, led by Staf de Clercq.

Freikorps = Free Corps. In Germany during 1919–20, nationalist paramilitary squads active against left and border minorities.

Francistes Small French fascist and later collaborationist movement, founded in 1933 and led by Marcel Bucard.

Führerprinzip = Leadership principle. German term for general fascist and nazi belief in the importance of leadership, authority, obedience, and 'top-down-wards' decision-making.

Gleichschaltung = Co-ordination. Euphemistic term for Nazi takeover of German power-centres in 1933–34.

Heimwehr, -en = Home Army, -ies. Austrian extreme right-wing and eventually fascist organizations, officially suppressed in 1936 by Schuschnigg regime.

IKL People's Patriotic Movement: largely unsuccessful Finnish fascist organization formed after suppression of Lapua (q.v.).

Imperial Fascist League Extreme British fascist and racist movement founded in 1920s by Arnold Leese.

Integralismo Lusitano = Lusitanian (i.e. Portuguese) Integralism. Important Portuguese authoritarian-nationalist movement, founded before the First World War and strongly influencing aspects of the Estado Novo (q.v.).

Iron Guard Popular name for Romanian Legion (q.v.).

Iron Wolf (Gelezinis Vilkas) Semi-clandestine organization of Lithuanian army officers, founded 192′ and suppressed 1934.

Jeunesses Patriotes = Patriotic Youth. French nationalist league, founded in 1924 by Pierre Taittinger.

JONS (Juntas de Ofensiva Nacional-Sindicalista) = Committees for National-Syndicalist Offensive. Spanish fascist movement founded in 1931 by Ramiro Ledesma and Onésimo Redondo; merged in 1934 with Falange Española (q.v.).

Kampfzeit Time of struggle: Nazi term for Nazism's years in opposition.

Korneuberg Oath Oath sworn in 1930 by Austrian Heimwehr (q.v.), committing it to an essentially fascist programme.

LANC (League for National Christian Defence) Romanian ultra-nationalist and antisemitic party led by A.C. Cuza, to which Corneliu Codreanu, founder of Romanian Legion (q.v.), belonged until 1927.

Lapua Finnish fascist movement, founded in 1929 and banned after unsuccessful rising in 1932; reformed as IKL (q.v.).

Ligue des Patriotes = Patriotic League. French late-nineteenth-century nationalist league, led by Paul Déroulède and active in Boulangism (q.v.).

Machtergreifung The Nazi 'seizure of power'.

Moçidade = Youth. Youth movement of the Salazar 'New State' in Portugal.

MSVN Voluntary Militia for National Security: Italian Fascist militia.

Nasjonal Samling = National Unity. Norwegian fascist party led by Vidkun Quisling.

National Fascist Community (NOF) Czech fascist movement founded in 1926 and led by General Rudolf Gajda.

National Radical Camp (ONR) Polish successor, more radical and influenced by nazism, to Camp of Great Poland (q.v.).

National Socialist Movement (NSB) Dutch nazi party led by Anton Mussert.

National Syndicalism, -ists Fascist organization led by Rolão Preto and operating within Salazar's Portugal. It was suppressed in 1934.

New European Order Hitler's supposed vision for a German-dominated Europe following victory in Second World War.

Partito Nazionale Fascista (PNF) = National Fascist Party. The official party of Italian Fascism and single party of the Fascist state, founded in November 1921.

Parti Populaire Français = French Popular Party. French fascist party led by former communist Jacques Doriot.

Parti Social Français = French Social Party. French ultra-nationalist party with fascist overtones, founded in 1936 as successor to the Croix de Feu (q.v.) and led by Colonel de la Rocque.

Ras Fascist regional 'boss' during Italian Fascism's rise to power. (The term is an Ethiopian word for 'chief'.)

Ratnitsi = Warriors. Bulgarian fascist-style movement of the 1920s and 1930s.

Renovación Española = Spanish Renovation. Spanish authoritarian monarchist party, founded in 1933 and strongly influenced by Italian Fascism.

Rex, Rexism (see *Christus Rex*)

Romanian Legion   Romanian fascist movement, founded in 1927 as Legion of the Archangel Michael. Led until 1938 by Corneliu Codreanu, then by Horia Sima. See also Iron Guard; TPT.

Salò republic   Officially Italian Social Republic: puppet regime installed under Mussolini's presidency at Salò in 1943 following collapse of Fascism throughout non-German-occupied Italy.

Scythe Cross   Also known as Hungarian National Socialist Workers' Party: movement founded in 1931 and led by Böszörmény; suppressed in 1936 following rebellion.

Slovak People's Party   Catholic populist party with fascist overtones in 1930s Slovakia; became mainstay of Tiso's collaborationist regime after 1939.

social Darwinism   Misapplication of Darwin's ideas to social theory, arguing the inevitability and virtue of struggle throughout human existence; enthusiastically embraced by many fascists, notably Mussolini and Hitler.

SA (Sturmabteilung)   = Stormtroopers. Brownshirted paramilitary wing of Nazi movement.

SS (Schutzstaffel)   = Defence Corps. Elite Nazi organization established 1925–26 and led after 1929 by Heinrich Himmler. Became core of Nazi regime during Second World War.

Solidarité Française   French Solidarity: French fascist movement founded in 1933 and led by François Coty.

squadristi   Members of Italian Fascist squads (It.: *squadre*) which spearheaded Fascism's attacks on left in 1920–22.

Strength Through Joy   Nazi leisure and recreational organization; equivalent to Italian Fascist Dopolavoro (q.v.).

Sudeten German Party   Main party of Sudeten Germans in Czechoslovakia. Led by Karl Henlein, it fell increasingly under Nazi influence and after 1938 was absorbed in NSDAP.

Szeged fascism   Assortment of far-right organizations and individuals in Hungary during 1920s and early 1930s, whose leading figure was Gyula Gömbös.

Third Hellenic Civilization   The 'big idea' of Metaxas's dictatorship in Greece (1936–41). (The first two Hellenic civilizations were the Classical and the Byzantine.)

Third Way   Idea of a social, economic and political programme avoiding both socialism and unrestrained capitalism; adopted in early twentieth century by Catholic corporatists and primitive 'national socialists', the term has recently (and ignorantly) been taken up by 'Blairite' centrists.

Thunder Cross   Latvian fascist/nazi movement of the 1930s, dissolved by Ulmanis regime.

TPȚ (Totul Pentru Țara)   = All for the Fatherland: political party formed by Romanian Legion to fight elections.

Unión Patriótica = Patriotic Union: 'Single party' of the Spanish dictatorship of Miguel Primo de Rivera.

União Nacional = National Union: 'Single party' of the Portuguese dictatorship of Salazar.

Ustaša = Uprising. Croat fascist party within pre-1941 Yugoslavia, and single party of collaborationist Croatian state under Ante Pavelić.

Vaps Estonian Veterans' League: well-supported right-wing, paramilitary organization, founded in 1929 and suppressed in 1934 by Päts. Strongly influenced by Nazism and by Lapua (q.v.).

Verdinaso Acronym for Federation of National Solidarists of the Low Countries. Belgian fascist-style movement, founded (1931) and led by Joris van Severen; advocated recreation of medieval Burgundian state.

Vlajka Czech nazi-style and antisemitic party of the 1930s.

Volksgemeinschaft = People's community. German term, made official by Nazis, suggesting social unity based on patriotism and transcending social divisions.

Zbor = Convention. Serb fascist-style party in pre-1941 Yugoslavia.

Zentrum German Catholic Centre Party.

Zveno = The Link. Pressure group of elitist fascists in 1930s Bulgaria; suppressed by Boris III in 1934.

WHO'S WHO

NB this list does not include major figures (Franco, Hitler, Mussolini, Pétain, Salazar, etc.)

Antonescu, Ion   Romanian army marshal and dictator ('Conducator') 1940–44. Head of short-lived 'Legionary State' 1940–41.

Balbo, Italo   Leading Italian Fascist. *Squadrista* and *ras* of Ferrara during rise of Fascism; later renowned aviator and governor of Libya.

Barrès, Maurice   Eminent and influential late nineteenth- and early twentieth-century French nationalist writer and propagandist.

Bianchi, Michele   Italian anarchist-turned-fascist; first secretary of the Fascist Party (1921–25).

Boris III   King of Bulgaria from 1918. In 1934 established non-fascist authoritarian regime. Died suddenly 1943.

Böszörmény, Zoltán   Hungarian national-socialist leader of 1930s. Founder (1931) and leader of Scythe Cross movement.

Bottai, Giuseppe   Leading Italian Fascist. Minister of corporations 1929–32; minister for national education 1939–43.

Bucard, Marcel   French fascist and wartime collaborator; founded (1933) and led Francistes.

Carol II   King of Romania from 1927. In 1938 suppressed fascist Romanian Legion and established personal, fascist-influenced dictatorship. Forced to abdicate 1940.

Codreanu, Corneliu   Founder (1927) and leader ('Capitanul') of fascist Romanian Legion. Murdered by forces of King Carol II (q.v.) 1938.

D'Annunzio, Gabriele   Italian poet and adventurer. In 1919, at head of volunteer army, seized, and for a year ruled, city of Fiume under regime that offered foretastes of Fascism. Later marginalized by Mussolini.

Déat, Marcel   French socialist-turned-fascist. In 1932 founded 'néo-socialisme'. Collaborated during Second World War, founding and leading Rassemblement National Populaire.

Degrelle, Léon   Belgian Catholic fascist. Founded (1935) and led Christus Rex or Rexism. Collaborated during Second World War, and fought on Russian front with Waffen SS.

Doriot, Jacques   French communist-turned-fascist. Founder and leader of Parti Populaire Français. Collaborated during Second World War.

Drumont, Edouard   French antisemitic writer and journalist; author of *La France Juive* (1886).

Farinacci, Roberto   Italian Fascist leader of radical and antisemitic outlook; *squadrista* and *ras* of Cremona 1920–22; secretary of PNF 1925–26.

Feder, Gottfried   German nationalist and economist; one of authors of early Nazi economic and financial policy.

Gajda, Rudolf   Czech general; founder (1926) and leader of National Fascist Community (NOF).

Gömbös, Gyula   Leading Hungarian 'Szeged' fascist; as prime minister 1932–36, attempted to introduce authoritarian and corporatist system; died suddenly 1936.

Henlein, Karl   Leader of Sudeten German Party in 1930s Czechoslovakia.

Horthy, Miklós   Ultra-conservative leader, effectively dictator, of Hungary, 1919–44.

Imrédy, Béla   Leading figure within fascist-influenced Hungarian extreme right throughout 1930s.

Ledesma, Ramiro   Spanish fascist; co-founder (with Onésimo Redondo) of JONS, and later (1934), with José Antonio Primo de Rivera, of Falange Española y de las JONS.

Marinetti, Filippo   Leader of Futurism, Italian cultural and artistic movement, and early supporter of Italian Fascism.

Maurras, Charles   Distinguished French nationalist and monarchist intellectual from 1890s to d. in 1952; co-founder and intellectual leader of Action Française.

Metaxas, Ioannis (or John)   Greek army officer and right-wing politician. Seized power 4 August 1936 and ruled as dictator until death in 1941. Rejected Italian ultimatum 1940.

Mosca, Gaetano   Italian early twentieth-century elitist social theorist.

Mosley, Sir Oswald   British fascist leader; after leaving Labour Party, founded and led New Party 1931–32 and British Union of Fascists (BUF) 1932–40; interned 1940–45; after Second World War founded and led neo-fascist Union Movement.

Mussert, Anton　Founder and leader of Dutch National Socialist Movement (NSB); collaborator and puppet leader of Netherlands 1942–45; executed 1946.

Nedić, Milan　Yugoslav general and Serb puppet leader under Germans, 1941–44.

Nietzsche, Friedrich　German philosopher (1844–1900); author (1883–85) of *Also sprach Zarathustra*; ideas concerning 'will' and 'superman' inspired Nazis.

Pareto, Vilfredo　Italian early twentieth-century elitist social theorist.

Päts, Konstantin　Semi-authoritarian leader of Estonia, 1934–40.

Pavelić, Ante　Leader of Croat fascist Ustaša in 1930s Yugoslavia; as wartime collaborationist dictator of Croatia, responsible for mass murders of Serbs and Jews.

Preto, Rolão　Founder (1932) and leader of fascist National-Syndicalist movement in Salazar's Portugal; led unsuccessful coup attempt 1935.

Primo de Rivera, José Antonio　Spanish fascist leader and son of Miguel Primo de Rivera (q.v.); founder (1933) and leader of Falange Española; executed in Republican Spain 1936.

Primo de Rivera, Miguel　Spanish general and father of José Antonio Primo de Rivera (q.v.); overthrew parliamentary system 1923; dictator 1923–30.

Redondo, Onésimo　Spanish fascist; co-founder (with Ramiro Ledesma) of JONS.

Rocco, Alfredo　Italian Nationalist, later leading Fascist; as minister of justice from 1925 a leading architect of the Fascist state.

Rosenberg, Alfred　Nazi racial theorist; author (1930) of *The Myth of the Twentieth Century*; minister for eastern occupied territories 1941–44; executed for war-crimes 1946.

Rossoni, Edmondo　Italian revolutionary syndicalist-turned-fascist; head of Fascist trade union confederation until this was broken up by Mussolini in 1928.

Salazar, António Oliveira　Ultra-conservative premier and dictator of Portugal, 1932–68; died 1970.

Sima, Horia　Romanian fascist; succeeded Codreanu (q.v.) as leader of Romanian Legion; collaborated with Antonescu (q.v.) in brief 'Legionary Regime' of 1940–41.

Smetona, Antanas　Authoritarian president of Lithuania, 1926–40.

Sorel, Georges　French early twentieth-century social theorist, much admired by Mussolini; author (1906–8) of *Reflections on Violence*.

Spann, Othmar　Leading theorist of Austrian Catholic corporativism; inspired Heimwehr.

Szálasi, Ferenc Hungarian national socialist; founder (1937–38) and leader of Hungarian National Socialist Party (= Arrow Cross); collaborationist leader of Hungary 1944–45.

Stojadinović, Milan Semi-authoritarian leader of Yugoslavia, 1935–39.

Tiso, Joséf Slovak Catholic cleric; president of Slovakia as German satellite, 1939–44.

Tsankov, Aleksandûr Bulgarian professor and leader of nazi National Socialist Movement in 1930s.

Ulmanis, Karlis Semi-authoritarian premier of Latvia, 1934–40.

Voldemaras, Augustinas Extreme right-wing interwar Lithuanian intellectual and politician.

Valois, Georges Early French fascist, formerly militant of Action Française; founded (1925), led and dissolved (1928) Faisceau; later abandoned fascism, fought in Resistance, and died in German concentration camp.

von Schönerer, Georg Late nineteenth-century leader of Austrian pan-Germanism, much admired by Hitler.

von Stahremberg, Prince Ernst Rüdiger Leader of Austrian Heimwehr; co-operated with Dollfuss–Schuschnigg regime.

Zog Originally Ahmed Zogolli, then Ahmed Zogu; Albanian politician; president of Albania 1925–28; king of Albania 1928–39.

BIBLIOGRAPHY

With a single exception this bibliography is limited to works published in, or translated into, English. The place of publication is London unless otherwise stated.

PROBLEMS OF STUDYING FASCISM

1   Allardyce, G., 'What fascism is not: thoughts on the deflation of a concept', *American Historical Review*, 84, 2, 1979, pp. 367–88.

2   Griffin, R., *International Fascism. Theories, Causes and the New Consensus*, Arnold, 1998.

FORETASTES OF FASCISM IN PRE-1914 EUROPE

3   Balfour, S., *The End of the Spanish Empire*, Clarendon Press, Oxford, 1997.

4   Bergson, H., *Creative Evolution*, Modern Library Edition, New York, 1944.

5   Blinkhorn, M., *Carlism and Crisis in Spain, 1931–1939*, Cambridge University Press, Cambridge, 1975.

6   Carsten, F.L., *Fascist Movements in Austria. From Schönerer to Hitler*, Sage Publications, 1977.

7   Clark, M., *Modern Italy*, Longman, 1984.

8   De Grand, A., *The Italian Nationalist Association and the Rise of Fascism in Italy*, University of Nebraska Press, Lincoln, Nebr., 1978.

9   Drake, R., *Byzantium for Rome. The Politics of Nostalgia in Umbertian Italy, 1878–1900*, University of North Carolina Press, Chapel Hill, N.C., 1980.

10 Eley, G., 'The Wilhelmine Right: how it changed', in R.J. Evans (ed.), *Society and Politics in Wilhelmine Germany*, Croom Helm, 1978, pp. 112–35.

11 Eley, G., *Reshaping the German Right. Radical Nationalism and Political Change after Bismarck*, Yale University Press, New Haven, Conn.,1980.

12 Fogarty, M., *Christian Democracy in Europe 1820–1953*, Routledge and Kegan Paul, 1957.

13 Gregor, A.J., *Young Mussolini and the Intellectual Origins of Fascism*, University of California Press, Berkeley, Calif., 1979.

14 Howard, W., 'Nietzsche and Fascism', *History of European Ideas*, 11, 1989, pp. 893–99.

15 Levy, R.S., *The Downfall of the Anti-Semitic Parties in Imperial Germany*, Yale University Press, New Haven, Conn., 1975.

16 Lyttelton, A. (ed.), *Italian Fascisms from Pareto to Gentile*, Jonathan Cape, 1973.

17 McClelland, J.S., *The French Right from de Maistre to Maurras*, Jonathan Cape, 1970.

18   Martins, H., 'Portugal', in S.J. Woolf (ed.), *European Fascism*, Weidenfeld and Nicolson, 1968, pp. 302–36 (esp. pp. 302–12).

19   Mayer, A.J., *The Persistence of the Old Regime. Europe to the Great War*, Croom Helm, 1981.

20   Mazgaj, P., *The Action Française and Revolutionary Syndicalism*, University of North Carolina Press, Chapel Hill, N.C., 1979.

21   Misner, P., *Social Catholicism in Europe. From the Onset of Industrialization to the First World War*, Darton, Longman and Todd, 1991.

22   Mosse, G.L., 'The French Right and the working classes: Les Jaunes', *Journal of Contemporary History*, 7, 3–4, 1972, pp. 229–52.

23   Nye, R.A., *The Anti-Democratic Sources of Elite Theory. Pareto, Mosca, Michels*, Sage Publications, 1977.

24   Pulzer, P.G.J., *The Rise of Political Anti-Semitism in Germany and Austria*, Wiley, 1964.

25   Roberts, D.D., *The Syndicalist Tradition and Italian Fascism*, Manchester University Press, Manchester, 1979.

26   Rogger, H., 'Russia', in H. Rogger and E. Weber (eds), *The European Right. A Historical Profile*, Weidenfeld and Nicolson, 1965, pp. 443–500.

27   Roth, J.J., *The Cult of Violence. Sorel and the Sorelians*, University of California Press, Berkeley, Calif., 1980.

28   Rutkoff, P.M., 'The Ligue des Patriotes: the nature of the radical right and the Dreyfus Affair', *French Historical Studies*, 8, 1974, pp. 584–603.

29   Searle, G., *The Quest for National Efficiency*, Oxford University Press, Oxford, 1971.

30   Soucy, R., *Fascism in France. The Case of Maurice Barrès*, University of California Press, Berkeley, Calif., 1972.

31   Stachura, P.D., *The German Youth Movement, 1900–1945. An Interpretative and Documentary History*, Macmillan, 1981, ch. 1.

32   Sternhell, Z., *Neither Right nor Left. Fascist Ideology in France*, University of California Press, Berkeley and Los Angeles, Calif., 1986.

33   Stuart Hughes, H., *Consciousness and Society. The Reorientation of European Social Thought 1890–1930*, MacGibbon and Kee, 1958.

34   Weber, E.J., *Action Française. Royalism and Reaction in Twentieth Century France*, Stanford University Press, Stanford, Calif., 1962.

35   Weber, E.J., *The Nationalist Revival in France, 1905–1914*, University of California Press, Berkeley and Los Angeles, Calif., 1968.

36   Whiteside, A., *The Socialism of Fools. Georg von Schönerer and Austrian Pan-Germanism*, University of California Press, Berkeley and Los Angeles, Calif., 1975.

INTERWAR EUROPE IN CRISIS

37   Aldcroft, D.H., *The European Economy*, Croom Helm, 1978, ch. 3.

38   Beetham, D., *Marxists in Face of Fascism. Writings by Marxists on Fascism from the Inter-war Period*, Manchester University Press, Manchester, 1983.

39   Blinkhorn, M., 'Conservatism, traditionalism and fascism in Spain, 1898–1937', in M. Blinkhorn (ed.), *Fascists and Conservatives. The Radical*

Right and the Establishment in Twentieth-Century Europe, Unwin Hyman, 1990, pp. 118–37.

40   Childers, T., 'The social bases of the National Socialist vote', *Journal of Contemporary History*, 11, 4, 1976, pp. 17–42.

41   Diehl, J.M., *Paramilitary Politics in Weimar Germany*, University of Indiana Press, Bloomington, Ind., 1977.

42   Geary, D., *Hitler and Nazism*, Routledge, 1993.

43   Lackó, M., 'The social roots of Hungarian fascism: the Arrow Cross', in S.U. Larsen, B. Hagvet and J.P. Myklebust (eds), *Who Were the Fascists? Social Roots of European Fascism*, Universitetsforlaget, Bergen/Oslo/Tromsø, 1980, pp. 395–400.

44   Ledeen, M., *The First Duce. D'Annunzio at Fiume*, Johns Hopkins University Press, Baltimore, Md., 1977.

45   Livezeanu, I., 'Fascists and conservatives in Romania: two generations of nationalists', in M. Blinkhorn (ed.), *Fascists and Conservatives. The Radical Right and the Establishment in Twentieth-Century Europe*, Unwin Hyman, 1990, pp. 218–39.

46   Lyttelton, A., *The Seizure of Power. Fascism in Italy 1919–1929*, Weidenfeld and Nicolson, 1973.

47   Maier, C., *Recasting Bourgeois Europe. Stabilization in France, Germany, and Italy in the Decade after World War I*, Princeton University Press, Princeton, N.J., 1975.

48   Payne, S.G., *Politics and the Military in Modern Spain*, Stanford University Press, Stanford, Calif., 1967.

49   Peukert, D.J.K., *The Weimar Republic. The Crisis of Classical Modernity*, Penguin Books, 1991.

50   Skidelsky, R., *Politicians and the Slump*, Macmillan, 1967.

51   Stengers, J., 'Belgium', in H. Rogger and E. Weber (eds), *The European Right. A Historical Profile*, Weidenfeld and Nicolson, 1965, pp. 128–67.

52   Weber, E., 'The men of the Archangel', *Journal of Contemporary History*, 1, 1, 1966, pp. 101–26.

53   Wheeler, D., *Republican Portugal. A Political History 1910–1926*, University of Wisconsin Press, Madison, Wis., 1975.

FASCIST AND RIGHT-WING MOVEMENTS, 1919–1939

54   Abse, T., 'Italian workers and Italian Fascism', in R. Bessel (ed.), *Fascist Italy and Nazi Germany. Comparisons and Contrasts*, Cambridge University Press, Cambridge, 1996, pp. 40–60.

55   Allardyce, G.D., 'The political transition of Jacques Doriot', *Journal of Contemporary History*, 1, 1966, pp. 56–74.

56   Baker, D., 'The extreme right in the 1920s: fascism in a cold climate or "Conservatism with knobs on"?', in M. Cronin (ed.), *The Failure of British Fascism. The Far Right and the Fight for Political Recognition*, Macmillan, 1996, pp. 12–28.

57   Barbu, Z., 'Psycho-historical and sociological perspectives on the Iron Guard, the fascist movement of Romania', in S.U. Larsen, B. Hagvet and J.P. Myklebust (eds), *Who Were the Fascists? Social Roots of European Fascism*, Universitetsforlaget, Bergen/Oslo/Tromsø, 1980, pp. 379–94.

58 Blinkhorn, M., 'The Iberian states', in D. Mühlberger (ed.), *The Social Basis of European Fascist Movements*, Croom Helm, 1987, pp. 320–48.

59 Bracher, K.D., *The German Dictatorship. The Origins, Structure and Consequences of National Socialism*, Weidenfeld and Nicolson, 1971, ch. 2.

60 Childers, T., *The Nazi Voter*, University of North Carolina Press, Chapel Hill, N.C., 1983.

61 Clogg, R., *A Concise History of Greece*, Cambridge University Press, Cambridge, 1992.

62 Corner P., *Fascism in Ferrara 1915–25*, Oxford University Press, Oxford, 1975.

63 Crampton, R.J., *Eastern Europe in the Twentieth Century*, Routledge, 1994.

64 De Grand, A., *Italian Fascism. Its Origins and Development*, University of Nebraska Press, Lincoln, Nebr., 1982.

65 Deák, I., 'The peculiarities of Hungarian Fascism', in R.L. Braham and B. Vago (eds), *The Holocaust in Hungary. Forty Years Later*, Columbia University Press, New York, 1985, pp. 43–51.

66 Delzell, C.F. (ed.), *Mediterranean Fascism, 1919–1945*, Macmillan, 1970.

67 Djordević, D., 'Fascism in Yugoslavia: 1918–1941' and I. Avakumovic, 'Yugoslavia's fascist movements', in P.F. Sugar (ed.), *Native Fascism in the Successor States*, ABC-Clio, Santa Barbara, Calif., 1971, pp. 125–44.

68 Douglas, A., 'Violence and fascism: the case of the Faisceau', *Journal of Contemporary History*, 19, 1984, pp. 689–712.

69 Edmondson, C.E., *The Heimwehr and Austrian Politics 1918–1936*, University of Georgia Press, Athens, Ga., 1978.

70 Ellwood, S.M., *Spanish Fascism in the Franco Era*, Macmillan, 1987.

71 Erös, J., 'Hungary', in S.J. Woolf (ed.), *Fascism in Europe*, Methuen, 1981, pp. 117–50.

72 Gallagher, T., 'Conservatism, dictatorship and fascism in Portugal, 1914–45', in M. Blinkhorn (ed.), *Fascists and Conservatives. The Radical Right and the Establishment in Twentieth-Century Europe*, Unwin Hyman, 1990, pp. 157–75.

73 Gordon, H.J., *Hitler and the Beer Hall Putsch*, Princeton University Press, Princeton, N.J., 1972.

74 Hamilton, A., *The Appeal of Fascism. A Study of Intellectuals and Fascism, 1919–1945*, Anthony Blond, 1971.

75 Hamilton, R.F., *Who Voted for Hitler?*, Princeton University Press, Princeton, N.J., 1982.

76 Hiden, J. and P. Salmon, *The Baltic Nations and Europe. Estonia, Latvia and Lithuania in the Twentieth Century*, Longman, 1991.

77 Hitler, A., *Mein Kampf* (with introduction by D.C. Watt), Hutchinson, 1969.

78 Jelinék, Y., 'Clergy and fascism: the Hlinka party in Slovakia and the Croatian Ustasha movement', in S.U. Larsen, B. Hagvet and J.P. Myklebust (eds), *Who Were the Fascists? Social Roots of European Fascism*, Universitetsforlaget, Bergen/Oslo/Tromsø, 1980, pp. 367–78.

79 Kater, M.H., *The Nazi Party. A Social Profile of Members and Leaders, 1919–1945*, Harvard University Press, Cambridge, Mass., 1983.

80 Kershaw, I., *Hitler*, Longman, 1991.

81 Lannon, F., *Privilege, Persecution, and Prophesy. The Catholic Church in Spain, 1875–1975*, Clarendon Press, Oxford, 1987.

82   Larsen, S., 'Conservatives and fascists in the Nordic countries: Norway, Sweden, Denmark and Finland, 1918–45', in M. Blinkhorn (ed.), *Fascists and Conservatives. The Radical Right and the Establishment in Twentieth-Century Europe*, Unwin Hyman, 1990, pp. 240–63.

83   Lewis, J., 'Conservatives and fascists in Austria, 1918–34', in M. Blinkhorn (ed.), *Fascists and Conservatives. The Radical Right and the Establishment in Twentieth-Century Europe*, Unwin Hyman, 1990, pp. 98–117.

84   Lindström, U., *Fascism in Scandinavia 1920–1940*, Almqvist and Wiksell International, Stockholm, 1985.

85   Linehan, T.P., *East London for Mosley. The British Union of Fascists in East London and South-West Essex 1933–40*, Frank Cass, 1996.

86   Lyttelton, A.,'Fascism in Italy: the second wave', *Journal of Contemporary History*, 1, 1966, pp. 75–100.

87   Manning, M., 'The Irish experience: the Blueshirts', in S.U. Larsen, B. Hagvet and J.P. Myklebust (eds), *Who Were the Fascists? Social Roots of European Fascism*, Universitetsforlaget, Bergen/Oslo/Tromsø, 1980, pp. 557–67.

88   Mastny, V., *The Czechs under Nazi Rule. The Failure of National Resistance, 1939–1942*, Columbia University Press, New York, 1971.

89   Misiunas, R.J., 'Fascist tendencies in Lithuania', *Slavonic and East European Review*, 48, 1970, pp. 88–109.

90   Noakes, J., 'German Conservatives and the Third Reich: an ambiguous relationship', in M. Blinkhorn (ed.), *Fascists and Conservatives. The Radical Right and the Establishment in Twentieth-Century Europe*, Unwin Hyman, 1990, pp. 71–97.

91   Orlow, D., 'A difficult relationship of unequal relatives: the Dutch NSB and Nazi Germany, 1933–1940', *European History Quarterly*, 29, 3, 1999, pp. 349–80.

92   Parming, T., *The Collapse of Liberal Democracy and the Rise of Authoritarianism in Estonia*, Sage Publications, 1975.

93   Payne, S.G., *Falange. A History of Spanish Fascism*, Oxford University Press, Oxford, 1962.

94   Pollard, J., 'Conservative Catholics and Italian fascism: the Clerico-Fascists', in M. Blinkhorn (ed.), *Fascists and Conservatives. The Radical Right and the Establishment in Twentieth-Century Europe*, Unwin Hyman, 1990, pp. 31–49.

95   Preston, P., *The Politics of Revenge. Fascism and the Military in 20th Century Spain*, Unwin Hyman, 1990.

96   Ránki, G., 'The Fascist vote in Budapest in 1939', in S.U. Larsen, B. Hagvet and J.P. Myklebust (eds), *Who Were the Fascists? Social Roots of European Fascism*, Universitetsforlaget, Bergen/Oslo/Tromsø, 1980, pp. 401–16.

97   Rawnsley, S., 'The membership of the British Union of Fascists', in K. Lunn and R.C. Thurlow (eds), *British Fascism. Essays on the Radical Right in Inter-War Britain*, Croom Helm, 1980, pp. 150–67.

98   Rosenhaft, E., *Beating the Fascists? The German Communists and Political Violence, 1929–1933*, Cambridge University Press, Cambridge, 1983.

99   Salvemini, G., *The Origins of Fascism in Italy*, Harper & Row, 1973.

100 Sarti, R., 'Italian Fascism: radical politics and conservative goals', in M. Blinkhorn (ed.), *Fascists and Conservatives. The Radical Right and the Establishment in Twentieth-Century Europe*, Unwin Hyman, 1990, pp. 14–30.

101 Schepens, L., 'Fascists and nationalists in Belgium, 1919–40', in S.U. Larsen, B. Hagvet and J.P. Myklebust (eds), *Who Were the Fascists? Social Roots of European Fascism*, Universitetsforlaget, Bergen/Oslo/Tromsø, 1980, pp. 501–16.

102 Skidelsky, R., *Oswald Mosley*, Macmillan, 1975.

103 Snowden, F., *Violence and the Great Estates in the South of Italy: Apulia 1900–1922*, Cambridge University Press, Cambridge, 1986.

104 Soucy, R., *French Intellectual: Drieu La Rochelle*, University of California Press, Berkeley, Calif., 1979.

105 Soucy, R., 'Centrist fascism: the Jeunesses Patriotes', *Journal of Contemporary History*, 16, 1981, pp. 349–68.

106 Soucy, R., *French Fascism: The First Wave*, Yale University Press, New Haven, Conn., 1986.

107 Soucy, R., 'French Fascism and The Croix de Feu: a dissenting interpretation', *Journal of Contemporary History*, 26, 1, 1994, pp.155–84.

108 Soucy, R., *French Fascism: The Second Wave*, Yale University Press, New Haven, Conn., 1995.

109 Stachura, P.D., 'The NSDAP and the German working class, 1925–1933', in M.N. Dobkoski and I. Wallimann (eds), *Towards the Holocaust. The Social and Economic Collapse of the Weimar Republic*, Greenwood Press, 1983, pp. 131–54.

110 Sternhell, Z., with M. Snazder and M. Asheri, *The Birth of Fascist Ideology*, Princeton University Press, Princeton, N.J., 1994.

111 Tilton, T.A., 'The social origins of Nazism: the rural dimensions', in M.N. Dobkoski and I. Wallimann (eds), *Towards the Holocaust. The Social and Economic Collapse of the Weimar Republic*, Greenwood Press, 1983, pp. 61–74.

112 Tucker, W.R., *The Fascist Ego. A Political Biography of Robert Brasillach*, University of California Press, Berkeley, Calif., 1975.

113 Turner, H.A., *German Big Business and the Rise of Hitler*, Oxford University Press, Oxford, 1985.

114 Upton, A.F., 'Finland', in S.J. Woolf (ed.), *Fascism in Europe*, Methuen, 1981, pp. 191–223.

115 Wallef, D., 'The composition of Christus Rex', in S.U. Larsen, B. Hagvet and J.P. Myklebust (eds), *Who Were the Fascists? Social Roots of European Fascism*, Universitetsforlaget, Bergen/Oslo/Tromsø, 1980, pp. 517–23.

116 Weber, E., 'Rumania', in H. Rogger and E. Weber (eds), *The European Right. A Historical Profile*, Weidenfeld and Nicolson, 1965, pp. 501–74.

117 Wereszycki, H., 'Fascism in Poland' and Wandycz, P.S., 'Fascism in Poland: 1918–1939', in P.F. Sugar (ed.), *Native Fascism in the Successor States*, ABC-Clio, Santa Barbara, Calif., 1971, pp. 83–98.

118 Zacek, J.F., 'Czechoslovak fascisms', in P.F. Sugar (ed.), *Native Fascism in the Successor States*, ABC–Clio, Santa Barbara, Calif., 1971, pp. 56–62.

FASCIST AND RIGHT-WING REGIMES

119   Andreski, S., 'Poland', in S.J. Woolf (ed.), *Fascism in Europe*, Methuen, 1981, pp. 171–90.

120   Austin, D., 'The conservative right and the far right in France, 1934–44: the search for power', in M. Blinkhorn (ed.), *Fascists and Conservatives. The Radical Right and the Establishment in Twentieth-Century Europe*, Unwin Hyman, 1990, pp. 176–99.

121   Ben-Ami, S., *Fascism from Above. The Dictatorship of Primo de Rivera in Spain*, Oxford University Press, Oxford, 1983.

122   Ben-Ami, S., 'The forerunners of Spanish fascism: Unión Patriótica and Unión Monárquica', in M. Blinkhorn (ed.), *Spain in Conflict. Democracy and its Enemies*, Sage Publications, 1986, pp. 103–32.

123   Braham, R.L., *The Politics of Genocide. The Holocaust in Hungary*, 2 vols, Rosenthal Institute for Holocaust Studies/City University of New York and Social Science Monographs, Boulder, Col., 1994.

124   Broszat, M., *The Hitler State. The Foundations and Development of the Internal Structure of the Third Reich*, Longman, 1981.

125   Burleigh, M., *Death and Deliverance. 'Euthanasia' in Germany, c.1900–1945*, Cambridge University Press, Cambridge, 1994.

126   De Felice, R., *Fascism. An Informal Introduction to its Theory and Practice*, Transaction Books, New Brunswick, N.J., 1977.

127   De Grand, A., 'Cracks in the façade: the failure of Fascist totalitarianism in Italy, 1935–1939', *European History Quarterly*, 21, 1991, pp. 515–35.

128   De Grazia, V., *The Culture of Consent. Mass Organization of Leisure in Fascist Italy*, Cambridge University Press, Cambridge, 1981.

129   De Grazia, V., *How Fascism Ruled Women in Italy: 1922–1945*, University of California Press, Berkeley, Calif., 1992.

130   Delzell, C.F., *Mussolini's Enemies. The Italian Anti-Fascist Resistance*, Princeton University Press, Princeton, N.J., 1961.

131   Ellwood, D.W., *Italy 1943–1945*, University of Leicester Press, Leicester, 1985.

132   Fenyő, M.D., *Hitler, Horthy, and Hungary*, Yale University Press, New Haven, Conn., 1972.

133   Gentile, E., 'The problem of the party in Italian Fascism', *Journal of Contemporary History*, 19, 1984, pp. 251–74.

134   Gordon, B.M., *Collaborationism in France during the Second World War*, Cornell University Press, Ithaca, N.Y., 1980.

135   Gregor, A.J., *Italian Fascism and Developmental Dictatorship*, Princeton University Press, Princeton, N.J., 1979.

136   Hauner, M., 'Did Hitler want world dominion?', *Journal of Contemporary History*, 13, 1978, pp. 15–32.

137   Hayes, P.M., *Quisling. The Career and Political Ideas of Vidkun Quisling 1887–1945*, David and Charles, Newton Abbot, 1971.

138   Higham, R. and T. Veremis (eds), *The Metaxas Dictatorship. Aspects of Greece 1936–40*, ELIAMEP, Athens, 1993.

139   Hutchings, R., 'Albania's inter-war history as a forerunner to the Communist period', in T. Winnifrith (ed.), *Perspectives on Albania*, Macmillan, 1992, pp. 115–22.

140 Jelinek, Y., *The Parish Republic. Hlinka's Slovak People's Party, 1939–1945*, East European Quarterly/Columbia University Press, Boulder, Col., 1976.

141 Kershaw, I., *The Hitler Myth. Image and Reality in the Third Reich*, Oxford University Press, Oxford, 1987.

142 Knox, M., *Mussolini Unleashed 1939–1941. Politics and Society in Fascist Italy's Last War*, Cambridge University Press, Cambridge, 1982.

143 Koon, T.H., *Believe, Obey, Fight. Political Socialization of Youth in Fascist Italy*, University of North Carolina Press, Chapel Hill, N.C, 1985.

144 Marrus, M.R, *The Holocaust in History*, Penguin Books, 1989.

145 Mason, T.W., *Social Policy in the Third Reich. The Working Class and the 'National Community'* (ed. J. Caplan), Berg, Oxford, 1993.

146 Mommsen, H., 'National Socialism. Continuity and change', in W. Lacqueur (ed.), *Fascism. A Reader's Guide*, Wildwood House, 1976, pp. 179–210.

147 Nagy-Talavera, N.M., *The Greenshirts and the Others*, Stanford University Press, Stanford, Calif., 1970.

148 Noakes, J., 'German Conservatives and the Third Reich: an ambiguous relationship', in M. Blinkhorn (ed.), *Fascists and Conservatives. The Radical Right and the Establishment in Twentieth-Century Europe*, Unwin Hyman, 1990, pp. 71–97.

149 Paxton, R.O., *Vichy France. Old Guard and New Order, 1940–1944*, Barrie & Jenkins, 1972.

150 Payne, S.G., *The Franco Regime*, University of Wisconsin Press, Madison, Wis., 1987.

151 Peukert, D.J.K., *Inside Nazi Germany. Conformity, Opposition and Racism in Everyday Life*, Penguin Books, 1989.

152 Pollard, J.F., *The Vatican and Italian Fascism, 1929–32. A Study in Conflict*, Cambridge University Press, 1985.

153 Preston, P., *Franco*, HarperCollins, 1993.

154 Rath, J. and C.W. Schum, 'The Dollfuss–Schuschnigg regime: fascist or authoritarian?', in S.U. Larsen, B. Hagvet and J.P. Myklebust (eds), *Who Were the Fascists? Social Roots of European Fascism*, Universitetsforlaget, Bergen/Oslo/Tromsø, 1980, pp. 249–56.

155 Sarti, R., *Fascism and the Industrial Leadership in Italy, 1919–1940. A Study in the Expansion of Private Power under Fascism*, University of California Press, Berkeley, Calif., 1971.

156 Schneider, H.W., *Making the Fascist State*, Oxford University Press, New York, 1928.

157 Smith, D. Mack, *Mussolini*, Weidenfeld and Nicolson, 1981.

158 Smith, D. Mack, *Italy and its Monarchy*, Yale University Press, New Haven, Conn., 1989.

159 Stephenson, J., *Women in Nazi Society*, Croom Helm, 1976.

160 Stokes, L., 'Anton Mussert and the NSB', *History*, 56, 1971, pp. 387–407.

161 Wright, G., *The Ordeal of Total War 1939–45*, Harper & Row, 1968.

THEORIES AND INTERPRETATIONS

162 Adorno, T. *et al.*, *The Authoritarian Personality*, Harper and Row, 1950.

163 Arendt, H., *The Origins of Totalitarianism*, Harcourt, Brace and World, New York, 1951.

164 Bosworth, R.J.B., *The Italian Dictatorship. Problems and Perspectives in the Interpretation of Mussolini and Fascism*, Arnold, 1998, pp. 45–6, 88–9.

165 Botz, G., 'Austro-Marxist interpretation of fascism', *Journal of Contemporary History*, 11, 4, 1976, pp. 129–56.

166 Dimitrov, G., *For the Unity of the Working Class against Fascism. Report to the 7th Congress Communist International 1935*, Red Star Press, 1973.

167 Dülffer, J., 'Bonapartism, fascism and national socialism', *Journal of Contemporary History*, 11, 4, 1976, pp. 109–28.

168 Eatwell, R., *Fascism. A History*, Chatto & Windus, 1995.

169 Friedrich, C. and Z. Brzezinski, *Totalitarian Dictatorship and Autocracy*, Praeger, New York, 1961.

170 Fromm, E., *The Fear of Freedom*, Routledge and Kegan Paul, 1942.

171 Gentile, E., *The Sacralization of Politics in Fascist Italy*, Harvard University Press, Cambridge, Mass., 1996.

172 Germino, D.L., *The Italian Fascist Party in Power*, University of Minnesota Press, Minneapolis, Minn., 1959.

173 Gregor, A.J., *The Fascist Persuasion in Radical Politics*, Princeton University Press, Princeton, N.J., 1974

174 Griffin, R., *The Nature of Fascism*, Routledge, 1991.

175 Kershaw, I, *The Nazi Dictatorship*, Edward Arnold, 1985.

176 Lipset, S.M., *Political Man*, Heinemann, 1959.

177 Loewenberg, P., 'The psychohistorical origins of the Nazi Youth cohort', *American Historical Review*, 76, 1971, pp. 1457–502.

178 Loewenberg, P., 'The unsuccessful adolescence of Heinrich Himmler', *American Historical Review*, 76, 1971, pp. 612–41.

179 Mosse, G.L., *Nazism. A Historical and Comparative Analysis of National Socialism*, Basil Blackwell, 1978.

180 Mühlberger, D., 'Germany', in D. Mühlberger, *The Social Basis of European Fascist Movements*, Croom Helm, 1987, 40–139.

181 Müller, K.-J., 'French fascism and modernization', *Journal of Contemporary History*, 11, 4, 1976, pp. 75–108.

182 Nolte, E., *Three Faces of Fascism. Action Française. Italian Fascism. National Socialism*, Weidenfeld and Nicolson, 1963.

183 Nolte, E., *Die europäische Bürgerkrieg, 1917–1945. Nationalsozialismus und Bolschewismus*, Propyläen Verlag, Berlin, 1989.

184 Ortega y Gasset, J., *The Revolt of the Masses*, Allen and Unwin, 1951.

185 Parsons, T., 'Some sociological aspects of the fascist movements' and 'Democracy and social structure in pre-Nazi Germany', in T. Parsons, *Essays in Sociological Theory*, Free Press, New York, 1950, pp. 104–41.

186 Paxton, R.O., 'The five stages of fascism', *Journal of Modern History*, 70, 1, 1998, pp. 1–23.

187 Payne, S.G., *A History of Fascism, 1914–1945*, University of Wisconsin Press, Madison, Wis., 1995.

188 Reich, W., *The Mass Psychology of Fascism*, Souvenir Press, 1972.

189 Roseman, M., 'National Socialism and modernisation', in R. Bessel, (ed.), *Fascist Italy and Nazi Germany. Comparisons and Contrasts*, Cambridge University Press, Cambridge, 1996, pp. 197–229.

190 Thurlow, R.C., 'The return of Jeremiah: the rejected knowledge of Sir Oswald Mosley in the 1930s', in K. Lunn and R.C. Thurlow (eds), *British Fascism. Essays on the Radical Right in Inter-War Britain*, Croom Helm, 1980, pp. 100–13.

191 Vajda, M., *Fascism as a Mass Movement*, Allison and Busby, 1976.

192 Waite, R.G.L., *'The Psychopathic God!' Adolf Hitler*, Basic Books, New York, 1977.

193 Wistrich, R.S., 'Leon Trotsky's theory of fascism', *Journal of Contemporary History*, 11, 4, 1976, pp. 157–84.

UNDERSTANDING FASCISM

194 Eley, G., 'Conservatives and radical nationalists in Germany: the production of fascist potentials, 1912–28', in M. Blinkhorn (ed.), *Fascists and Conservatives. The Radical Right and the Establishment in Twentieth-Century Europe*, Unwin Hyman, 1990, p. 52.

195 Luciano Cheles, Ronnie Ferguson and Michalina Vaughan, *The Far Right in Western and Eastern Europe*, Longman, 1995.

INDEX

STUART BRITAIN

Social Change and Continuity: England 1550–1750 (Second edition)
Barry Coward   0 582 29442 8

James I (Second edition)
S J Houston   0 582 20911 0

The English Civil War 1640–1649
Martyn Bennett   0 582 35392 0

Charles I, 1625–1640
Brian Quintrell   0 582 00354 7

The English Republic 1649–1660 (Second edition)
Toby Barnard   0 582 08003 7

Radical Puritans in England 1550–1660
R J Acheson   0 582 35515 X

The Restoration and the England of Charles II (Second edition)
John Miller   0 582 29223 9

The Glorious Revolution (Second edition)
John Miller   0 582 29222 0

EARLY MODERN EUROPE

The Renaissance (Second edition)
Alison Brown   0 582 30781 3

The Emperor Charles V
Martyn Rady   0 582 35475 7

French Renaissance Monarchy: Francis I and Henry II (Second edition)
Robert Knecht   0 582 28707 3

The Protestant Reformation in Europe
Andrew Johnston   0 582 07020 1

The French Wars of Religion 1559–1598 (Second edition)
Robert Knecht   0 582 28533 X

Phillip II
Geoffrey Woodward   0 582 07232 8

The Thirty Years' War
Peter Limm   0 582 35373 4

Louis XIV
Peter Campbell   0 582 01770 X

Spain in the Seventeenth Century
Graham Darby   0 582 07234 4

Peter the Great
William Marshall   0 582 00355 5

EUROPE 1789–1918

Britain and the French Revolution
Clive Emsley   0 582 36961 4

Revolution and Terror in France 1789–1795 (Second edition)
D G Wright   0 582 00379 2

Napoleon and Europe
D G Wright   0 582 35457 9

Nineteenth-Century Russia: Opposition to Autocracy
Derek Offord   0 582 35767 5

The Constitutional Monarchy in France 1814–48
Pamela Pilbeam   0 582 31210 8

The 1848 Revolutions (Second edition)
Peter Jones   0 582 06106 7

The Italian Risorgimento
M Clark   0 582 00353 9

Bismark & Germany 1862–1890 (Second edition)
D G Williamson   0 582 29321 9

Imperial Germany 1890–1918
Ian Porter, Ian Armour and Roger Lockyer   0 582 03496 5

The Dissolution of the Austro-Hungarian Empire 1867–1918 (Second edition)
John W Mason   0 582 29466 5

Second Empire and Commune: France 1848–1871 (Second edition)
William H C Smith   0 582 28705 7

France 1870–1914 (Second edition)
Robert Gildea   0 582 29221 2

The Scramble for Africa (Second edition)
M E Chamberlain   0 582 36881 2

Late Imperial Russia 1890–1917
John F Hutchinson   0 582 32721 0

The First World War
Stuart Robson   0 582 31556 5

EUROPE SINCE 1918

The Russian Revolution (Second edition)
Anthony Wood   0 582 35559 1

Lenin's Revolution: Russia, 1917–1921
David Marples   0 582 31917 X

Stalin and Stalinism (Second edition)
Martin McCauley   0 582 27658 6

The Weimar Republic (Second edition)
*John Hiden*0 582 28706 5

The Inter-War Crisis 1919–1939
Richard Overy   0 582 35379 3

Fascism and the Right in Europe, 1919–1945
Martin Blinkhorn   0 582 07021 X

Spain's Civil War (Second edition)
Harry Browne   0 582 28988 2

The Third Reich (Second edition)
D G Williamson   0 582 20914 5

The Origins of the Second World War (Second edition)
R J Overy   0 582 29085 6

The Second World War in Europe
Paul MacKenzie   0 582 32692 3

Anti-Semitism before the Holocaust
Albert S Lindemann   0 582 36964 9

The Holocaust: The Third Reich and the Jews
David Engel   0 582 32720 2

Britain and Europe since 1945
Alex May   0 582 30778 3

Eastern Europe 1945–1969: From Stalinism to Stagnation
Ben Fowkes   0 582 32693 1

The Khrushchev Era, 1953–1964
Martin McCauley   0 582 27776 0

NINETEENTH-CENTURY BRITAIN

Britain before the Reform Acts: Politics and Society 1815–1832
Eric J Evans   0 582 00265 6

Parliamentary Reform in Britain c. 1770–1918
Eric J Evans   0 582 29467 3

Democracy and Reform 1815–1885
D G Wright   0 582 31400 3

Poverty and Poor Law Reform in Nineteenth-Century Britain, 1834–1914:
From Chadwick to Booth
David Englander   0 582 31554 9

The Birth of Industrial Britain: Economic Change, 1750–1850
Kenneth Morgan   0 582 29833 4

Chartism (Third edition)
Edward Royle   0 582 29080 5

Peel and the Conservative Party 1830–1850
Paul Adelman   0 582 35557 5

Gladstone, Disraeli and later Victorian Politics (Third edition)
Paul Adelman   0 582 29322 7

Britain and Ireland: From Home Rule to Independence
Jeremy Smith   0 582 30193 9

TWENTIETH-CENTURY BRITAIN

The Rise of the Labour Party 1880–1945 (Third edition)
Paul Adelman   0 582 29210 7

The Conservative Party and British Politics 1902–1951
Stuart Ball   0 582 08002 9

The Decline of the Liberal Party 1910–1931 (Second edition)
Paul Adelman   0 582 27733 7

The British Women's Suffrage Campaign 1866–1928
Harold L Smith   0 582 29811 3

War & Society in Britain 1899–1948
Rex Pope   0 582 03531 7

The British Economy since 1914: A Study in Decline?
Rex Pope   0 582 30194 7

Unemployment in Britain between the Wars
Stephen Constantine   0 582 35232 0

The Attlee Governments 1945–1951
Kevin Jefferys   0 582 06105 9

The Conservative Governments 1951–1964
Andrew Boxer   0 582 20913 7

Britain under Thatcher
Anthony Seldon and Daniel Collings   0 582 31714 2

INTERNATIONAL HISTORY

The Eastern Question 1774–1923 (Second edition)
A L Macfie   0 582 29195 X

The Origins of the First World War (Second edition)
Gordon Martel   0 582 28697 2

The United States and the First World War
Jennifer D Keene   0 582 35620 2

Anti-Semitism before the Holocaust
Albert S Lindemann   0 582 36964 9

The Origins of the Cold War, 1941–1949 (Second edition)
Martin McCauley   0 582 27659 4

Russia, America and the Cold War, 1949–1991
Martin McCauley   0 582 27936 4

The Arab–Israeli Conflict
Kirsten E Schulze   0 582 31646 4

The United Nations since 1945: Peacekeeping and the Cold War
Norrie MacQueen   0 582 35673 3

Decolonisation: The British Experience since 1945
Nicholas J White   0 582 29087 2

The Vietnam War
Mitchell Hall   0 582 32859 4

WORLD HISTORY

China in Transformation 1900–1949
Colin Mackerras   0 582 31209 4

US HISTORY

America in the Progressive Era, 1890–1914
Lewis L Gould   0 582 35671 7

The United States and the First World War
Jennifer D Keene   0 582 35620 2

The Truman Years, 1945–1953
Mark S Byrnes   0 582 32904 3

The Vietnam War
Mitchell Hall   0 582 32859 4